WHAT ARE NORMS?

WHAT ARE

A Study of Beliefs

FRANCESCA M. CANCIAN

Assistant Professor of Sociology
Stanford University

NORMS?

and Action
in a Maya Community

Cambridge University Press

Published by the Syndics of the Cambridge University Press
Bentley House, 200 Euston Road, London NW1 2DB
American Branch: 32 East 57th Street, New York, N.Y. 10022

© *Cambridge University Press 1975*

Library of Congress Catalogue Card Number: 74-77833

ISBN: 0-521-20536-0

First published 1975

Printed in the United States of America

CONTENTS

TO FRANK

PREFACE

THE QUESTION 'What are norms?' can be answered in many ways. In this book, I give three kinds of answers. First, I present a method for describing the norms of a community. Second, I examine the relation between norms and social organization in the Maya community of Zinacantan. Third, I contrast two theoretical approaches to norms and social action: the Parsonian theory of the socialized actor and the social identity approach.

The book is written from the perspective of my current theoretical position, which focuses on how people define social identities, and how these definitions relate to what people do. However, when I began the research that is described in this book, my theoretical orientation was different. The history of this study is also the history of my change from a Parsonian to a 'social construction of reality' sociologist.

I began the research, in 1965, as an ambivalent Parsonian. I have always been committed to interpreting society from the actor's point of view, and Parsons' theory of the internalization of norms seemed to be the best way to explain social order from this perspective. On the other hand, I had serious doubts about whether people usually act in accordance with what they believe is right – doubts that were based on informal observation and a few studies done by others. However, the negative findings in some of these studies were unconvincing because I did not have confidence in their measures of norms and actions.

For these reasons I decided to do a study in Zinacantan that would carefully measure norms and action and would test some of the implications of Parsonian theory. I had done research in Zinacantan before, and this small, relatively homogeneous community seemed to be a good setting in which to examine whether and how the normative beliefs of individuals affect their actions.

I assumed that norms were culturally specific conceptions of good and bad action. Therefore, before I measured variation in norms I wanted to describe the norms of Zinacantecos and find out what categories of good and bad actions are important to them. No one before had rigorously described the norms of a community from the actor's point of view. However, I was familiar with some new methods for describing native category systems that were being developed by anthropologists in the field of 'ethnoscience.' In addition, I was intrigued with the possibility of using the ethnoscience approach to describe a complex and theoretically important domain like norms.

Therefore, I developed a new method for describing norms and used it to construct a model of the norms of Zinacantecos. The model provided a solid basis for measuring variation in normative beliefs among Zinacantecos.

I decided that the measures of action should focus on activities that are important to Zinacantecos and that are not strongly influenced by a person's wealth. I expected that the effect of an individual's beliefs would be most apparent in this type of situation. Moreover, there had to be sufficient variance in behavior so that I could examine whether individuals with different normative beliefs behaved differently. The three activities that met these criteria best were situations where Zinacantecos had to choose between a modern and a traditional behavior alternative, e.g., going to a Western doctor or to a native curer. Thus I had the opportunity to study modernization, as well as to examine the relation between norms and action.

In 1967, the description of Zinacanteco norms was essentially completed. So I proceeded to conduct a survey of several hundred Zinacantecos to find out how variation in norms related to modern v. traditional behavior. The survey data showed that there was no relationship between an individual's normative beliefs and his actions. The data also indicated that 'being modern' was not a unified concept, since there was little relationship between adopting one modern practice and adopting the others.

At this point, some social psychologists at Cornell introduced me to the vast number of previous studies on attitudes and behavior. Most of these studies had found little relationship between what people do and what people say is right and proper. An extensive re-analysis of my Zinacantan survey data convinced me that my data, also, showed no relation between norms and action.

When I joined the sociology department at Stanford in 1969, I was in search of a theoretical paradigm that would explain these negative findings and suggest a more fruitful way of thinking about norms and social action. I found the paradigm when I read Peter Berger's work and discussed the 'social construction of reality' approach with some colleagues and students who were committed to that perspective.

The first part of this book has not been greatly affected by my intellectual odyssey. The method for describing norms seems just as valid now as it did when I originally developed it. The analysis of how norms relate to social organization in Zinacantan is not dependent on either theoretical perspective, although some of the more interesting ideas in the analysis did not occur to me until after I had articulated the social identity approach. However, the survey that is described in the second part of the book would be different if I were to design it now. I would expand the survey so that it would provide data to test both the Parsonian and the social identity approach. It would include a different way of conceptualizing and measuring 'variance in norms,' and different criteria for selecting the behavioral alternatives.

The study has been a collective enterprise in many ways. The research in Zinacantan would not have been possible without the Harvard Chiapas Project and the steady, lighthanded support of its director, Evon Z. Vogt. Throughout my field work, I received a great deal of advice, help and support from Frank Cancian, George and Jane Collier and Robert Laughlin. The task of collecting the data depended on the hard work of many Zinacanteco assistants, especially Domingo de la Torre Perez, Jose Hernandez, Guillermo Perez Nuh, Chep Nuh, Romin Perez and Manuel Perez. I am also grateful to the many Zinacantecos who were willing to answer questions and provide the data I needed. I am indebted to the National Science Foundation (GS-1341) for providing the necessary funds.

Interpreting the data and writing this book also depended on the ideas and assistance of many people. Each draft was carefully criticized by Frank Cancian, who both pointed out major flaws and shortcomings, and gave me the encouragement to continue. I also benefited from the comments of Albert Bergesen, Jane Collier, Nancy Donham, Michael Hannan, John Meyer, Stephen Olsen, and Michele and Renato Rosaldo. I developed my conception of the social identity approach in the context of many discussions with John Meyer, and Albert Bergesen also helped me to develop new ways of thinking about norms in society. I received valuable assistance in analyzing the data from Susan Almey, Jane Badger, Bonnie Parke and Pamela Oliver, and the Stanford Committee on Latin American Studies provided some funds for data analysis. Finally, I am indebted to the Center for Advanced Study in the Behavioral Sciences, where I wrote the first draft of this book.

Besides this professional help, I was sustained throughout this project by a rich network of personal relationships that I will always treasure. I especially appreciate my fellow field-workers and my friends in San Cristobal and Zinacantan, in particular George and Jane Collier, Bob and Mimi Laughlin, Graciela Alvarado Vda de Villatoro, Domingo de la Torre, and Juan Vasques and his family. My family is in a special category. Frank Cancian is central to my life and my work in many ways – as a loving person, an esteemed colleague, and a worthy opponent. And my children, Maria and Steven, have made the entire enterprise more fun by enjoying our travels and accepting me as I am.

F.M.C.

1974

1

INTRODUCTION TO THE STUDY OF NORMS

THE CONCEPT OF 'norms' is central to sociology, but we know very little about what norms are and how they relate to social action. Norms can be loosely defined as shared conceptions of appropriate or expected action. This study attempts to advance our understanding of norms by analyzing the norms of a particular community and by considering two theories of how norms affect action.

The first part of the book presents a systematic description of the normative system of a Mexican community. A new method of describing norms is used to construct a model of the norms of Zinacantan, a Maya Indian township in southern Mexico. The model identifies Zinacantan categories of good and bad action, and suggests that the structure of norms corresponds to the major institutions and formal organizations of the community.

The second part of the book contrasts two theoretical perspectives on norms and social action. The Parsonian theory of the socialized actor is restated, and I show that this theory is not supported by previous research and that it does not explain the relation between norms and action in Zinacantan. An alternative perspective, based on the concept of social identity, seems to provide a better explanation of how norms function in society.

The concept of norms

Social scientists have proposed many different definitions of norms. According to Williams, 'Norms ... are rules of conduct; they

1

specify what should and should not be done by various kinds of social actors in various kinds of situations ...' (1960:24-5). Sherif defines social norms as 'frames of reference' or standardized ways of regulating activities and perceiving the world (1965:24-5). Others have defined norms as standards, patterns, statements or prescriptions that govern people's conduct or specify what people ought to do (Gibbs, 1965). Most definitions also include the idea that people are rewarded if they conform to norms and are punished if they deviate.

The concept of norms is ambiguous because it has been used to refer to most of the social and cultural part of human action, including values, laws, moral codes, customs, expectations for behavior and shared meaning. However, for the purposes of this study, it is not necessary to distinguish all the types and aspects of norms.

This chapter presents a working definition of norms that is useful for achieving the two goals of the study: developing a method for describing the norms of a community, and comparing two theories of the relation between norms and action. These goals require a definition of norms that includes part of the traditional meaning of the concept and that fits both theories of norms and action. The definition also should suggest a method for describing norms independently of action.

The following discussion distinguishes three types of normative beliefs that I label ranking norms, reality assumptions and membership norms. Then I consider the interpretation of norms in the theory of the socialized actor and the social identity approach. Finally, I discuss how to define norms independently of action. The chapter concludes with an outline of the book.

Three types of normative beliefs

The central theme in most discussions of norms is that norms are standards for evaluating or ranking people as good or bad, better or worse. This type of normative belief, which I label *ranking norms,* is the main focus of this book.

Ranking norms are used to evaluate differentially actions or individuals, on the basis of how well they conform to some standard.[1] They define the actions and attributes that distinguish a particular rank or status. For example, among professors, the belief that 'good professors publish high-quality papers' is a ranking norm.

Ranking norms focus on behavior that *varies* within the community, because without variation, differential evaluation is logically

---

[1]For an interesting interpretation of norms in terms of ranking or stratification, see Dahrendorf's essay, 'The Origin of Inequality' (1968).

impossible.[1] These norms are the basis for the everyday process of evaluating and justifying behavior, and selecting among alternative courses of action. They are constantly restated in daily gossip and in instructing children and others how to behave; therefore, the members of a community tend to be fairly conscious of them.

Reality assumptions are taken-for-granted understandings about what good and bad actions are meaningful or possible in a given context.[2] For example, according to the reality assumptions of my culture, a professor who appears at his lecture course and sings for an hour is engaging in meaningless or crazy behavior.

Reality assumptions affect behavior by restricting the sphere of meaningful acts. Actions that are defined as meaningful or possible will be noticed and taken seriously, and will elicit a response that is determined by the particular meaning of the act. Meaningless behavior is like a message in a private language. Such behavior will either be ignored or it will be treated as not serious (crazy, silly, mistaken) and will elicit responses appropriate for all crazy behavior. By definition, reality assumptions are taken for granted. If people begin to consider and discuss behavior that previously was meaningless, the behavior ceases to be meaningless. For this reason, it is very difficult to measure reality assumptions.

The third type of normative conception, called *membership norms,* combines some of the characteristics of ranking norms and reality assumptions. Membership norms are the standards for including or accepting a person within a group or social position. They apply equally to all group members and are not the basis for ranking.[3] An example of a membership norm for professors is the belief that 'professors are skilled at reading and writing.' This belief is not a ranking norm

[1] The distinction between ranking norms and other shared beliefs about behavior first emerged in the early stages of this study, when I attempted to elicit normative beliefs by asking people to complete sentences like, 'He is good because ...' To my surprise, the three men who produced thousands of normative statements in completing the sentences, never once mentioned a behavior pattern that did not vary in the community.

[2] These beliefs are labeled 'reality assumptions' instead of 'norms' for two reasons. First the term 'assumption' conveys the idea that these beliefs are more general than ranking or membership norms. Second, the term 'norm' is traditionally defined as a standard or rule that is applied to a (meaningful) act or object. However, reality assumptions are beliefs that constitute or define social reality; it seems misleading to conceive of them as standards applied to this reality. See the discussion in Chapter 9.

[3] This phrase concerning 'equal applicability' needs to be qualified to allow for different membership norms for different roles. Thus, the beliefs about being a member in good standing of a church are likely to be different for men and women. The distinction between ranking and membership norms is similar to Kimberley's (n.d.) distinction between task norms and non-task norms.

because there is not enough variance in literacy to differentiate among professors. Deviation from this norm is rare, and literacy tends to be taken for granted as a customary part of the professor role.

The distinction between ranking and membership norms often depends on what social system the researcher or community member is using as a reference point. For instance, within the university, writing a Ph.D. thesis is a membership norm for professors. However, from the perspective of the larger educational system, writing a thesis is a ranking norm that differentiates professors from school teachers.

These three types of normative beliefs have been defined to fit the particular emphases of this book. First, the book focuses on normative beliefs about particular roles or identities. It does not consider beliefs about people or society in general, for example, the belief that 'stores expect payment in money, not in kind,' or 'cars should be driven on the right side of the road.' Second, the book focuses on norms, or beliefs about specific situations. It does not explicitly consider values, or more abstract beliefs that have no clear implications for particular actions (see Kluckhohn, 1961; Blake and Davis, 1964). However, some of the measures and findings are also useful for understanding values. For other typologies of normative beliefs, see Gibbs (1965), Rokeach (1968) and Cicourel (1972).

My study of norms in Zinacantan focuses on ranking norms in particular because of the goals of the study. One goal was to develop a rigorous method for describing the norms of a community independently of behavior. To achieve this, it seemed preferable to consider ranking norms and avoid the difficulties of trying to describe normative beliefs that Zinacantecos are unaware of and take for granted.

The second goal of the study was to compare two theoretical perspectives on norms and action in the light of the evidence from the Zinacantan study and previous research: the theory of the socialized actor and the social identity approach. The theory of the socialized actor attempts to explain why people conform to ranking norms and has little to say about reality assumptions and membership norms. In addition, almost all previous research on norms and action considers only ranking norms. For these reasons, this study focuses on ranking norms, although the other types of beliefs will be considered in the last chapter.

Two theories of norms and action

Before going on to consider the definition of ranking norms in more detail, the two theoretical perspectives will be briefly summarized. The summary previews the major issues in the second part of the book. It also provides a basis for showing that my definition and measures of ranking norms are 'theoretically neutral' in the sense that they fit both theories of norms and action.

The theory of the socialized actor is the most influential conception of norms and social action in contemporary sociology. The starting point for this approach is the conception of the individual actor, who orients himself to the situation and then makes decisions so as to maximize his personal goals. This potentially anarchic individual is harnessed to society through the internalization of norms and values. During childhood socialization and throughout life, individuals develop needs and goals that correspond to social expectations. As a result of this process, the individual members of a society are motivated to conform to shared norms; they want to do what they are supposed to do.

One basic assumption in this theory is that action is a process in which individuals choose between alternatives so as to satisfy their goals and wants. A second assumption is that norms affect action by becoming integrated with an individual's goals and wants. People's actions conform to the norms insofar as they believe that conformity is good and deviance is bad, and at the same time, they want to conform and feel guilty or frustrated if they deviate.

The first assumption leads to a focus on ranking norms or standards for evaluating alternative actions. Since the theory focuses on choice among possible actions, it tends to minimize the importance of the taken-for-granted beliefs that delimit possible actions and define the minimal criteria for group membership. The second assumption leads to interpreting conformity to norms as the result of an individual's personal beliefs and motives. For example, according to the theory of the socialized actor, a woman will conform to the norm that she should enter a 'nurturant' occupation like nursing or teaching insofar as she has a need to be nurturant and believes that for her being nurturant is morally good.

The social identity approach starts with the conception of the collective definition and maintenance of social identities. Action is viewed as a process in which individuals communicate to each other that they are particular kinds of people. Action also includes collectively defining new identities. Norms are interpreted as shared conceptions about what identities or roles exist and what actions and attributes define a person as a member in good standing with a particular rank.

This perspective leads to a focus on reality assumptions and membership norms as well as ranking norms. It also suggests that individuals conform to norms insofar as the norms specify how to obtain validation for an important identity. For example, from this perspective, a woman will conform to the norms about being a teacher or nurse if she perceives that significant others will validate her identity as a woman if she enters these occupations. In the social identity approach, the woman's personality is not important; she may or may not have strong personal beliefs or feelings about being nurturant. What is important is her perception of the identity implications of different occupations.

These two theoretical perspectives lead to different ways of defining and talking about norms. The theory of the socialized actor suggests that ranking norms should be defined as shared standards for evaluation, or as beliefs about what actions and attributes are good and bad. From this perspective, a description of the norms of university professors would include statements like: 'Most professors believe that they ought to publish high quality papers.'

The social identity approach suggests that ranking norms be defined as shared perceptions about what actions or attributes will cause others to validate the identity of being a high-ranking person or a low-ranking person. Norms would be described in a different language, e.g., 'Most professors perceive that they must publish high quality papers in order to be defined as good, high-ranking professors.'

The definition and description of ranking norms that is presented in the first part of this book tries to encompass both theoretical perspectives. Ranking norms are defined as *shared beliefs about what actions and attributes bring respect and approval (or disrespect and disapproval) from oneself and others.*[1] The method for describing the norms of Zinacantan can be interpreted as measuring beliefs about what is good, or as measuring perceptions about what actions validate the identity of being a respected, high ranking person.

Distinguishing ranking norms from action

The relation between ranking norms and action cannot be considered unless the two concepts are defined independently from one another. Norms cannot be directly observed; therefore they must be inferred from some verbal or non-verbal act. However, if the relation between norms and action A is being examined, norms cannot be inferred from action A.

---

[1] In discussions of ranking norms throughout this book, I often refer only to positive evaluations (respect, approval, high rank) and do not mention negative evaluations (disrespect, disapproval, low rank). I do this to simplify the exposition, but readers should remember that ranking norms include negative evaluations.

The distinction between norms and action is often unclear in sociological discussions. Bierstedt defines a norm as 'a rule or standard that governs our conduct . . .' (1963:222). Harry Johnson defines a norm as 'an abstract pattern, held in the mind, that sets certain limits for behavior' (1960:8). Statements like these imply that norms, by definition, govern conduct, limit behavior or affect action. Other definitions of norms, and the closely related concept of role, equate norms with predictions of behavior. Predictions or expectations about how another person will behave are based on information about the past actions of the person, or others like him. Therefore, as Gross *et al.* point out (1958:58-9), if norms are defined as predictions, there will obviously be a positive relationship between norms and action insofar as action is consistent over time.

These problems are avoided by defining ranking norms as shared *beliefs*. My usage follows the suggestions of Homans, who defines a norm as 'an idea in the minds of the members of a group, an idea that can be put in the form of a statement specifying what the members or other men should do, ought to do, are expected to do, under given circumstances . . .' Norms 'are not behavior itself, but what people think behavior ought to be' (1950:124). A similar definition is used by Blake and Davis, who define a norm as 'any standard or rule that states what human beings should or should not think, say, or do under given circumstances' (1964:456).

However, defining norms as shared beliefs about appropriate action raises a major problem because it is too broad. It includes beliefs that obviously are not taken seriously and do not affect action, such as 'automobile drivers should not exceed the exact speed limit.' In addition, it provides no criteria for distinguishing beliefs that clearly seem to be norms, such as 'mothers should provide food for their children,' from beliefs that seem more difficult to categorize, such as 'girls ought to act dumber than boys' or 'you should get eight hours of sleep every night.'

The definition of norms must include some reference to action or sanctions in order to resolve these problems. The working definition of ranking norms accomplishes this by limiting the concept of norms to those beliefs that are perceived to be related to a particular kind of sanction: the granting of respect and approval by oneself and others. According to this definition, 'girls ought to act dumber than boys' is a norm insofar as people believe that conforming to that statement will bring approval and respect, or will validate a person's identity as a high ranking member of a group.

The definition of ranking norms refers to people's perceptions or beliefs about a particular kind of sanction.[1] In contrast, most definitions of norms refer to actual, observable sanctions. For example, Broom and Selznick's textbook, *Sociology,* introduces the concept as follows: 'All societies have rules or norms specifying appropriate and inappropriate behavior, and individuals are rewarded or punished as they conform to or deviate from the rules' (1963:68). And Homans qualifies his definition of norms, that was cited previously, as follows: 'A statement of the kind described is a norm only if any departure of real behavior from the norm is followed by some punishment' (1950:123). The typical definition of norms is a combination of two elements: (1) shared rules or beliefs about how people should act, (2) that are backed by sanctions, or are the criteria for reward and punishment (Blake and Davis, 1964:456).

There is a major drawback in identifying norms with actual sanctioning patterns. If norms are defined as the criteria for reward and punishment, then the hypothesis of a positive relation between norms and action looks very much like a behaviorist learning theory. The statement 'people tend to behave in conformity with the norms' becomes equivalent to the statement 'people tend to behave so as to maximize reward and minimize punishment.' This can easily degenerate into a tautology, given the difficulty of defining punishment and reward for an individual independent of the individual's behavior.

A behaviorist approach to norms has been proposed by John Finley Scott.[2] He defines a norm as 'a pattern of sanctions. More exhaustively, a norm consists of changes in the rates of emission of activities susceptible to reinforcement by social reinforcers' (1971:72). In other words, norms are equivalent to socially determined behavior. One problem with this approach is that it makes it almost impossible to examine the relation between norms and social action.[3] Another problem

[1] If ranking norms were defined as the criteria for the actual allocation of approval, then, since people may not be aware of their norms, the best way of measuring norms would be to observe the distribution of approval in daily interaction. With this approach the statement that norms determine behavior becomes equivalent to Homans' behaviorist theory, which asserts that rewards determine behavior and that social approval is a very important reward (1961:34-5).

[2] Scott rejects the usefulness of defining norms as beliefs or shared conceptions because he thinks that a phenomenological approach must depend on the method of introspection, and that it is impossible to verify scientifically statements about what people think. This book presents a method that shows how people's beliefs can be measured. See the discussion in Chapter 2, also Cancian (1971).

[3] Scott states that norms are not identical with behavior because rates of activity are also affected by other factors besides norms, such as non-social reinforcers and metabolism.

is that it is misleading to lump all social determinants of action together, under the concept of social reinforcers. After accomplishing this theoretical simplification, Scott proceeds to distinguish many types of reinforcers, including super-empirical sanctions, and reinforcers that continue to affect behavior years after they occur.

The translation of phenomenological sociology into learning theory does serve to remind us that most social action is 'learned' or is caused by past and present experience.[1] But it leaves us with the task of explaining how particular types of social actions, including the statement of shared beliefs, affect other actions.

In sum, in order to achieve the goals of this study, the following definition of norms will be used: Ranking norms are shared beliefs about what actions and attributes bring respect and approval from oneself and others. This definition is consistent with the traditional interpretation of norms as standards of evaluation. It fits with the conception of norms in both the theory of the socialized actor and the social identity approach. Finally, it suggests that norms can be measured independently of action by asking people to state their beliefs about how approval, respect and rank are obtained in their community.

Outline of the book

The first part of this book (Chapters 2 through 6) presents a new method for describing the ranking norms of a community, and applies this method to analyze the normative system of Zinacantan. Chapter 2 reviews previous methods for measuring norms and values, and argues that adequate measures should be based on a description of norms from the actor's point of view. In particular, a researcher should describe the actions that members of a community view as good and bad, before attempting to measure variation in norms across individuals.

Following a brief description of the community of Zinacantan in Chapter 3, a new method for describing norms is presented in detail in Chapter 4. This method provides a systematic way of describing how the members of a community define good and bad actions. The method includes two major steps. First, the domain of norms is identified by asking Zinacantecos to complete part-sentences like 'He is good because ...' Then subjects are asked to sort the norms according to similarity. The results of the sorting task identify the major clusters of norms in the community.

[1] See Campbell (1961) for an excellent, convincing presentation of the argument that the statements in learning theory can be translated into cognitive-phenomenological theory, and vice versa.

This method produced a model of the norms of Zinacantan, which is analyzed in Chapter 5. The model consists of nine clusters of norms that define the major ways of being a good, high-ranking man or a bad low-ranking man. For example, one cluster focuses on being religious, and one concerns being drunk and violent.

The model provides, for the first time, a rigorous description of the norms of a community from the actor's point of view. The model also suggests some general hypotheses about the relation between norms and social structure. In particular, the most important norms seem to refer to the major formal organizations of the community.

Chapter 6 describes three independent tests that confirmed the validity of this model of Zinacanteco norms. The tests include a repetition of the sorting task with a new set of norms, a survey questionnaire on norms and action, and an interview in which particular individuals were rated on some of the traits described by the norms. The results of these tests show that the norm clusters represent stable cognitive categories that Zinacantecos use in a variety of situations. Readers who are primarily interested in the structure of Zinacanteco norms can skip Chapters 2 and 6, and will be most interested in Chapter 5. Readers who are concerned with the methodology of describing norms should focus on Chapters 2, 4, 5 and 6.

The second part of the book (Chapters 7 through 9) compares two theoretical approaches to norms and social action. Chapter 7 outlines the theory of the socialized actor, and shows that previous research on norms, attitudes and behavior do not confirm the theory. However, these data are usually ignored by sociologists, because rarely do studies explicitly focus on the major norms of a community.

The results of the survey of norms and action in Zinacantan, described in Chapter 8, are more relevant to the theory of the socialized actor. Valid questions about norms were constructed on the basis of the model of norm clusters, and the measures of action concerned important decisions in Zinacanteco life. Thus, some of the important deficiencies of previous studies have been eliminated. The results of the survey do not support the theory, and show that the norms and actions of individuals are not positively correlated. These negative findings imply that the theory should be substantially revised or rejected.

The final chapter discusses the social identity approach to norms. This approach implies that norms are attributes of groups, not individuals, and can change rapidly without intensive interaction or internalization. The major propositions of the social identity approach are supported by some previous studies and they suggest some promising new lines of research on norms and social action.

2

STRATEGIES FOR DESCRIBING AND MEASURING NORMS

NORMS AND VALUES are culturally specific beliefs about what actions and attributes bring respect and approval. Before attempting to measure variation in norms within a community, a researcher must describe the categories of actions and attributes that are important to the members of that community. Norms must be described from the actors point of view. Research that begins with general ideas about important actions and attributes, rather than locally defined ones, is in serious danger of producing an invalid picture of the local normative system.

For example, a description of beliefs in a group of high school students might show that their norms focus on good personality, physical attractiveness and participation in sports. Thus, a valid measure of differences between different types of students should concentrate on beliefs in these three areas. Without a description of norms from the students' point of view, a researcher might assume that students' norms focus on cars and getting good grades, and this assumption would reduce the validity of all the subsequent research.

Previous studies of norms have been severely hampered by the absence of adequate methods for describing the content of norms from the actor's point of view. There has been no systematic way to find out what beliefs are treated as norms in a particular community or culture, and how these beliefs are structured. As a result, some investigators, of an anthropological bent, abandon rigor in order to capture the native world view. Others, who are committed to the 'hard-nosed' methodology of the social sciences, either ignore this major weakness in their research design or do some superficial field work to get a 'sense' of what questionnaire items might correspond to important norms and values.

The lack of adequate methods has also reinforced the traditional separation between 'soft phenomenologists' and their more hard-nosed colleagues. The argument that it is important to consider the actor's point of view is often rejected on the grounds that these topics cannot be studied scientifically. Thus, in a recent book on norms, Scott devotes a section to demonstrating 'The Impossibility of Scientific Phenomenology' (1971:21), and argues that the actor's point of view can only be studied by the method of introspection, which is a non-scientific method.

The study reported in this book rejects these restrictive arguments. It uses a combination of research approaches to develop a rigorous method that begins with the actor's point of view and permits measurement of variance of norms within a culture or community. This chapter first outlines the criteria for an adequate method for measuring norms, and then reviews the strategies developed by ethnographers, comparativists and survey researchers. The final section describes the methodological approach of ethnoscience, which represents a great advance toward solving the problem of constructing rigorous descriptions of the actor's system of beliefs.

Criteria of an adequate method for measuring norms

An adequate method for describing and measuring norms obviously must meet the scientific standards applied to any method: it should be reliable, that is, it should consist of specified procedures that yield the same results for different investigators, and it should be valid and lead to an accurate, unbiased representation of what is being measured.

A measure of norms, in particular, must be based on a description or model of the actor's normative belief system. According to almost every definition of norms or values, these concepts necessarily imply a phenomenological or subjective approach. They are defined as an aspect of culture or as certain types of beliefs or conceptions held by members of some community. Therefore, a valid method must attempt to represent the cognitive structure of the population being studied, and must avoid confounding their categories and beliefs with those of the investigator.

When researchers freely use their own cognitive principles to formulate questions and generalize from responses, they introduce a potentially alien logic that defeats the effort to describe a particular belief system. A question is implicitly or explicitly derived from a theory, or from assumptions about relevant dimensions and possible alternative answers; and the structure and content of a question largely determine the kinds of statements that can be made in response. If a model of the actor's normative beliefs has not been constructed, then the questions will reflect the assumptions of the investigator's own culture or of the social science community, and they may not be valid measures.

The first step in constructing a model of the actor's normative beliefs is to define the domain, or specify the boundary area that separates those things that will be called 'norms' from other things. After determining what beliefs tend to be treated as norms in a particular community, the structure of the domain should be investigated by using systematic, inductive procedures for identifying the major dimensions or categories of the normative system. Finally, the validity of the model should be tested by determining how well it predicts the cognitive judgments or other actions of community members.

It should be noted that a model of a belief system is not a photograph of the insides of people's heads or of what they really think. A set of judgments or other actions can often be explained by several alternative models, and it is always possible that new evidence will show that a model must be revised (see discussions by Burling, Hymes, Frake, 1964). Moreover, procedures for constructing and verifying such a model, like all procedures, ultimately rest on some *a priori* assumptions about reality and knowledge. However, within these limits, it is important to use empirical investigations instead of *a priori* assumptions in the description of normative beliefs. The following discussion shows how previous studies have failed to construct adequate measures of norms and values because the measures are either unreliable or they are not based on a valid model of the actor's belief system.

Intensive studies of communities

The methods that have been used in past studies of normative beliefs can be arranged in a rough continuum from the intuitive, holistic approach typically used by anthropoiogists to survey methods favored by sociologists and psychologists.[1] Opler's work on themes is a good example of the holistic method. He defines a theme as 'a postulate or position, declared or implied, and usually controlling behavior or stimulating activity, which is tacitly approved or openly promoted in a society' (1945:198). Themes are discovered by acquiring a thorough understanding of all aspects of a culture. Formalized expressions of

---

[1]For a discussion of possible methods of measuring values, see C. Kluckhohn (1951:403-9). See Labovitz and Hagedorn (1973) for a review of methods of measuring norms.

themes 'are relatively simple to note: a full outline of the traditional aspects of a culture usually throws most of them into relief ... But for the identification of unformalized expressions of a theme, close observation, accounts of personal experiences, and autobiographical materials must be utilized in addition' (1945:201). Opler adds that it requires a very good 'acquaintance with the culture to interpret symbolic expressions correctly' (1945:201). He suggests other clues to identifying themes, such as counting the number of expressions of a theme and noting 'the intensity of the reaction and the character of the sanction involved' (1945:201) when the terms of a theme are violated.

A similar approach is used in most anthropological monographs and in community studies by sociologists. For example, in Hollingshead's study of *Elmtown's Youth* (1949), and Whyte's book on *Streetcorner Society* (1955), the values and norms of the community are inferred primarily from the investigator's day-to-day contact with community members, supplemented by relatively unstructured interviews.

The major asset of this kind of method is that the resulting description of norms gives a convincing and integrated representation of the attitudes of the community. The major defect is that the method is not reliable or replicable; when two investigators independently study the same community, the results are often very different.[1]

The cross-cultural questionnaire

The primary goal of some studies of values has been to compare the values of different communities or cultures. Comparative research requires a single set of categories that can be used to describe the norms or values of different cultures. Because of the absence of careful descriptions of particular normative systems, these general categories cannot be formulated inductively. Therefore, the categories have been deduced from theoretical or philosophical assumptions, and then they have been applied to particular cultures, to see how well they fit. The problem with this approach, as one might expect, is that they often seem to fit very poorly with the native world view.[2]

Florence Kluckhohn's work on value orientations is the outstanding example of the cross-cultural questionnaire approach to studying values. Others have proposed general categories or dimensions for

[1]Redfield's and Lewis's different interpretations of the Mexican community of Tepotzlan are a classic example. See Foster (1960).

[2]See Vogt and Albert (1966:11-21) for a brief but incisive discussion of the problem of cross-cultural comparisons of values and how different researchers attempted to deal with the problem in the Harvard Study of Values in Five Cultures.

describing all value systems (Albert, 1956; C. Kluckhohn, 1958) but she is the only investigator who has developed a measuring instrument and used it in many cultural settings.

The Kluckhohn method for measuring values is based on an explicit theory. The theory asserts, first, that 'there is a limited number of common human problems for which all peoples at all times must find some solution' (Kluckhohn and Strodtbeck, 1961:10). Second, there are only a few solutions to these problems and the values of a community can be described in terms of the rank order of their preferences for these solutions. The five universal problems (value orientations) and the possible solutions to each (range of variation) are represented in Table 2-1.

Table 2-1 The five value orientations and the range of variations postulated for each

Orientation	Postulated range of variations		
man – nature	subjugation-to-nature	harmony-with-nature	mastery-over-nature
time	past	present	future
activity	being	being-in-becoming	doing
relational	lineality	collaterality	individualism
human nature	evil	neutral	mixture of good and evil	good
	mutable immutable	mutable immutable	mutable immutable

*Source: Taken from Kluckhohn and Strodtbeck (1961:12)

Specific value orientations are measured by a series of questions which describe a situation and ask the subject to rank order three responses to the question. For example, there are five questions for measuring temporal orientation. One of them is:

'Three young people were talking about what they thought their families would have one day as compared with their fathers and mothers. They each said different things.

(Future) The first said: I expect my family to be better off in the future than the family of my father and mother or relatives if we work hard and plan right. Things in this country *usually* get better for people who really try.

(Present) The second one said: I don't know whether my family will be better off, the same, or worse off than the family of my father and mother or relatives. Things always go up and down *even if* people do work hard. So one can never really tell how things will be.

(Past)   The third one said: I expect my family to be about the same as the family of my father and mother or relatives. The best way is to work hard and plan ways to keep up things as they have been in the past.

Which of these people do you think had the best idea?
Which of the other two persons had the better idea?
Which of these three people would most other ... your age think had the best idea'? (Kluckhohn and Strodtbeck, 1961:82.)

The rank orderings that are given in response to this type of question are then averaged over all subjects, to determine the value orientations of the community.

The Kluckhohn method of measuring value orientations is valid insofar as the responses to these questions have the same meaning for the subjects and for the investigator. If the responses have a different meaning, i.e., if the subjects understand them in terms of a cognitive model that is quite different from Kluckhohn's theory, then the questionnaire can produce a very distorted picture of the normative system. For example, in the above question about time orientation, people in some subcultures of the United States might interpret the alternative responses in terms of categories like political conservatism v. radicalism, instead of past, present and future time orientation. This might lead them to treat the 'future' and 'past' alternatives as basically the same, since both imply a conservative viewpoint: the 'future' alternative suggests approval of the current political system, and the 'past' alternative suggests support of the *status quo*. The 'present' alternative might be treated as politically neutral. Imagine what would happen if the question were asked in a politically active community that was evenly split between conservatives and radicals. Most of the radicals would choose the politically neutral 'present' response and the conservatives would divide evenly between the 'past' and 'future' responses. The misguided social scientist would report that the questions measuring values about time showed that this community has a present-time orientation. In fact, the questions were measuring political orientation and the responses showed an even split in the community between radicals and conservatives.

Cross-cultural comparison requires using the same categories or dimensions to describe the individual cultures that will be compared.

For those who are interested in comparing norms or values across cultures, the central question is: how should these general categories be constructed? Kluckhohn uses a deductive strategy. She begins with theoretical assumptions about the basic dimensions that underlie all value systems, and then devises questions that measure these dimensions, taking care to translate the questions appropriately and use situations that are meaningful to the respondents.[1] A similar approach is often used in comparative studies of modernization or achievement values (Rosen, 1971; Smith and Inkeles, 1966). The weakness of this strategy is that questions derived from *a priori* theories often are not valid measures; they may fail to mesh with the important distinctions and categories of a particular community, and therefore produce the kind of distortion described in the above example of values about time and politics. Several researchers have found that for this reason the Kluckhohn interview could not be used to describe the values of the community in which they were working.[2]

An alternative strategy is to construct the categories more inductively, and begin with careful descriptions of particular normative systems. Then general categories or dimensions can be formulated that reflect the similarities between these systems, or subsets of them.[3]

This is the approach to comparative studies of values that is suggested by Vogt and Albert, in their summary of the Harvard Study of Values in Five Cultures, which included much of Florence Kluckhohn's work. After reviewing the methodological strategies that were used in this immense project, they conclude:

> Were we now, in the middle 1960's, to undertake another values study, we could proceed quite differently. Our approach to data collection could be

[1] The meaning of 'translating the questions appropriately and using situations that are meaningful' is ambiguous. This phrase could mean that the questions would be formulated on the basis of a careful analysis of the particular culture, and would reflect the distinctions that are important in that culture. But if this were done, the questions might not measure the dimensions derived from the theory. Kluckhohn (1960) has proposed translating the question back into the original language as one way of checking the appropriateness of the translation.

[2] In a personal communication, Frank Cancian reported the inadequacy of the Kluckhohn questions for describing values in a southern Italian town. He found that after the individual items were independently translated into Italian, different items designed to measure the same value orientation elicited very different responses. This indicates that the items were understood in terms of a native category system that did not mesh with Kluckhohn's theory.

[3] If there were no similarities among the systems, no way of ordering them in terms of a single set of concepts or meta-language, then the descriptive strategy would be of no use for comparative research. Such a result would suggest that it is impossible to make valid comparisons.

based upon a type of elicitation and analysis that utilizes models for determining significance and distinctive characteristics explicitly derived from each culture. After describing the value systems of each culture, we would then, and only then, undertake comparative analysis of the basic conceptual systems of each culture. As Hymes has remarked of linguistics, 'One need not stop with the individual systems, but one must pass through them.' (1966:20)

The methods that Vogt and Albert have in mind for describing each culture are those 'developed by linguists and ethnographers who specialize in "componential analysis" or "ethnoscience" (1966:20). These methods, which are reviewed at the end of this chapter, formed the basis of the Frame-Sorting Method that I developed to describe the norms of Zinacantan.

Surveys of the norms and values of one culture

Most studies of norms and values consist of survey research done by sociologists and social psychologists, working in their own culture. The questions in these surveys are based on theoretical assumptions, previous questionnaires, superficial field-work and 'common sense.' The questions are not based on a systematic investigation of the actor's belief system, and since these studies are not comparative, there is little justification for this omission.

There seem to be several reasons for omitting a description of norms. Many researchers assume that they already know the culture and therefore it is not worthwhile to obtain more systematic data. In addition, there has been no available method for systematically describing the content and structure of normative beliefs.

Survey researchers who study norms and values within the United States often assume that they understand the normative system before they have collected any data (see Cancian, 1971). Their research typically focuses on the relative importance of different norms or changes in norms over time, and these issues are investigated with a questionnaire that is constructed with little or no input from the population being studied. When the research is written up for publication, there is no mention at all of how the particular questions were selected, even though the goal of these studies is to describe a particular normative system and the researchers are very careful about other aspects of their research design.

Some examples of this type of research are Coleman's study of the culture of several high schools (1961), Walter L. Wallace's study of *Student Culture* (1966), and Stouffer's research on *Conflicting Social Norms*

(1949).[1] Coleman's study clearly illustrates the problems with this approach. A central objective of his research was to examine the adolescent community and 'discover just what the value systems are' (1961:12). Data was collected by a questionnaire that included 'sociometric questions and semi-projective items, as well as the usual kinds of attitude and background items...' (1961:336) – that is all that is said about formulating questions to measure values.

The lack of attention to the content and structure of the students' value system probably led to many serious distortions, although Coleman's analysis seems to be an important contribution to understanding the effects of different value systems. For example, one of the key questions for discovering values was the following (with the distribution of responses indicated): 'If you could be any of these things you wanted, which would you most want to be? Jet pilot (32%); nationally famous athlete (37%); missionary (5%); atomic scientist (26%).' Coleman concludes from these results that 'these adolescent attitudes seem to reflect the dominant themes and heroes in the mass media far more than the heroes their teachers would have them follow' (1961:28). In fact, it is difficult to draw any conclusions from these results because the meaning of the alternative responses is not known. Was 'missionary' rejected because missionaries are seen as prissy or poor or religious? Was 'atomic scientist' rejected by many students because of the 'atomic' component and its association with nuclear war, or did it seem dull compared to 'jet pilot' and obscure compared with 'nationally famous athlete'? Coleman does not know what components of these occupational categories are salient to the students,[2] so he cannot infer values from the choices.

Other researchers have tried to obtain some data on how the members of a community view their own normative system, but they have been severely hampered by the lack of appropriate methods. The usual procedure is to obtain some normative statements from 'the natives' by doing some quick field-work (e.g., Gross et al. 1958:112) or by consulting written materials produced by the community or transcripts of interaction (e.g., White, 1951; Bales, 1970:495). More rarely, some members of the population are systematically interviewed (Kahl, 1968:23-4). The normative items collected by these methods are then thrown

[1]The questionnaire items in Stouffer's study seem to be based, in part, on Parsons' Pattern Variables. The Pattern Variables are intended to be a general set of dimensions for describing values cross-culturally and they have been used for this purpose by several researchers (see Simpson, n.d.).

[2]See Gusfield and Schwartz (1963), for a method of analyzing the semantic components of occupational categories.

together with a large bunch of items that are taken from previous questionnaires or are derived from theoretical interests. The final questions are selected by doing a pre-test and picking sets of questions that are correlated and seem to form a scale. It is unlikely that this method will produce questions that are valid measures of norms, since the statements from the 'natives' are unsystematically elicited; they are mixed up with a larger number of items taken from other sources and are often grouped into categories based on *a priori* assumptions (Kahl, 1968, chapter 2).

Several researchers have commented, in passing, on the possible inadequacy of these methods. In his study on measuring modern values in Brazil and Mexico, Kahl discusses a finding that suggests the possibility of a serious methodological problem. According to his measure of modern values, politically radical men are more likely to be traditionalists than modernists, holding social status constant. This finding suggests that the measure of modernity may not be valid. Perhaps, he states, 'our own concept of modernism contains some biases; the stereotype of the modern man from which it was derived referred to an urban, middle-class man who sought personal advancement through individualistic effort' (1968:117).

Other researchers, such as Rokeach, have commented on the lack of systematic procedures for sampling 'randomly or representatively ... from the total universe of beliefs' (1968:57). Gross *et al.* worry about the unknown representativeness of the norms in their questionnaire (1958:112), and take refuge in Guttman's assertion that this problem plagues all survey researchers: 'Questions are *constructed* by the research worker ... It is not as if there were available a list of all possible questions and their variations from which those used in the study were drawn at random' (quoted in Gross, 1958:113).

A few innovative social scientists have experimented with non-survey methods for defining the domain of norms from the natives' point of view. However, no methods have been devised for determining the structure or underlying dimensions of this domain, after it has been defined.[1] Banfield has used T.A.T. pictures to elicit normative beliefs (1958) and Goldschmidt and Edgerton (1961) have developed a picture test. But these researchers do not suggest any method for determining the structure of norms, after they have been elicited, and Ban-

[1]The structure of the domain of personal attributes, which is related to norms, has been analyzed by factor analysis and other correlational techniques. Following Leary's analysis (1957) many researchers have found that in the United States this domain is organized around two dimensions: love – hate and dominance – submission (see D'Andrade, 1965; references in Cancian, 1964).

field simply categorizes the responses into predetermined categories, like 'calamity' or 'misfortune,' that are based on his interpretation of the norms of the community. William A. Scott has used open-ended questions like 'What is it about any person that makes him good'? to elicit moral ideals. But the norms are then grouped into categories on the basis of *a priori* assumptions or unsystematic inspection of the corpus of norms (1965:19, 1959:302).

Finally, one might expect some methodological innovations from two prominent sociologists whose work is concerned with the actor's point of view: Garfinkel and his field of ethnomethodology, and Goffman. 'Ethnomethodology' is the study of people's 'practical skills,' their category systems and their own explanations of how they behave. However, ethnomethodologists have not been concerned with developing methods for reliably describing how people explain their behavior. Garfinkel's book, *Studies in Ethnomethodology* (1967), presents several empirical studies but does not suggest any systematic method for constructing models of the actor's belief system (Swanson *et al.,* 1968).[1] Goffman's work also fails to suggest better methods for describing norms, because he is not concerned with this problem. The goal of his work seems to be to develop general models of meaningful behavior in face-to-face interaction. These models are concerned with universal processes, and not with culturally specific categories and meanings.[2]

None of the approaches reviewed thus far has developed a method for systematically describing the domain and structure of norms from the actor's point of view; and without this type of description, it is unlikely that valid measures of norms can be constructed. However, methods for describing belief systems have been developed by a group of anthropologists interested in the area of 'ethnoscience.' Their work will now be briefly reviewed.

Methods of describing cognitive content from ethnoscience

Since the early 1950s, a number of anthropologists have been developing methods for describing the cognitive systems of other

[1]See Cancian (1971) for a critical analysis of Egon Bittner's ethnomethodological description of policemen on skid row.

[2]Goffman states, at the conclusion of his paper 'On Face-Work': 'Throughout this paper, it has been implied that underneath their differences in culture, people everywhere are the same.' Universal human nature consists of moral rules. 'These rules, when followed, determine the evaluation [a person] will make of himself and of his fellow-participants in the encounter, the distribution of his feelings, and the kinds of practices he will employ to maintain ... ritual equilibrium' (1967:44-5).

cultures. Their area of interest is usually labeled 'ethnoscience,' meaning the study of native systems of knowledge, classification and inference. The most elegant studies in ethnoscience concern kinship terminology, but the methods have also been used to investigate category systems in the domains of diseases, colors, firewood, linguistic prefixes, and rituals (see reviews in Sturtevant, 1964; Colby, 1966; Tyler, 1969; Cancian, 1971). The description of Zinacanteco norms attempts to use this methodological approach for describing normative beliefs, a domain that is more elusive and more relevant to sociologists.

The general procedure of an 'ethnoscientist' usually includes the following steps: (1) defining the cognitive domain or area; (2) describing the objects, events or words included in the domain; (3) determining which objects are grouped into one category or term and which are discriminated; and (4) formulating the rules for grouping and discriminating objects.

The basic methodological orientation consists of emphasizing 'emic' distinctions (from *phoneme,* i.e., distinctions that are made by the natives of a particular culture) and trying to avoid 'etic' distinctions (from 'phonetics,' i.e., distinctions made by scientists and applicable to all culture). Because of this effort to avoid *a priori* categories based on scientific theories or on the investigator's culture, there is a great stress on using the language of the subculture being studied. It should be noted that, in this context, the emic – etic contrast is a question of relative emphasis, rather than an either/or choice, because it is impossible to avoid completely the use of etic or scientific categories. 'Ethnoscientists' typically use scientific language and assumptions in defining the domain, describing the objects within the domain and communicating their findings.

An excellent example of the methods of ethnoscience is Metzger and Williams' 'A formal ethnographic analysis of Tenejapa Ladino weddings' (1963)–Ladinos are non-Indian Mexicans. Metzger and Williams describe Ladino weddings 'in terms of the ways in which they [the Ladinos] perceive weddings to differ in form, as well as the kind of inferences which they draw on the basis of the occurrence of one form rather than another ...' Their methodological goal is to produce a description and employ procedures that are 'free of the distortion introduced by investigators' own implicit perception or assumption of descriptive units' (1963:1076).

Metzger and Williams begin by defining the domain or area to be studied. The domain is equated with a native phrase: *fiesta de matrimonio.* The relevance of any particular event to the domain is judged by asking members of the village (or informants) if it is part of a *fiesta de matrimonio*.

Then they record conversations that informants say are part of a *fiesta de matrimonio*. From these recordings, they select phrases to be used as 'substitution frames,' i.e., incomplete sentences which are completed by informants. For example, one of the phrases in the recordings was 'let's appoint nine male attendants.' Several frames were developed from this phrase to obtain different kinds of information. The ways in which informants completed the frame 'Let's appoint _____ male attendants' indicated possible variation in the number of male attendants. The responses to other frames indicated the kinds and number of other ritual roles at weddings (Let's appoint nine _____) or the interdependence between one role and another (Let's appoint _____, and let's appoint _____).

The responses to many such frames resulted in a description of the objects or events that are included in weddings and how the objects are grouped into units or categories (steps two and three). For example, the frames described above identified the category of 'ritual role' and the kinds of people included in this category. Other frames led to a description of the sequence of ceremonies, meals and music, how the forms of these units could vary and how these variations were evaluated by people in the village.[1]

Metzger and Williams' approach resulted in a description of the cognitive domain of weddings that is primarily based on empirical research, not on *a priori* assumptions. However, their description is not completely 'free of the distortion introduced by investigators' own implicit perception or assumption of descriptive units.' (1963:1076). First of all, some (unreported) criteria had to be used to select the frames from the recordings, and they probably selected the frames that they thought would elicit 'important' data. For example, one of the frames they selected was '(the music) was good, de luxe.' This frame probably influenced informants to mention the attributes of a wedding that are relevant to judging people's social class. If other frames had been selected, then a somewhat different description of the domain would probably have resulted. Secondly, Metzger and Williams had to use some criteria for selecting informants and interpreting disagreements between informants. Finally, they used English terms such as 'friend' and 'ceremony' to communicate their findings to social scientists. In

[1]Metzger and Williams' paper does not include the fourth step of an ethnoscience analysis: formulating the rules for grouping objects. The reason may be that the domain of weddings is complex and its organization may shift in different social contexts.

sum, their method minimizes *a priori,* etic assumptions, but it does not eliminate them.

Ethnoscience has developed a variety of methods for describing cognitive domains, besides substitution frames (see Sturtevant, 1964; Tyler, 1969; Wallace, 1970; Romney *et al.,* 1972). Sorting tasks and other procedures have been used to obtain subjects' judgments on the similarity and differences among the items in a domain. Studies of kinship terminology often use the method of componential analysis, whereby the grouping of kinsmen in a particular language is represented by a model of the least number of dimensions necessary to generate these groupings (dimensions such as sex and generation). Finally, some researchers have developed methods for determining which of several descriptive models is the most valid representation of a cognitive domain (Romney and D'Andrade, 1964; Frank Cancian, 1963).

The methods developed in ethnoscience suggest that it is possible to construct a model of normative beliefs from the actor's point of view, thereby solving a major problem in the study of norms and values. The following chapters will show how substitution frames and sorting tasks were used to construct a model of the norms of Zinacantan.

Criticisms of ethnoscience

Ethnoscience can be criticized in two ways. First, in most ethnoscience descriptions there has been little attempt to collect data from a representative sample of informants. The possibility of variation in cognitive structure across subgroups or situations is usually ignored, and the boundary and structure of a domain is often treated as if it were as clear and determinate as a blueprint. In fact, the structure of many domains is probably quite variable and ambiguous, as is suggested by the description of Zinacanteco norms in the following chapters. The study of Zinacanteco norms deals with this problem by considering variation in norms across individuals and across situations.

The second type of criticism is more fundamental. Some students of norms and values may argue that the ethnoscience approach is not adequate for describing normative beliefs because it depends on artificial verbal techniques. However, there are good grounds for rejecting this argument. The objection to using verbal statements to describe norms can be dismissed on the grounds that norms have been defined as a type of *belief* about behavior. It is extremely difficult to measure beliefs without using verbal statements. The objection to describing norms on the basis of an artificial task like completing substitution frames can also be rejected. This argument is based on the following false assumption: people behave in the same way in all natural situations and behave in a different way in artificial situations; therefore, insofar as social scientists are concerned with explaining day-to-day natural behavior, they must measure behavior in natural situations. The assumption of greater similarity across natural situations than between natural and artificial situations is obviously false in some cases. For example, the natural situation of talking with your friends is probably more similar to the artificial situation of talking with a peer in a laboratory experiment, than it is to the natural situation of talking with your boss.[1]

The important problem is not the difference between 'natural' and 'artificial' situations. The real problem is that social scientists do not understand what kinds of differences among situations affect particular actions. Regardless of what type of method is used, researchers in most fields do not know what variables must be controlled or what conditions must obtain, in order for their findings to be replicated. Therefore, we must continue to do research in some specific situation, and the generalizability of the findings will not be known until the research is replicated in many other settings.

Unfortunately, there will probably continue to be little research done in certain 'natural' situations, because they present many difficulties, regardless of whether one is using an ethnoscience-type method or some other approach. For example, if one attempted to measure norms in 'natural' gossiping situations, it would be very difficult to identify expressions of norms, and to sample these situations. Studies done in such 'natural' settings would be extremely valuable, not because they are particularly 'real' or general, but because they are inherently interesting situations about which we have little systematic data.

Summary

The norms or values of a community are a culturally specific system of beliefs. The domain and structure of this belief system must be systematically described, before it is possible to construct valid measures of variation in norms. If questions or other measures of

---

[1]Moreover, the meaning of 'artificial' is unclear. It seems to refer to the unfamiliarity or novelty of the situation, but for some people, for example a college freshman, filling out a questionnaire may be a great deal more familiar than many of the 'natural' situations he encounters.

norms are based on the investigator's assumptions, and not on a careful description, then the results may be very misleading.

Previous studies of norms or values have not been based on a systematic description of the actor's normative beliefs, in large part because of the absence of methods to produce such a description. However, ethnoscience has developed several methods for describing belief systems. The domain of normative beliefs can be defined by using substitution frames to elicit normative statements. The structure of the domain can be identified by asking individuals to judge the similarities among norms. As the next chapters will show, these methods produce a valid model of a community's normative system and provide a basis for constructing valid questions to measure variation in norms.

The next four chapters focus on the description of Zinacanteco norms. Chapter 3 provides some background information on the community of Zinacantan. The method for constructing a model of Zinacanteco norms is presented in Chapter 4. Then the content of the model is discussed and the relation between the normative system and the social organization of Zinacantan is analyzed in Chapter 5. Chapter 6 presents several tests of the validity of the model of Zinacanteco norms.

3

RESEARCH SETTING: THE MAYA COMMUNITY OF ZINACANTAN[1]

THE STUDY OF norms and social action was carried out in the Maya Indian community of Zinacantan, Mexico. The description of norms and the survey that are presented in the following chapters focus on the particular activities that are important to Zinacantecos, such as corn farming, service in the religious offices and family life. These activities are briefly described below, after a discussion of previous research in Zinacantan.[2]

Research in Zinacantan

Zinacantan has been extensively studied by the Harvard – Chiapas Project since the late 1950s. Under the leadership of Professor Evon Z. Vogt, dozens of students and professionals have done research in the community.[3] By 1965, when the study of norms began, we knew a great deal about Zinacantan, and almost all Zinacantecos knew about the Project and were willing to cooperate with us. Some traditions of doing research had been established over the years, such as paying Zinacan-

[1]This chapter draws heavily from the detailed description of Zinacantan by Evon Z. Vogt (1969), and also from Frank Cancian's description of the system of religious offices (1965).

[2]This description was written for the explicit purpose of elucidating the clusters of norms that emerged from the Frame-Sorting Method of describing norms. Therefore, there is little in the description that conflicts with the results of this method. To obtain an independent description of Zinacantan that might provide some grounds for evaluating the success of the method for measuring norms, the reader should consult the excellent and extensive general monograph by Vogt (1969) or his shorter description (1970).

[3]For references to early publications on Zinacantan, see Vogt (1969). Recent publications include Frank Cancian (1972); Jane Collier, 1973; George Collier, in press.

tecos to come to our offices for intensive interviewing, and several
Zinacantecos had been trained to be very able research assistants.

In addition to the Harvard – Chiapas Project, the study of norms
drew on my own past work in Zinacantan. In the course of a previous
study of family interaction (Cancian, 1964), I had spent about fifteen
months in Zinacantan and had acquired a fair mastery of Tzotzil, the
native Maya language.[1] Knowing the language was essential to studying normative beliefs, especially because most men and almost all
women in Zinacantan are monolingual in Tzotzil.

The community of Zinacantan

Zinacantan is a township of about 9,000 Indians and 350 Ladinos[2]
in the state of Chiapas, Mexico. In Mexico, Indians are distinguished
from Ladinos by language and dress. Ladinos speak Spanish and Indians speak aboriginal languages. Ladinos wear European clothing
while Indians wear regional costumes.

There are many distinct groups of Maya Indians in the Chiapas
highlands, and each has some special cultural patterns and a distinctive
costume. Zinacantecos can be quickly distinguished from the others by
their clothing – the men in wide-brimmed hats festooned with multi-
colored ribbons, the women in navy skirts and white and red shawls.

Ten kilometers east of Zinacantan lies San Cristobal, a city of
about 23,000 people, which has been the largest Ladino center in the
highlands since the sixteenth century. San Cristobal is the center for
marketing and services for more than 100,000 highlanders, most of
them Indians. It contains many stores, two markets, and a variety of
bars, churches, government offices and clinics. Every morning, several
hundred Zinacantecos come to the city by foot, truck or bus to buy and
sell, deal with government officials or baptize a child. In the evening,
they all return to their one-room adobe homes in Zinacantan.

Zinacantan is spread over about 120 square kilometers of mountains and small valleys, on both sides of the Pan American highway. It
is divided into a Center and fifteen hamlets that vary in size from 121
people to 1,227. Some are densely populated valleys where all houses
can be seen from any house top, while others are widely dispersed in

---

[1]My knowledge of Tzotzil enabled me to understand and participate in most conversations. I only failed to understand jokes, ritual language, and long utterances in
which the speaker was rapidly describing an event.

[2]According to the 1960 Mexican census, there were 7,760 Indians and 350 Ladinos
in Zinacantan. Frank Cancian estimates that by 1966 there were 9,000 Indians, since the
population is growing rapidly and Indians are under-enumerated.

the forests of pine and oak. The Center is a densely populated valley surrounded by the sacred mountains, where curing ceremonies are performed. The Center contains the town hall, which is the locus of the political and legal organization, and two churches, where the religious office holders celebrate the big fiestas and perform an annual cycle of rituals. There are also several schools, including a recently opened boarding school, and some tiny stores and bars.

Zinacantecos maintain an evolving but distinct culture, in spite of 400 years of close contact with the Western world. The following sections outline the organization of economics, religion, law and kinship in Zinacantan, and discuss some prominent themes of social interaction.

The economic system[1]

The main source of food and income in Zinacantan is corn farming. Almost all men farm corn in the highlands on land controlled by their family, or in the lowlands on land rented from Ladinos. Lowland farming is by far the most important and is the major source of corn and money. When they farm in the lowlands, Zinacantecos form groups, often composed of kinsmen, that are led by one man. This group leader or representative must speak some Spanish and be skilful in locating good land and dealing with the Ladino landlord. Land is rented annually, and there is a constant search for better land that has not been farmed for many years. Such 'new' land requires more work to clear, but produces much higher yields. A lot of new land has become available to Zinacantecos in recent years, because of the development of a network of roads.

The organization of work follows the demands of growing corn, with the peak work periods occurring at the time of weeding and at harvest. At these times, Zinacantecos employ others to work with them, at a daily wage (in 1965) of 8 pesos plus meals. Throughout most of the year, Zinacanteco men go on trips to their lowland fields for several days or weeks, usually leaving the women and children behind. Most men spend a total of about three to four months a year away from home working on their cornfields in the lowlands.

Corn farming provides almost all households with their basic food supply and the cash that is needed for curing ceremonies and religious offices and for buying thread, salt, rum, hoes, machetes, etc. Some men also grow beans, which is a risky crop that can bring very high profits.

[1]See Frank Cancian (1972) for a detailed description of corn farming in Zinacantan.

A handful of adult Zinacantecos have other full-time occupations besides farming. A few men sell salt; about a dozen buy corn from Zinacantecos and resell it at the San Cristobal market, and a few grow flowers commercially. Also, during the slack season when there is little work to be done on their corn fields, many men look for ways to supplement their income. Some grow and sell flowers; some work as agricultural day laborers or work on the roads; others trade in peaches, and in recent years, some have found employment with anthropologists. But the main occupation, source of income and focus of concern is corn.

The Zinacanteco attitude toward work and money is a combination of dedication to community service and commitment to individual achievement. Vogt concludes that 'in important respects Zinacantecos appear to have "the Protestant Ethic" without being Protestants' (1969:613). Zinacantecos tend to be hard-working and punctual. Even those who are wealthy employers do their own portion of work and usually seem to take pride in being fast and industrious laborers. Being lazy is condemned, and men who are poor are often held in contempt and treated as if they were responsible for their poverty. However, a man's wealth actually seems to be determined in large part by his father's wealth, the number of kinsmen and other contacts he has, and his health. On the other hand, an intelligent, hard-working man can probably achieve a sound economic position on the basis of his own effort, and a little luck.

The first responsibility of a man is to provide for his own family; if they are hungry it is his fault. But beyond that, a man who accumulates wealth is expected to spend a good part of it on taking religious offices and performing rituals that benefit the entire community. He is also expected to lend money, without interest, to others who need the funds for their religious offices or for curing ceremonies.

Stratification and the religious offices

Zinacantan, like many other Middle American Indian communities, has a complex system of religious offices (see Frank Cancian, 1965, for a detailed description). Each office is dedicated to the service of a particular saint and is occupied by a different man every year. During his year of service, the man pays for the rum, meals, candles, firecrackers and other things required for the rituals he must perform. For the most expensive offices, these costs add up to about 14,000 pesos, or the equivalent of 1,750 days of work as a laborer; many offices cost between 3,000 and 5,000 pesos.

The religious offices are hierarchically arranged into four levels, with forty positions at the first level, and only two at the fourth and final level. A man begins by taking an office at the first level, then 'rests' for a few years before taking an office at the second level, and so on. At each level, the positions are ranked from the cheapest, lowest prestige position to the most expensive one that brings the highest prestige, and usually only those who take the high prestige positions at one level proceed to the next.[1] The most visible sign of a man's social status is the religious offices he has taken, and men who have passed prestigious offices are held in high esteem by the community.

The office holders are helped by a variety of auxiliary personnel in carrying out the rituals for their saints. Each office holder has a Ritual Advisor, a man who has passed two positions himself, and who tells the office holder what to do. Many rituals require musicians, and also a variety of cooks, drink pourers, men who set off firecrackers, errand boys, etc. The largest number of helpers appear for the two big fiestas of San Lorenzo and San Sebastian. On these occasions, half the population of Zinacantan comes to the Center to observe the office holders carry out the rituals, to drink with their kinsmen and to look over the marriageable girls and boys. In the meantime, the office holders carry out many ritual activities, such as parades, horseback races, or dances, each of which requires some helpers.

This system of religious offices represents the public, community-wide part of religion in Zinacantan. It includes some features of official Catholicism: the saints' calendar, churches, masses, and sacristans are essential parts of the ritual of the office holders. These elements have been woven into a Maya institution that forms the basis of the stratification system by converting individual wealth into community prestige. The religious office holders perform and finance rituals that benefit the entire community; in return they receive public recognition and prestige.

Other religious activities

Other religious activities in Zinacantan are carried out privately by individuals, households and groups of households. The most elaborate religious activity in the hamlets occurs in May and January, when the related households that share a waterhole perform complex rituals to safeguard themselves, their land and their water supply. Each household head supports the community-wide fiestas by paying a tax, and

[1]The expense and the prestige of different religious offices are highly correlated, but not perfectly correlated (see Frank Cancian, 1965).

during Easter week, the adults in every household are expected to comply with certain restrictions on eating and drinking.

The most important rituals for individual families are curing ceremonies. When a Zinacanteco is sick, a member of his family will call a curer to diagnose the illness and cure him by performing the proper rituals. Zinacanteco curers are called to their position by having certain dreams and they have a special relationship with the Lord of the Earth and the ancestral gods. Sickness is usually explained as the result of a disturbed relationship between a person and the ancestral gods. The curer re-establishes a good relationship by praying at the sacred mountains, sacrificing a rooster, and offering the gods candles, incense, and rum (see Vogt, 1969:297ff.).

Curers are also capable of causing sickness through witchcraft, because of their special relations with the Lord of the Earth; and other Zinacantecos, who are not curers, are also sometimes accused of witchcraft. The object of witchcraft usually seems to be a relative who is envied because of his wealth or is hated because he cheated his kinsmen out of their rightful portion of land.

The commitment to traditional beliefs and practices about illness is very strong in Zinacantan. As will be shown later, virtually all Zinacantecos go to the curer when they are ill, even though this may be followed by a visit to a modern clinic.

The political – legal system

Zinacantan has its own system of roles and procedures for making political decisions and settling disputes (see J. Collier, 1973, for an intensive study of Zinacanteco law). In the hamlets, extended disputes are handled by bringing the case before a respected man, usually someone who is old and wealthy and has passed several prestigious religious offices. This man will listen to both sides and then settle the dispute through his wise counsel. Major cases and community-wide disputes are taken to the president and other political officers of Zinacantan who hold court at the town hall in the Center (except that Mexican law requires that some offenses such as murder, be handled by Ladino officials in San Cristobal). Besides settling legal disputes, the officials at the town hall also make political decisions about public works and relations with the Ladino world. For major decisions, dozens or hundreds of important Zinacanteco men will meet in front of the town hall to work out a common course of action or split off into rival factions.

In addition to the leaders in the hamlets, and the political officials in the Center, there are several committees with political functions. The most important of these is the Ejido Committee, which is in charge of administering the farm land that is part of the national land distribution program. These political – legal organizations are in the hands of Zinacantecos, to handle in their own way, as long as they do not conflict with Mexican law and come to the attention of outsiders. Ladino officials and others with a strong interest in Zinacantan often succeed in influencing internal politics, but the day-to-day decisions are made by Zinacantecos.

Dealing with the Ladino world requires somewhat different skills from those valued in a local leader. Zinacantecos who can influence Mexicans to make the proper decisions must appear to have local support; but in addition, they must speak Spanish fairly well, understand something about government bureaucracies and be able to say the appropriate things and bribe the appropriate officials. It is also helpful to be somewhat literate in Spanish. Men who have these skills are often asked to help obtain the release of a Zinacanteco from a Ladino jail, to talk to government officials about financing public works projects like roads, and to perform other services. These favors can build up an important political constituency, and along with the man's influence among Ladino officials, they can give a man considerable political power within Zinacantan. These same skills, however, make it possible for him to drop his native language for Spanish and change into European clothes, thereby becoming a Ladino instead of remaining a Zinacanteco. This possibility arouses the suspicion of many Zinacantecos, since Ladinos have been exploiting them for centuries.

Kinship and ritual kinship

Participation in the system of religious offices and in politics, law and lowland farming, bring Zinacanteco men in contact with a large number of others in their community. The rest of the time, they interact primarily with the members of their household. For the women and children, the household is most of their social world. Most households are fairly independent, although several patrilineally linked households may cooperate on some occasions. The members of a household usually include a nuclear family, and if the sons of the couple have recently married it may also include the son's wife and small children. The women of the household are responsible for child care and making food and clothing, while the men are responsible for providing corn for food and cash. Ideally, a man should also be good tempered and generous. He should bring treats of candy or fruit for his children, take his family to fiestas, and when they are sick, arrange to have elaborate and expensive curing ceremonies.

The long courtship in Zinacantan tests the generosity and good humor of most men. The courtship begins with the relatives of the prospective groom and a go-between forcing entry into the girl's home and obtaining an agreement for a formal courtship. After this the young man brings gifts of fruit, rum and soft drinks to his prospective in-laws over a period of two years or longer. However, this ideal way of conducting a courtship often is not followed, and many men spend much less time and money on obtaining a bride (see J. Collier, 1968, for a description of Zinacanteco courtship).

In addition to blood and marriage, Zinacantecos are linked to each other through ritual kin ties formed at baptism, confirmation and marriage. When a Zinacanteco couple baptize their child, they form an enduring relationship between themselves and the couple that takes the role of the child's godparents. The relationship between the two couples will be expressed in visiting each other, drinking together at fiestas, lending each other money, and in general showing the same loyalty and helpfulness that one would expect of a close kinsman. Confirmation of children is used primarily to form ties with Ladinos, and during a proper marriage ceremony a Zinacanteco couple can acquire a vast number of ritual kinsmen.

Themes of social interaction

The social institutions that have just been described, such as religion and kinship, are cross-cut by some pervasive 'themes' of interaction. They include rank and ritual, speaking well, as well as drinking and violence. These relationships and personal attributes are of central importance to Zinacantecos in all spheres of activity.

A major theme in Zinacanteco interaction is the representation of relative rank through ritual (see Rosaldo, 1968). From the perspective of a native of the United States, much of Zinacanteco social interaction is expressed in ritual ways – in bowing, exchanging particular greetings, and drinking in a prescribed order while uttering the prescribed toasts. Virtually every contact between Zinacantecos who are not close kinsmen begins with ritual greetings and bowing. And every time a Zinacanteco asks someone to do him a favor, such as lend him money or help with a religious office, this is preceded by the supplicant's offering a bottle of rum in the prescribed manner.

As Vogt points out, 'the Zinacantecos are very rank-conscious people' (1969:329), and almost all of these ritual forms signify the relative status of all people who participate in them. For example, the low status person bows to the high status person, and in a drinking situation, people receive their portion in order of decreasing rank. In most cases, age and sex determine status, with older men having higher rank than younger women, but sometimes a person with great wealth, political power or a distinguished career of religious offices will receive more deference than a slightly older man.

A related theme in Zinacantan might be called 'pride in appearance,' and it is especially evident among men younger than forty or fifty, who give a great deal of attention to how they look. The day-to-day costume of men is rather elaborate, including a white and pink 'vest,' a beribboned hat and a hand-tooled leather bag. A man who wants to be respected tries to be clean, well-dressed, well-groomed and comport himself with dignity. Zinacantecos seem to be very concerned with self-discipline in the area of appearance, as well as in the area of work.

Ritual and appearance express a man's relative status. 'Talking well or talking badly' indicates whether a man obtains status by being intelligent and helpful, or by being crafty and self-serving. A virtuous man is able to listen calmly and talk intelligently and reasonably; these are the qualities of leaders who are able to settle disputes. Men of little virtue do not settle disputes; they create them through gossiping and informing on the real or imagined wrong-doings of their neighbors. Such men lie and connive to cheat their relatives out their rightful land inheritance. They are angry, envious and crafty, and intensify disputes by siding with whatever position serves their interests best.

Another way to 'talk badly' is to be incompetent. Men who are shy and fearful and cannot make impressive public speeches are not admired. However, the incompetent are not powerful, by definition; thus it is the crafty intriguer who is most condemned in Zinacantan.

'Drinking and violence' is another major theme in Zinacantan. As mentioned above, offerings of rum and drinking ceremonies are crucial elements of almost every important social situation. However, drinking can lead to drunkenness which Zinacantecos view as a cause and an excuse for deviant behavior, especially violence. Severe conflicts between brothers or between husband and wife usually involve one party's being drunk and then abusing the other verbally or physically. Men who are too lazy or poor to provide for their family often act like 'town drunks,' spending a lot of time and money on liquor and making fools of themselves in public.

'Drinking and violence' and the other themes and institutions outlined above are all basic elements of the social organization of Zinacantan. Each of them is an important part of the normative system that is described in the following chapters.

4

THE FRAME-SORTING METHOD FOR DESCRIBING NORMS

WHAT ARE THE norms of Zinacantecos? I answered this question by developing a new method for identifying the ranking norms of a community. The method is based on the ethnoscience approach and it has two major components: (A) the domain of norms is defined by eliciting normative statements with substitution frames, and (B) the structure of the domain is examined with a sorting task that shows how these statements are organized into clusters of norms. The two parts together are labeled the Frame-Sorting Method, for convenience.

The outline below shows the major steps of the Frame-Sorting Method. Each step will then be presented in detail.

The Frame-Sorting Method

A. Defining the domain of norms with Substitution Frames
    Step
        One: Selecting the substitution frames
        Two: Eliciting normative statements with the frames
        Three: Eliminating redundant and idiosyncratic norms
B. Describing the structure of norms with the sorting task
    Step
        Four: Selecting 100 representative norms
        Five: Recording judgments of similarity with the sorting task
        Six: Analyzing the clusters of norms

A. Defining the domain of norms with substitution frames

The domain of Zinacanteco norms was defined by using some Tzotzil phrases as substitution frames. For example, one of the frames was the Tzotzil equivalent of 'He is respected because ...'[1] The statements that Zinacantecos produced to complete the frames represented the domain of norms, after eliminating idiosyncratic and redundant statements. This procedure identified a large set of statements that fit the concept of 'norms.' At the same time, it avoided using an *a priori* definition of norms that would include only those statements that North Americans perceive as relevant to a man's goodness.

I considered several other approaches to defining the domain of norms. One possibility was to observe interaction in a variety of settings and record actions that seemed to express norms. Another possibility was to work with texts written by Zinacantecos, and extract normative statements. Both methods were rejected because they depended too heavily on my own judgments in identifying norms. The identification could not be done by Zinacantecos because I was unable to explain my concept of norms to the native research assistants in either Tzotzil or Spanish. Using substitution frames avoided the problem of identifying particular normative statements, since all completions of the substitution frames were considered to be norms.

Step One: Selecting the substitution frames

The substitution frames were selected on the basis of my theoretical assumptions about norms and the results of a pretest. I began with a definition of norms as 'shared beliefs about what actions and attributes bring respect and approval from oneself and others.' Working with this definition, I and two Zinacanteco assistants selected eight frames that occurred frequently in conversations and tended to be followed by norm-like statements. These frames were tested by asking four Zinacantecos to produce twenty-five responses to each one. The best frames were then identified by determining which ones elicited the highest proportion of appropriate, norm-like responses.

A further restriction on the selection of frames was that the study of norms was limited to adult men. All participants in the study were men, and the substitution frames were intended to define the domain of norms relevant to men from the male perspective. This was done to simplify the task of describing Zinacanteco norms, since beliefs about

---

[1]A very similar method was used successfully by Scott (1959) to assess the 'moral ideas' of several midwestern communities in the U.S.A.

how one should behave probably vary by sex and age. In addition, it is much more difficult to do research with Zinacanteco women because they are much less free to come and go as they please, and because almost all women are illiterate.

Selecting the frames was inevitably a difficult task because of the problems inherent in defining any cognitive domain, especially one that is intended to correspond to some *a priori* category like 'norms.' When researchers attempt to define a domain from the actor's point of view they are caught in a dilemma. On the one hand, they clearly do not yet know the defining characteristics of the domain, and they are committed to avoiding the imposition of *a priori* definitions in order to discover the native category system. On the other hand, the researchers must have some conception of the domain in order to select a particular procedure as appropriate for defining it. Moreover, if the native domain is going to be identified with a scientifically defined domain like 'kinship terms' or 'norms,' there should be a firm basis for asserting that the two domains are the same or are similar.[1] This dilemma cannot be totally resolved.

In this study, the domain of norms was operationally defined by frames that were selected because they elicited responses that fit my *a priori* definition of norms. Norms were defined as beliefs about what actions elicit approval and disapproval. Therefore, I evaluated the results of the pretest in terms of my own general understanding of what was important to Zinacantecos in approving and disapproving of each other. On this basis, for example, I judged the statements 'he works hard,' 'he is a murderer' and 'he knows how to burn incense' to be appropriate, norm-like responses. The statement 'he fell down' seems irrelevant to approval; and the statement 'he knows how to be a servant' was rejected because it refers to an activity that is of minor importance in Zinacantan.

The evaluation of the pretest results was also guided by my interest in producing a description of Zinacanteco norms that fit the theory of the socialized actor. The theory of the socialized actor suggests that the domain of norms refers only to actions and attributes over which the

[1]The general issue of cross-cultural variance v. the equivalence of domains or units is still a central, unresolved problem in comparative research. It has received considerable attention in the context of cross-cultural research, where it is referred to as the 'problem of translation' or the 'problem of equivalence of units' (see discussion and references in Naroll and Cohen, 1970, parts I and VI). In this study the equivalence of the scientific domain of 'norms' and the corpus of statements elicited by the frames, depends on the meaning of the frames that were used. In order to demonstrate empirically the equivalence of these two domains, it would be necessary to have a method for assessing the meaning of the frames, independently of the responses they elicit.

actor has some control. In this theory, actors conform to norms because they are motivated or want to conform. If an attribute is not controlled by the actor, then conformity or having this attribute cannot be explained by the actor's motivation, for example, the attribute of 'being an orphan' in our culture. The social identity interpretation of norms includes attributes over which the actor has no control, as will be discussed in Chapter 9. However, I relied primarily on the assumptions of the theory of the socialized actor in defining the domain of Zinacanteco norms.[1]

For these reasons, some responses in the pretest were judged to be inappropriate because they referred to behavior over which the actor has no control, e.g., 'his father just died,' 'his wife is barren.' This type of response was fairly frequent for the fifth and sixth frames in the list below.

The following eight frames were pretested:

English translation	Tzotzil[2]
1. John is good because ...	Lek li Marian yu? un ...
2. John is bad because ...	Copol li Marian yu? un ...
3. He is respected because ...	Lek p'isbil ta vinik yu? un ...
4. He is not respected because ...	Muk' p'isbil ta vinik yu? un ...
5. He has a good heart because ...	Lek yo? on yu? un ...
6. He has a bad (heavy) heart because ...	Copol yo? on yu? un ...
7. He is useful (competent, an asset) because ...	Lek xtun yu? un ...
8. He is of no use (no good) because ...	Mu xtun yu? un ...

The pretest identified the first four frames as the best ones. They elicited an average of three inappropriate responses out of every twenty-five while the other frames elicited a much higher proportion of inappropriate responses.[3]

---

[1] At the time that I selected the frames, I was strongly influenced by the theory of the socialized actor and had not yet articulated the social identity approach.

[2] In writing Tzotzil, an apostrophe indicates a glottalized consonant and a question mark indicates a glottal stop.

[3] The fifth frame seems to mean 'he is happy,' since it elicited many responses about good things happening, such as, 'he is well fed at home,' 'he doesn't have any brothers (to fight with).' The sixth one seems to mean 'he is unhappy,' and elicited responses such as: 'he broke his leg,' 'his wife is barren.' The seventh and eighth frames elicited a large number of responses referring to occupation, such as: 'he knows how to castrate horses,' 'he is a good carpenter.'

The frames that were selected by this procedure seem to have produced a fairly undistorted definition of the domain of Zinacanteco norms. The normative statements elicited by the four frames were very redundant and appear to be exhaustive, in the judgment of myself and several other experienced field-workers in Zinacantan. However, one of the theoretical assumptions that was used in evaluating the pretest turned out to be incorrect. I assumed that I could define a domain of Zinacanteco norms that excluded attributes over which the actor has little or no control. But the four frames elicited many statements of this type and they make up one of the nine major clusters of norms that emerged from the Frame-Sorting Method.

This result can be interpreted in two ways: (1) the procedure was successful in discovering some of the special ways in which Zinacantecos define the domain of norms, or (2) the procedure was not entirely successful because the domain that was defined by the frames is broader than 'norms' insofar as it includes these unexpected statements. I believe that the first interpretation is more fruitful because it makes it possible to examine variation in the definition of domains across cultures. This interpretation also raises some interesting questions about the theory of the socialized actor, which will be discussed in Chapter 9.

Step Two: Eliciting normative statements with the frames

The completions of the frames were used to define the domain of norms. Therefore, it was important that respondents considered all areas of Zinacanteco life when they completed the frames, and did not limit themselves to the statements that happened to come to their minds at the moment. This problem has been a major obstacle in previous attempts to elicit norms with a sentence-completion technique. As William A. Scott has pointed out, in reference to his own effort to use this method, 'a respondent's answers are likely to be unduly affected by momentary, transient concerns ...' (1965:19).

This methodological problem was solved by using a dictionary as a standard stimulus for suggesting completions to the frames. A fairly complete Tzotzil dictionary of about 16,000 words was available (Laughlin, n.d.), and since it was an almost exhaustive list of all Tzotzil words, it was an excellent tool for ensuring that all aspects of Zinacanteco life were considered in completing the substitution frames.

The following procedure was used to elicit the normative statements: each respondent was told to go through the dictionary and look for words that could be used to complete the sentence in a meaningful way, with or without the use of additional words. For example, a man working with the frame 'John is good because ...' might come to the word for 'children' in the dictionary and complete the sentence with the normative statement 'he doesn't beat his children.' He then would write this statement on a slip of paper.

Another important consideration in eliciting the statements was to minimize the bias that might be introduced by the particular Zinacantecos who completed the frames. It was impossible to select these men randomly, since very few Zinacantecos are literate enough to write many statements in a reasonable amount of time.[1] Instead, I employed two highly trained Zinacanteco assistants who had worked with the Harvard Project for years, and reduced bias by selecting a third man who was quite different from them; he was fifteen years older, barely literate and had not participated in much research previously. In addition, bias was minimized by eliminating statements that were produced by only one informant, as will be discussed shortly. The three informants varied in residence, wealth, political power and personality. However, all three knew Spanish well and all had fathers who had either died or left home when the informant was a child (being fatherless in Zinacantan often results in working for Ladinos and thereby learning Spanish).

These three men were employed to work on completing the frames in their spare time, during a year when I was absent from the field. Each man worked independently of the others. They followed instructions with few exceptions,[2] and produced an unexpectedly large number of normative statements.

[1] If a larger group of randomly selected informants were used, the work involved in processing all the statements would be staggering. In this case it would probably be best to revise the method and use a word list instead of an entire dictionary, so that each informant would produce fewer statements.

[2] The first exception was that one of the informants changed the frames slightly. He altered the frame 'he is respected because ...' to 'John is respected because ...' and occasionally changed 'John is bad because ...' to 'John is very bad because ...' It seems unlikely that these minor changes would have much effect on the statements that he constructed to complete the frames. Second, the two highly trained informants ignored the instruction that they work with one frame at a time and do all the completions for that frame before going on to the next. The purpose of this instruction was to maximize the variance in the completions for different frames, but these two men altered the procedure so as to maximize their working speed. They worked with one section of the dictionary at a time (all the words starting with the same letter) and completed all the frames, using the words in that section. Then they went on to the next section of the dictionary. This change almost certainly reduced the variance between the frames, since an informant who had just written 'John is good because he farms well' would be very likely to complete the sentence 'he is respected because ...' with 'he farms well.' Given this change in the procedure, it could be argued that actually only one frame was used, not four. However, the completions to different frames were very similar for all the informants, including the one who did follow the instructions.

The two men who could read and write well took about three months to complete the task and produced about 3,500 statements each, while the third man took most of the year to produce 7,000 barely legible statements, for a grand total of about 14,000. The statements were translated and, where necessary, explained by informants, so that I could be relatively confident that I understood the Tzotzil.

These normative statements describe evaluated actions or attributes that vary among Zinacantecos (ranking norms). Some examples are: 'he has taken four religious offices,' 'he steals horses,' 'he is cross-eyed.' They are the kind of statements that are often heard in Zinacanteco conversations, and almost all of them clearly imply approval or disapproval by using Tzotzil words that mean that one is doing something well *(lek)* or excessively *(toh, tol).*[1]

None of the normative statements refers to actions or attributes that do not vary among Zinacantecos. Thus, there is no norm like 'he wears pants,' since all Zinacanteco men wear pants; it is part of being a man.[2] But there are norms about aspects of dress that vary, such as 'he doesn't wear a hat.' This perfect uniformity in the norms elicited by the substitution frames is striking. It shows the usefulness of distinguishing between ranking norms and reality assumptions; and it indicates that when people make normative judgments and distinguish between good and bad, respected and not respected, they will only consider actions that vary or that have meaningful alternatives within their community.[3]

Step Three: Eliminating redundant and idiosyncratic norms

The corpus of 14,000 statements was reduced in two ways, so that it would constitute an adequate definition of the domain of norms. First, I eliminated 1,700 normative statements that were redundant, that is, they exactly replicated another statement produced by the same infor-

---

[1] The two 'good' frames, referring to respect and goodness, appeared to elicit almost identical norms, as did the two bad frames. Therefore, the analysis does not attempt to distinguish norms on the basis of which frames elicited them.

[2] The only occasion when men appear in public in skirts, instead of pants, is when they are 'being women' and impersonate females during rituals (see Vogt, 1969).

[3] Possibly, other substitution frames may elicit reality assumptions, for example, a frame like: 'when a man wakes up in the morning, it is appropriate to . . .' On the other hand, these assumptions may be completely taken for granted, because they are always followed; perhaps no substitution frame will elicit many of them. Other researchers have argued that when respondents are asked to make any kind of report, they are more likely to report characteristics that vary rather than constant ones (Rommetveit, 1960).

mant.[1] Secondly, I eliminated all norms that appeared to reflect the idiosyncratic interests of a particular informant. If a normative statement was produced by only one informant, it was excluded from the domain of norms. If the same statement was produced by two or three informants, it was retained. I used explicit rules to decide what statements were 'the same,' but in most cases the decision was simple because two or three of the men had written identical statements, word for word.[2]

This procedure concerns the important issue of variation in the definition of norms within a community, and it deserves some comment. The procedure is based on the assumption that there is *a* domain of norms in Zinacantan. I assume that Zinacantecos agree, more or less, on their conception of what aspects of behavior are relevant in evaluating each other. In a larger, more differentiated society, it is probable that the definition of the domain of norms varies across subcultures or statuses. But in Zinacantan, where all men participate in the same activities of family life, corn farming, and religious service, it is reasonable to expect considerable consensus among men. In addition to variativities of family life, corn farming, and religious service, it is reasonable to expect considerable consensus among men. In addition to variapossibility was not explored because of the complex problems involved

---

[1] At this stage of the study, I underestimated the importance of distinguishing between positive and negative statements of the same behavior, e.g., 'he beats his wife,' 'he does not beat his wife.' In some cases I eliminated some positive statements if the informant had already written the statement in the negative, and vice versa. This results in biasing the description of norms so that it is less likely that good behavior will look like the negative mirror image of bad behavior. However, there was so much redundancy in the norms that this bias probably was not very strong. An attempt was made to correct it in the second sorting task, as will be described later in Chapter 6.

[2] The normative statements were first sorted into twenty-one *ad hoc* categories, to facilitate the location of identical statements. Then the following rules were applied:
1. A norm was selected if it had been produced by two or three of the men, using statements that had the same key words and the same meaning. Words and phrases were treated as having the 'same' meaning if: (1) they were given English translations in Laughlin's Tzotzil – English Dictionary (n.d.) that I judged to be synonymous, or (2) if I understood the words and judged that they would be used interchangeably by Zinacantecos to convey the same information.
2. A norm was selected if it had been produced by two or three men, using statements that had the same meaning; unless a norm with the same translation had already been selected.
3. A norm was selected if it had been produced by two or three men, using the criteria stated in 1 and 2 above, except that one statement described doing an act and the other described not doing it; in such a case the statement describing doing the act would be selected as a norm, unless a norm with the same translation had already been selected.

in devising a typology of situations and defining a multiplicity of normative domains.

There was considerable consensus among the three informants. They virtually always agreed on what behavior was good or bad. That is, the same normative statement was never used by one man to complete a 'good' frame ('John is good because ...,' and 'he is respected because ...') and by another man to complete a 'bad' frame. The only two exceptions are (1) wearing shoes, which is a sign of becoming a non-Indian or Ladino, and (2) taking a low-status religious office, which is both a sign of being poor and of caring more about religious service than social prestige. Both of these norms refer to major points of conflict or strain in Zinacantan.

The three men were also quite similar in the number of statements they produced about different aspects of Zinacanteco life. A classification of the statements into twenty-one *ad hoc* categories showed that all three produced a very large number of normative statements concerning the system of religious offices, politics, and law (see Appendix 1). However, the classification also revealed some striking differences. One of the informants, Chep, produced a very large number of norms concerning personal appearance, which fits in with the fact that he is the most careful dresser of the three. Romin was more concerned with kinship than were the other two, which may be related to his history of living alone with his mother for much of his life, without a father and siblings. Shun, the oldest and least literate of the three, produced the largest proportion of norms concerning aggression and violence. He is a controversial political leader in Zinacantan, and, according to gossip, he and the leader of the opposing faction have been involved in some lurid political murders.

The domain of Zinacanteco norms was defined as the corpus of 775 statements that remained, after eliminating redundant and idiosyncratic statements. The rest of this chapter presents the method for analyzing the structure of the domain.

B. Describing the structure of norms with the sorting task

The structure of Zinacanteco norms was analyzed by discovering how the normative statements are organized into clusters. The clusters were identified by a sorting task, in which individuals were given a deck of 100 cards, each one with a Tzotzil statement typed on it, and were asked to place similar norms in the same pile. For example, many subjects placed the norms about growing corn, organizing agricultural workers and being wealthy in the same pile; these norms formed part of a set that was labeled the Economic Cluster.

This method of describing the structure of norms is based on the assumption that normative statements are grouped on the basis of general dimensions or ideal types.[1] When individuals make judgments about the similarity among statements, they will use whatever dimensions or types are most salient in that situation. Insofar as the members of a community make the same judgments of similarity, it can be inferred that they are using the same underlying dimensions.

A great deal of variance among individuals can be expected in most domains, because many alternative dimensions may be salient and because several different kinds of relationships can be involved in judgments of similarity.[2] Consider, for example, how Zinacantecos would respond to the following three statements, if they had to judge which two were most similar: (1) he is rich, (2) he lends money, (3) he has taken expensive religious offices. Each pair seems to refer to a common underlying dimension, i.e., (1) and (2) refer to economic actions, (2) and (3) refer to service; and (1) and (3) refer to wealth and status. One might expect Zinacantecos to divide equally among these three pairings. In fact, most subjects grouped 'he is rich' with 'he lends money,' as will be shown in the next chapter. This indicates that the dimension of 'economic activity' is more salient in the structure of Zinacanteco norms than the dimensions of 'service' or 'status.'

It was possible to identify distinct clusters of norms in Zinacantan because there was considerable consensus in judging the similarity among normative statements in the sorting task. Each cluster consists of norms that were placed in the same pile by many subjects, and were not placed together with a norm from another cluster by many subjects.

The clustering is assumed to be generated by underlying general dimensions that constitute the similarity among the particular statements that were placed together. This assumption was tested and verified by conducting a second sorting task, as will be described in Chapter 6. The second sorting task included new statements that were

---

[1]For a discussion of the assumptions implied by using judgments of similarity to analyze cognitive structure, see Romney *et al.* (1972).

[2]Previous research indicates that judgments of similarity among pairs of terms are determined not only by the synonymous relationship between the terms (e.g., big – large) but also by other relationships such as 'whole – part' (e.g., bird – wing) and 'object – attribute' (e.g., mouse – small). For studies of the basis for making similarity judgments, see Flavell (1959) and Flavell and Stedman (1961). These references are discussed in D'Andrade (1970).

designed to represent the underlying dimensions of various clusters; the results show that these statements were placed in the predicted cluster by most subjects. The analysis of the structure of Zinacanteco norms also assumes that the dimensions that are identified by the sorting task are general and apply to many different situations. After all, it would be of little interest to identify the dimensions of meaning that Zinacantecos use only when they sort slips of paper! This assumption was tested and verified by examining the grouping of norms in several different situations (see Chapter 6).

The remainder of this chapter describes how the sorting task was conducted and how the results of the sorting task were analyzed to identify clusters of norms. The content of the norm clusters and their relation to the social structure of Zinacantan will be described in the next chapter.

Step Four: Selecting 100 representative norms

The sorting task required the selection of about 100 normative statements from the corpus of 775 that had been elicited by the substitution frames. This was necessary both because few Zinacantecos could read and remember many more than 100 statements, and because the computer programs for analyzing the resulting data could not handle more than that number of items. Procedures for data collection and computer analysis were being developed by a group of anthropologists studying semantic domains, and the sorting task was designed so that their techniques could be applied where they seemed useful.[1]

The 100 norms were selected by employing two highly literate informants to sort the 775 statements on the basis of similarity. Each statement was typed on a slip of paper, and the two men were instructed to sort the slips, using whatever criteria of similarity they wished. Afterwards, they explained to me the criteria they had used in grouping norms. The 775 statements included many that were almost synonymous, e.g., 'he doesn't know how to play the violin well,' and 'he doesn't know how to play songs on stringed instruments.' I expected that both men would group such similar norms together, and that we could then select one norm to represent the pile. In this way, a

---

[1] A. Kimball Romney and Roy D'Andrade, working with Michael Burton and John Brim, introduced me to sorting techniques and informed me about methods of computer analysis. For a discussion of different methods of analyzing the structure of semantic domains, see Romney (1972) and Romney *et al.* (1972).

smaller number of normative statements could be selected to represent the corpus of 775 norms.

In the end, the representative norms were selected on the basis of the work of one of the informants, called Palas. He completed the task in a day and formed his piles on the basis of similar types of behavior. For example, he placed into one pile all the twenty-one norms about illicit sex, e.g., flirting with girls, breaking into women's houses at night, incestual relations, etc. He explained this pile as consisting of norms about 'chasing women.' After he sorted the norms and explained his criteria for grouping, Palas was instructed to select one or more norms to represent each pile.[1] These 100 representative norms were used in the sorting task and they are listed in the next chapter.

As the list shows, Palas selected fifty-eight norms describing 'bad' actions and attributes and forty-two norms describing 'good' actions. This imbalance was caused by the fact that each of the informants who completed the substitution frames produced about 1.7 times as many completions for the two 'bad' frames than for the two 'good' frames. Some explanations for this pattern will be considered in the next chapter.

The other informant, Marian, was a much slower reader and did something very unexpected. He took a week to do the task and formed his piles on the basis of a reasonable sequence of events. For example, he placed the statement 'he molests girls' and 'he doesn't know how to present his case before court' into the same pile and then explained their similarity by telling a story about a man who got into trouble with girls and then couldn't defend himself when he was brought to court. Marian's work was not used in selecting the norms.[2]

The list of 100 norms appears to be a valid representation of the domain of Zinacanteco norms. Judging from my own knowledge of the community, the norms appear to be common expressions that refer to most of the attributes that are relevant to respect and rank among adult men. Other researchers in Zinacantan, who have studied the language,

[1]Palas had originally sorted the norms into seventy-six piles, with 2 to 41 norms in each pile, plus 33 norms which were not grouped with any others. He was then instructed to select one or more normative statements to represent each pile, with the general guidelines of an eventual total of 100 representative statements and a ratio of one representative statement for every seven slips. The representative statements were supposed to state the meaning of the slips in the pile on a more general level, or were to sample the slips. About 75 of the representative statements were among the original 775, 20 were made up by Palas, and 5 were made up by myself with his approval.

[2]Marian's conception of how norms are associated in terms of a *reasonable sequence* certainly deserves further exploration. However, it was too complex to consider in this first attempt to describe the structure of a normative system.

the process of settling disputes and the content of gossip, agree with this evaluation.[1]

However, the selection of the 100 norms has the methodological shortcoming of relying very heavily on the judgments of one man. Therefore, after the sorting task was completed and the major norm clusters were identified, the process of selecting representative norms was repeated, and the sorting task was done again. The procedures and results of this test are described in Chapter 6.

Step Five: Recording judgments of similarity with the sorting task

Thirty-five Zinacanteco men were employed to sort the 100 normative statements on the basis of similarity. Each man who did the sorting task was given a shuffled deck of 100 slips of paper, with a normative statement typed on each slip. He was asked to study the norms, with my help if necessary, until he could read them all. Some subjects spent four entire days learning to read or memorizing the norms, and two men could not learn to read them and did not complete the task. All the men were paid for their time, according to the customary wages paid by members of the Harvard Project. The pay included a meal, and ranged from eighty cents to two dollars a day depending on age, skill, and transportation costs.

Once the subject could accurately read aloud each norm, he was given a room to himself and was asked to sort the slips into ten to twenty piles according to similarity. No information was given on the type of similarity, except in a few cases where the men pushed for further clarification. In those cases, I pointed out two slips referring to stealing, 'he steals squash' and 'he steals horses,' and said something like: 'for example, you might think these two norms are similar.' No further clarification was ever given. All the men seemed to understand the instructions except for two who sorted the statements on the basis of whether the first word of each normative statement was the same; their results were not used.

After the sorting was finished, I interviewed each man about the criteria he had used in grouping the norms. This was done to ensure that the norms had not been sorted on a random or playful basis, and

[1] The list of norms has been inspected and found 'reasonable' by Laughlin, who is producing a Tzotzil – English dictionary (n.d.), Haveland (1971), who has analyzed gossiping in Zinacantan, and Jane Collier (1973), who has studied the legal system and has collected many descriptions of legal cases. We expect that a systematic content analysis of the legal cases or the gossiping texts would show a great deal of overlap with the 100 statements, but this has not yet been done.

also to learn if the men would talk about general categories of norms. In the interview, I read aloud the statements in each pile, and then asked what these norms had in common. Five men could not give any explanation of why they had grouped the norms the way they did, and they were asked to sort the norms again. Three of them were able to explain what they had done the second time. The other two men were given a test to determine whether they were sorting norms randomly or systematically.[1] In the end, I had useable results from thirty men, after eliminating the men who could not learn to read, or who sorted the statements randomly or on the basis of the first word in the statement.

The men who did the sorting task were not randomly selected because it was difficult to locate people who were literate enough to perform the task. However, an effort was made to overcome the most obvious source of bias by including some older men and restricting the number of young boys who had just finished school. The thirty men had a mean age of thirty; six of them were forty or older and six of them were twenty or younger. The men came from four different hamlets in Zinacantan, and all but seven were married. These subjects are probably fairly representative of Zinacanteco males over sixteen who are somewhat literate. Their consensus in judging the similarity among normative statements was used to analyze the structure of Zinacanteco norms.

Step Six: Analyzing the clusters of norms

The results of the sorting task were analyzed to identify what sets or clusters of norms had been placed together by many of the thirty subjects. The first step in the analysis was to construct a 100 by 100 matrix, and record the number of men who had placed every possible pair of normative statements in the same pile. For example, if one of the men had judged norms A, C, D and F to be similar and placed them together in a pile, then I would enter a '1' in the matrix in six cells: the cell where norms A and C intersect, and the cells for norms A and D, A and F, C and D, C and F, and D and F. After all the judgments of the thirty men had been entered, the entries in each cell were summed, to show how many men had placed each pair of normative statements in the same pile.

[1]The test consisted of reconstituting six of the man's piles, removing two norms from each pile and shuffling them up, and then asking him to place each of the twelve norms in one of the piles. If the man placed most of the norms in the same way that he had originally placed them, I assumed that he was sorting on some systematic basis and included him in the data analysis. One of the men passed this test and one failed.

It should be noted that with this method, subjects who grouped the 100 norms into a few large piles produced more entries in the matrix than subjects who grouped them into many small piles. For example, a pile with two statements would result in one entry in the matrix, while a pile of eight statements would result in twenty-eight entries. To reduce the differential sensitivity of the matrix to 'lumpers' and 'splitters,' all subjects were limited to making between ten and twenty piles.[1]

The information in the matrix is represented by 'cluster diagrams,' in which similar norms are placed close together and are joined by lines. As an example, the figure below shows part of the cluster diagram for norms about economic activity. The four normative statements on the left side of the figure are placed close together because many subjects judged them to be similar; they form part of the Economic cluster. There is a double line between 'he is rich' and 'he grows corn well' because seventeen or more subjects placed these two norms together; similarly, there is a double line between 'he is rich' and 'he lends money.' Norms that were placed together by twelve to sixteen subjects are linked by a single line, and norms that were placed together by fewer than twelve subjects are not linked by a line, e.g., 'he grows corn' and 'he treats poor well.' The norm 'he respects God' is placed far from these four norms and is not linked to any of them by lines, because it was not judged to be similar to any of these norms by twelve or more subjects. Therefore, 'he respects God' is not part of the Economic cluster; instead it is linked to other norms concerning religion.

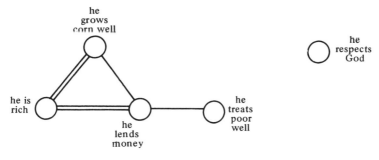

Figure 4.1

The degree of consensus represented by single and double lines on the cluster diagrams was set so as to maximize visual clarity. A trial-

[1]Seven of the thirty subjects made between 10 and 12 piles, while six made 18 to 20 piles.

and-error process showed that if consensus by a smaller number of subjects was represented by connecting lines, then the boundaries of individual norm clusters became blurred because there were many lines across clusters. If the level of consensus was raised, then many within-cluster connections were lost.

After determining the general range of consensus that would produce the clearest visual pattern, a standard set of rules for drawing lines between norms was devised. First, the number of subjects that could be expected to place any two norms together by random chance was calculated. This 'random number' is equal to the number of subjects (thirty) divided by the average number of piles into which the norms were grouped. Single lines were drawn between two norms if they were judged to be similar by 2.5 to 3.4 times the random number. Double lines were drawn if there was consensus by 3.5 times the random number. Finally, I checked the possibility that these arbitrary cutting points had distorted the definition of norm clusters; the consensus level was lowered and I found that most of the connections at this lower level were within clusters (indicating no distortion) and not across clusters.

These cluster diagrams are the basis for the analysis of Zinacanteco norms in the next chapter. The diagrams show the structure of norms in a form that is relatively easy to grasp. It is immediately apparent that some norm clusters are clearly separate from each other, i.e., there are no lines between them, while the boundary between other clusters is less clear. The relative centrality of particular normative statements can also be seen, i.e., some statements are linked to all the statements in the cluster, while others are more peripheral and are only linked to one or two statements in the cluster.

The major disadvantage of the diagrams is that the spatial location of norms is somewhat arbitrary. It was not possible to construct clear diagrams and at the same time place norms so that the distance between them exactly reflected the number of subjects that had judged them to be similar. It would be useful if computer methods could be developed that would produce such precise diagrams. Some of the available methods for computer analysis of the sorting data were tried out.[1] The results are consistent with the cluster diagrams, but they are much more difficult to represent.

[1]The matrix generated by the sorting task was analyzed by a computer program for hierarchical cluster analysis. The program is described in Johnson (1967). There has been a lot of recent work on programs for cluster analysis. Some of it is reviewed in Wallace (1968).

Summary

The Frame-Sorting Method was developed to produce a reliable description of Zinacanteco norms from the actor's point of view. The domain of norms was defined as the corpus of normative statements elicited by four substitution frames, excluding idiosyncratic and redundant statements. The structure of norms was analyzed by measuring the perceived similarity among a representative set of norms, and then constructing diagrams to show the sets or clusters of similar norms. This method resulted in a valid model of Zinacanteco norms, as will be shown in the following chapters.

5

ZINACANTECO NORMS
AND THE SOCIAL ORDER

THE FRAME-SORTING Method produced a model of the norms of Zinacantecos. It identified a series of norm clusters that represent the cognitive categories in terms of which Zinacantecos perceive and evaluate each other. This model provides, for the first time, an adequate empirical referent for the concept of 'the norms of a community.' Previous studies of norms or values have either ignored the problem of describing native categories of norms or have used unreliable methods (see Chapter 2).

The following two chapters constitute a detailed analysis of Zinacanteco norms. This chapter first analyzes the content and structure of the norm clusters that were defined by the sorting task, and presents some survey data on the hierarchical organization of norms. The second part of this chapter considers some of the relationships between the norms and social organization of a community. The next chapter describes several tests that confirm the validity and reliability of the model of Zinacanteco norms.

Part One: A model of Zinacanteco norms

The two cluster diagrams which follow represent the model of Zinacanteco norms that was produced by the sorting task. These diagrams show that the normative statements are divided into two distinct sets: norms about being good and norms about being bad. The two sets are subdivided into clusters of similar norms. My interpretations of the basis of similarity within each cluster suggest that 'good' clusters focus on the major institutions of Zinacantan, such as the religious and economic systems, while most of the 'bad' clusters refer to non-institutionalized, or personal attributes such as violence and incompetence. The hierarchical ordering of the norm clusters also suggests a correspondence between norms and social structure. The norm clusters that Zinacantecos perceive to be most important are those that refer to the major formal organizations of the community. The following discussion analyzes the 'good – bad' distinction, the content of the norm clusters and their hierarchical structure.

Table 5-1 Good Norms

Political cluster

P1* he knows how to talk Spanish well

P2* he is good at getting people released from jail

P3* he is good at settling disputes

P4* he is good at making intelligent, wise, reasonable statements at meetings

P5 he is good at giving orders at the town hall

P6 he is good at respecting and obeying the president of Zinacantan

P7 he is good at accepting orders and doing his duty in his community

P8 he has learned to read and write well

P9 he wants to become a Ladino (a non-Indian)

Religious cluster

R1* he respects God and performs his religious duties well

R2* he is good at accepting the duties of Ritual Advisor

R3* he takes religious offices and performs them well

R4 when he has a religious office, he is good at performing the rituals at the fiesta of San Sebastian

R5 he has taken all four religious offices and performed well in them

R6 he is good at accepting the duty of riding a horse for fiesta rituals

R7* when religious office holders ask his help, hs is good at accepting this duty

R8 he is good musician at the rituals of the religious office holders

R9 he is good at ringing the church bell when he is sacristan

R10 he is good at paying the tax for fiestas

Economic cluster

E1* he is good at growing beans

E2* he is good at being the representative of a group of farmers

E3* he is a good corn farmer

E4 he feeds his workers well (primarily farm workers)

E5* he is good in lending people money

E6 he treats the poor well

E7* he is rich

E8 he is a good farmer and gardener

Kinship cluster

K1*   he receives many presents (of liquor) from all his friends (who come to ask him favors)

K2*   he has a good heart and doesn't get angry

K3*   he is good at giving soda to his mother-in-law

K4   he conducted a proper courtship for his wife

K5*   he treats his wife and children well

K6   he takes good care of his godchild

K7   he is friendly with his ritual kinsmen

K8   he is a good, successful go-between for arranging marriages

K9   he calmly listens and hears the truth in what is said

K10   he doesn't chase the go-between out of his house when his daughter is asked for in marriage

K11   he talks with a very good heart (kind, generous, friendly)

Not in a cluster

01   he is a curer, good at stopping sickness due to witchcraft

02   he is good at accepting the duties of being a curer

03   he is a well-dressed man, his clothes are clean and well made

04   he is good at paying his debts

*An asterisk identifies the norms that were used in the second sorting task, which is discussed in Chapter 6.

Table 5-2   Bad norms

Violent cluster

V1*   he picks fights too much when he's drunk

V2*   he separates from his wife too much

V3*   he murders people too much, like a Jew

V4   he reprimands others to much

V5   he is a curer but can't cure sickness

V6   he is a witch and makes other sick

V7   he gets drunk too much

V8   he is always getting put in jail

V9   there is a lot of bad gossip about him

V10   he had intercourse with his ritual kinswoman

V11* he chases after women too much

V12   he makes a public spectacle of himself when he gets drunk

V13   he beats his wife too much

V14   he's always hitting people

V15* he whips his children too much

Lazy cluster

L1*   he is a lazy corn farmer

L2*   his children don't have enough to eat

L3*   he doesn't want to help people out by working for them

L4   he is too lazy, and unhappy when he works

L5   he doesn't have a penny

L6*   he doesn't pay his debts

L7   he spends the day sleeping

L8*   doesn't wash himself (he is dirty)

L9   he gives away his children; he doesn't want to raise them

Incompetent cluster

N1* he is deaf and can't understand when people talk

N2* he doesn't know how to talk to Ladino bureaucrats; he's too stupid (doesn't know Spanish)

N3 he stumbles and can't walk well, lame

N4* he can't play stringed instruments (violin, harp, guitar)

N5 he just shakes with fear when he talks at the town hall

Crafty cluster

C1* he informs too much on people's wrongdoings

C2* in a dispute he changes sides, according to which side is winning

C3 he gets people put in jail too much

C4 when disputes are being settled, he interferes and disrupts the settlement

C5* he lies too much

C6 he deceives and tricks people, goes back on his word

C7 he criticizes and mocks others too much

C8 when someone does wrong, he lies and gets them into worse trouble, falsely accuses them

C9 he cheats his relatives out of their land (steals their land)

Irreligious cluster

I1* he doesn't want to take a religious office

I2* when asked to help a religious office holder, he refuses to accept this duty

I3 he is arrogant and uncooperative when he has the position of setting off firecrackers at fiestas

I4* he won't lend people money

I5 he doesn't give out corn gruel properly when he has a religious office

I6 he doesn't want to pay his workers

I7 he doesn't respect God and perform his religious duties

Not in a cluster

05 he steals horses too much

06 he steals squash too much

07 he can't talk or listen with intelligence, with reason

08 he doesn't know how to settle disputes

09 he doesn't know how to take care of himself (poor clothes, and undignified behavior)

010 he doesn't care how he looks or behaves

011 he can't have children because he is sterile

012 he doesn't want to get married

013 he doesn't obey his father

014 he doesn't care if his relatives or friends are sick

015 he rejects his daughter's suitors too much

016 he doesn't want people to bow to him

*An asterisk identifies the norms that were used in the second sorting task, which is discussed in Chapter 6.

The Good – Bad distinction

The cluster diagrams clearly show the importance of the good – bad distinction for the Zinacanteco normative system (henceforth referred

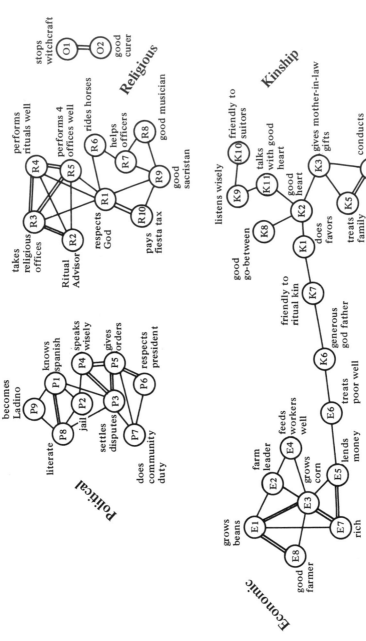

Diagram 5.1 Clustering of Good norms

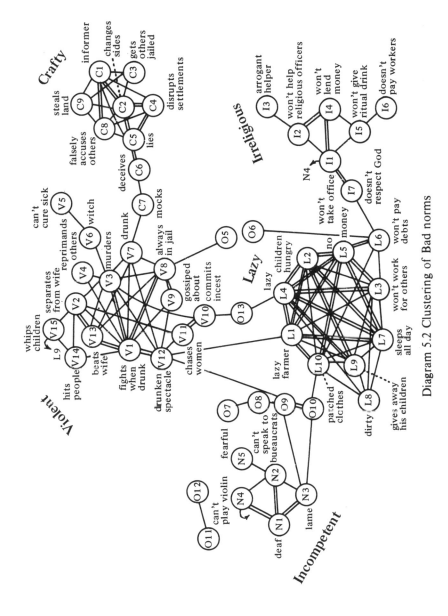

Diagram 5.2 Clustering of Bad norms

to as the Good and Bad sets of norms). On the diagrams, norms are placed close together and are joined by lines if they were judged to be similar by many subjects in the sorting task. As discussed in the previous chapter, norms are linked by a double line on the diagram if there is a strong connection between them (if the number of subjects who placed them together is at least 3.5 times larger than the number that would be expected from random placement of norms). Pairs of norms are linked by a single line if there is a moderate connection between them (if they were put in the same pile by 2.5 to 3.4 times the expected number of subjects). A strong or moderate connection among ·Bad norms requires consensus by fewer subjects than a strong or moderate connection among Good norms. This is because the sorting task included 58 Bad norms and only 42 Good norms.[1]

The Good and Bad norms are represented by two separate cluster diagrams because there was not one instance in which a Good and Bad norm were judged to be similar by many subjects. One diagram contains all the norms concerning obviously bad attributes, such as 'he is a murderer,' or 'he doesn't respect God' and the other diagram contains all the obviously good attributes, such as 'he is a good farmer' or 'he respects God.' Thus, the Bad norms are those that were grouped with obviously bad attributes, even though some of them are not obviously bad to Americans, e.g., 'he doesn't have a penny.'

The distinction between the Good and Bad norms was apparent from the beginning of my description of Zinacanteco norms. In completing the substitution frames, the three informants almost never used the same statement to complete a Good and a Bad frame, as was discussed in the last chapter. When I observed some of the subjects doing the sorting task, I noticed that they all began by placing the norms into two piles, one Good and one Bad. The results of the sorting task show that all the subjects agreed that none of the Good norms was similar to any of the Bad norms, with the exception of two Good norms about becoming a Ladino.[2] These findings are not surprising, since the Good – Bad distinction was built into the two pairs of substitution

---

[1]The number of subjects who would place two norms together, if placement were random, is equal to the number of subjects who performed the sorting task divided by ·the average number of piles into which the statements were partitioned. The mean number of statements per pile was the same for the 42 Good statements and the 58 Bad ones: 5.8 per pile. The Good statements were divided into an average of 6.2 piles. Therefore, there was about one chance in six that an individual subject would place any two Good statements in the same pile, and for the 30 subjects combined, the random number of subjects placing the two statements in the same pile would be 4.8, or 1/6.2 times 30. The Bad statements were divided into an average of 8.5 piles. For the Bad statements the random number is 3.5 or 1/8.5 times 30.

frames: 'Marian is good because ...', and 'Marian is not good because ...'; 'he is respected because ...' and 'he is not respected because ...'

The primacy of the Good – Bad distinction in the structure of Zinacanteco norms is also consistent with the findings of previous research on cross-cultural dimensions of meaning. Osgood and his associates (1964) have isolated three basic factors that can be used to define the meaning of concepts in different cultures: the 'Evaluative,' 'Potency' and 'Activity' factors. These dimensions emerged from independently factor analyzing the adjectives used in different languages. The evaluative dimension is the most powerful across cultures; it is 'represented by scales such as good – bad, pleasant – unpleasant and positive – negative' (1964:173).

This universal importance of moral evaluation as a component of meaning implies that few words or statements are evaluatively neutral; instead a crucial part of their meaning is the information they convey about the goodness or badness of what is being referred to. The universality of the Good – Bad component of meaning also suggests that there may be some corresponding universal component of social structure, such as stratification.

The extra-ordinary consensus in Zinacantan on how particular activities are evaluated is probably far from universal. Societies that include publicly recognized subcultures or divergent reference groups would probably show considerable disagreement in evaluating particular normative statements. Thus, if the Ladinos who live in Zinacantan had been included in this study, there would have been much less consensus. Or if such a study were conducted in the United States, there would probably be low consensus in evaluating statements like 'he is

---

[2] The norm, 'he wants to become a Ladino,' was grouped with Bad norms by 11 subjects and grouped with Good norms by 19 subjects. The age of the subject accounts for most of the variance in how this norm is treated. Of the 19 men who grouped the norm with Good norms, 13 were younger than thirty-one, while 9 of the 11 men who grouped it with the Bad norms were thirty-one or older. The other exception is a minor one and consists of one older subject who grouped the norms 'he knows how to talk Spanish well' and 'he wants to become a Ladino' with two Bad norms about being arrogant and heartless (I3 and O10 on the list in this chapter).

These exceptions suggest that the present homogeneous normative orientation of Zinacantecos may eventually split into two factions or reference groups, with the younger men approving of assimilation into the wider Mexican culture and the older men rejecting it. However, it is possible that the difference between age groups results from life cycle, not from changes over historical time. Young men in Zinacantan have relatively low status in the community and have not yet made a major investment in their status by financing their wedding and religious office. Therefore, the young may always be more open to assimilation than the old.

good at organizing anti-war demonstrations.' The high degree of consensus in Zinacantan is consistent with the absence of clearly defined subgroups in the Indian community.

Because of the absence of subcultures, Zinacantecos do not systematically reject the evaluative meaning of a statement on the ground that it originated from a group with opposing conceptions of good action. The evaluative meaning of most of the norms elicited by the substitution frames was clearly indicated by including the words *'toh'* or *'tol,'* meaning 'too much,' or the word *'lek'* meaning 'doing something well.' But even the norms that lacked these obvious evaluative markers were categorized in the same way by all subjects, e.g., 'he doesn't have a penny.'

The high level of consensus on the Good – Bad distinction does not mean that Zinacantecos never disagree on how to evaluate a particular concrete act; on the contrary, they devote considerable energy to justifying or condemning each other's actions and engaging in legal disputes. However, once an action is described by a particular set of words, these words define the act as Good or Bad and there is no disagreement on their evaluative meaning. Verbal statements give clear meaning to ambiguous events, therefore, Zinacantecos argue about how to describe 'what really happened' because they realize that the words used to describe an event may affect their lives more than the event itself. Verbal statements probably have this function in all societies, but they are particularly powerful in communities like Zinacantan, where there is a high degree of consensus on the evaluative meaning of statements, and where there are no clearly defined subcultures.

The four clusters of Good norms

Diagram 5-1 shows two clearly distinct Good clusters, labeled Political and Religious, and two clusters that are linked to each other, Economic and Kinship. The four clusters encompass all the major social institutions of Zinacantan. The Political cluster includes the political and legal system for resolving disputes and organizing collective action within Zinacantan and with the external society. The Religious cluster refers to participating in the community-wide system of religious offices, either by taking offices oneself or by assisting office-holders. The other clusters concern success in the agricultural economic system and generosity in participating in the kinship system.

According to the assumptions discussed in Chapter 4, each cluster consists of norms that share a common dimension, and this dimension was the basis for grouping the norms together in the sorting task. The label of each cluster and the discussion below present my interpretation of what these dimensions are. The dimensions were identified simply by inspecting the diagrams; the validity of these interpretations of the clusters was later tested, as will be described in the next chapter. The content and underlying dimensions of the Good clusters will now be examined in more detail, followed by a similar examination of Bad clusters.

The common dimension underlying the *Political cluster* concerns being an effective leader in political and legal affairs. The group of norms on the bottom of the cluster concern political leadership within Zinacantan; it includes giving orders at the town hall and respecting the local president (P6). The norms at the top of the cluster describe political relations with the outside Ladino society. They include speaking Spanish, being literate and using these skills to extricate Zinacantecos from Ladino jails in San Cristobal (P2). The fourth norm in this group refers to leaving Zinacantan and becoming a Ladino, which is the only Good norm that was placed with Bad norms by many subjects. This suggests some ambivalence about being skillful in dealing with the outside world. On the one hand, these skills can be used to benefit Zinacantan; on the other hand, they can lead to leaving the community or exploiting it.

Settling disputes is the central normative statement in the Political cluster. It has the largest number of connections to other norms in the cluster, and is linked to both external and internal political norms. In Zinacantan, settling disputes requires having the respect of the contending parties, being able to speak well and make convincing moral arguments, and in general, having the reputation for being a fair and important person.

In the *Religious cluster,* the underlying dimension is obvious. All ten norms, and only these, refer to participation in the Catholic – Maya religious system. The top four norms concern participation in the system of religious offices, and each one has strong or moderate connections with all of the others.[1] The other norms in the Religious cluster are less densely inter-connected and refer to specific roles involving helping religious office holders during fiestas (R6, R7, R8), assisting in carrying out church activities (R9), and paying the taxes that help finance religious ceremonies (R10). The central norm in the cluster (R1) can be literally translated as 'he knows how to behave in

[1]This high degree of consensus may not be significant, because two of the norms are very close in meaning (R3 and R4), and the other two (R2 and R5) refer to behavior that requires already having performed the behavior referred to in norms R3 and R4.

relation to God,' or 'he respects God and performs his religious duties well.' This norm has the largest number of connections and is also the only one in the cluster that is connected to both the norms concerning taking religious offices and to those concerning assisting religious office holders.

The *Economic cluster* focuses on being a successful, generous farmer. Three of the norms in this cluster concern skill and success in growing corn and beans and four concern wealth and generosity.[1] The link between farming and wealth is obvious, since selling surplus corn is the only way of obtaining wealth for most Zinacantecos (see Frank Cancian, 1972). The link between farming, wealth and generosity might be less obvious to an American. In their view of the moral universe, Zinacantecos seem to perceive personal or family resources as converted into benefits for the community. Thus, being rich is perceived as very similar to lending others money, at no interest; and being a good corn farmer is seen as similar to being generous in feeding one's agricultural workers. A similar pattern is evident in the Political cluster, where the ability to give orders (P5) is linked to accepting orders and doing one's duty for the community (P7).

The *Kinship cluster* is the weakest of the four. It is a loosely connected string of normative statements, and has only one set of three interconnected norms, whereas the other clusters have many such 'closed networks.' This cluster seems to focus on kinship relations; all norms about kinship are in this cluster and eight of the eleven norms in the cluster concern relations with current or prospective kinsmen.[2] The remaining three norms are about being helpful and friendly (K1, K2, K9), and many of the other norms in the cluster concern being friendly and generous to kinsmen. The common theme of generosity explains the links between the Economic and Kinship clusters.

The weakness of the Kinship cluster may be related to the absence of Good norms that refer to central kinship relations. There are only two Good normative statements about a man's relations with his wife, children or parents, but there are eight such Bad norms. This suggests that obligations to close relatives are membership norms and not ranking norms; therefore they were not elicited by the substitution frames.

[1] Norm E6, 'he treats the poor well,' is part of the chain of norms about generosity that links the Economic and the Kinship clusters. It was included in the Economic cluster because, at a reduced cut-off point, it has more connections with this cluster than with the Kinship cluster, while the reverse is true for the other norms in the chain.

[2] The number 'eight' includes the norm about being a go-between (K8); the go-between will become a ritual kinsman of the couple and their families at the wedding ceremony.

Perhaps everyone is expected to fulfill central kinship obligations and no one receives special respect for doing so; only failure to meet these obligations is noticed.

These four Good clusters were defined by the cluster diagram, which showed a connection between two statements if twelve or more subjects placed them in the same pile in the sorting task. The clusters include all but 4 of the 42 Good norms. Moreover, the same definition of clusters emerges if a lower cut-off is used (consensus by ten or eleven subjects, or 2 to 2.4 times the random rate). There are forty-eight connections between norms at this level and thirty-four of them link two norms from the same cluster; the other fourteen connections are across clusters with seven of them between the Kinship and Economic clusters.

In sum, the actions and attributes that define a respected Zinacanteco man are clearly organized into four clusters: Political, Religious, Economic and Kinship. The first two showed up most clearly in the diagram, reflecting the relatively high degree of consensus among subjects in placing political and religious norms. In later sections of this chapter, I will show that the degree of consensus in defining Good clusters is related to two factors: (1) the importance of the cluster to Zinacantecos, and (2) the extent to which the cluster refers to a community-wide, formal organization.

The five clusters of Bad norms

Five Bad clusters emerged from the sorting task: Violent, Crafty, Incompetent, Lazy and Irreligious. Their structure is shown in Diagram 5-2, and a quick examination of the diagram shows some obvious contrasts with the organization of the Good clusters. First, the clusters seem to focus on attributes that are personal or are not linked to particular organizations. The Bad clusters do not correspond to the institutions of Zinacantan, except for the Irreligious and Lazy clusters.

The second difference is that the Bad norms are less clearly organized into distinct clusters. Each Bad cluster has at least one direct connection with another cluster, for a total of four direct cross-cluster connections, compared to one for the Good norms.[1] Another complicating element is the presence of several norms that are not exclusively connected to any of the major clusters (05 through 016).

---

[1]In order to avoid further confusion, two of these four cross-cluster connections are not drawn in the diagram (V15 with L9, and N4 with I1).

Despite these complications, five major clusters can be identified.[1] Two of the most important ones are located at the top of the diagram. They are labeled Violent and Crafty and refer to the two major ways of causing conflict in Zinacantan: (1) through uncontrolled, drunken violence and (2) through willful malice. This same distinction between accidental disruption and intentional evil was independently identified in Jane Collier's detailed study of Zinacanteco legal cases (1973).[2]

The focus of the *Violent cluster* is shown by the two norms that have the largest number of internal connections: 'he picks fights when he's drunk' and 'he murders people' (V1 and V3). This cluster contains fifteen norms, more than any other cluster, and most of them concern harming others through irresponsible physical violence.

The theme of drunkenness appears in many of the norms and is indirectly involved in others. Thus, the two normative statements about conflict with one's wife actually involve drunkenness, since the sequence of events leading up to a marital separation is almost always that the husband gets drunk, then beats his wife, and then she leaves him. The cluster also includes several norms about sexual deviance and witchcraft.

The common dimension that seems to underlie these norms is committing deviant acts that involve physical violence, wildness, and the lack of self-control that Zinacantecos associate with getting drunk. Thus, stealing horses or craftily plotting to steal your neighbor's land are not part of this cluster, because they imply self-control, sobriety, and lack of violence. Similarly, norms about sexual deviance such as sterility or bachelorhood (011 and 012) are not included in the

[1]The Bad clusters were originally defined from the results of the first twenty subjects who did the sorting task. The questions for the survey had to be constructed at that time, and in this preliminary analysis, the boundaries between the five clusters were fairly clear. The results from all thirty subjects were used to construct Diagram 5-2, and in some cases it was necessary to use the following rules to determine to which cluster a norm belonged. The boundaries of the Bad clusters were defined by starting with the five clusters identified in the preliminary analysis, and including a norm in one of these clusters if it met one of two criteria: (1) more connections with that cluster than all other clusters combined, at the cut-off point of 2.5 times the random rate; or (2) the same number of connections with that cluster and all other clusters at the 2.5 level, and at least one more connection with that cluster than all others combined at the level of 2 to 2.4 times the random rate. According to these rules, the nine norms, 05 through 013, did not belong to any of the major clusters, and the chain of norms linking the Violent and Crafty clusters belonged to the Crafty cluster. Of the 58 Bad norms 3 were not linked to any norm at the 2.5 level. They are omitted from the diagram and are labeled 014, 015 and 016.

[2]Collier's book (1973) describes in detail the process by which different types of conflict are resolved by the Zinacanteco legal system. Her discussion of types of 'crimes' is especially relevant to the description of Bad clusters in this chapter. Her study and mine were done independently.

Violence cluster, but those concerning uncontrolled sexual activity, such as incest, are included. The only norms that do not fit with this interpretation are those about witchcraft, a planful, calculating activity, but these are the most peripheral norms in the cluster.

The *Crafty cluster* is difficult to label in one or two English words, although the unifying element in it seems clear. All the norms refer to controlled, verbal aggression, to harming others, and causing dissension by intrigue and deception. The basic elements of the cluster are well represented by the two key normative statements. One refers to informing on the wrongdoing of others (C1) which violates the Zinacanteco principle that it is up to the injured party to make complaints – others should not interfere and start trouble. The second norm, 'he changes sides in a dispute according to which side is winning' (C2), refers to a person who does not try to arrange a proper compromise, but intensifies the dispute by his self-serving position.

The *Lazy cluster* is the negative mirror image of the Economic Cluster, and describes the causes and consequences of economic failure. The ten norms in this cluster are the most densely interconnected of any cluster, which reflects high consensus on the similarity of each norm in the cluster to all of the others.[1] All ten norms refer to aspects of laziness and poverty; they concern unwillingness to work, unwillingness to care for one's children, slovenly appearance, and poverty. The cluster suggests a Calvinistic world view, where poverty is associated with laziness and not with exploitation or bad luck.

The *Irreligious cluster* consists of the negative side of the Good Religious cluster. Six of the seven norms in the cluster, and only those norms, refer to inability or unwillingness to perform religious obligations, especially those concerning taking religious offices or helping others who hold offices.

The final, *Incompetent cluster* is the most surprising of all the norm clusters. It seems peculiar to someone from our culture to include in the domain of norms statements that refer to incapacities over which the actor has little or no control, such as being deaf, lame, or fearful. If Americans were given the frame 'he is bad because ...' it is very unlikely that they would produce normative statements like 'he is deaf.'

A quick inspection of the norms in the Incompetent cluster might suggest that this cluster is the negative, mirror image of the Political

---

[1] Although the Lazy cluster has the largest number of internal connections, it also has many direct connections with other clusters and many indirect ones through the nine 'unattached' statements (labeled 05, 06, etc.). The only cluster with which it has no connections is the Crafty cluster.

cluster, since three of the five normative statements describe attributes that would make a person incapable of settling disputes and assuming political leadership (N1, N2, N5). However, the two statements that most directly concern political leadership are not included in the cluster: 'he can't talk or listen with intelligence' (07) and 'he doesn't know how to settle disputes' (08).

A more careful analysis indicates that the underlying dimension in the Incompetent cluster is various kinds of disabilities or inabilities. The dimension may be more specific, and refer to incompetence that has few anti-social implications, since none of the norms in the cluster concern behavior that injures others, or implies failure to meet the major role obligations of the average man. This interpretation accounts for the absence of strong links between the Incompetent cluster and the two norms about being sterile and unmarried (011 and 012), which do concern failure to meet role obligations. It also explains why the four norms about anti-social incompetence (07, 08, and 010) are not a part of the cluster, although they have two connections to it.

In sum, the model of norms indicates that Zinacantecos organize their negative evaluation of each other in terms of the disruption and conflict produced by uncontrolled violence and calculated deception. Failure to be economically successful or to participate in the system of religious offices are also major dimensions of the normative system. The final dimension concerns physical and mental incompetence.

Consensus in categorizing norms

The model of Zinacanteco norms that has just been discussed is based on the sorting task, that is, on consensus among subjects in their judgments of similarity among norms. The cluster diagrams show considerable variance among subjects in judging particular norms.[1] Of the 164 pairs of Good norms that are in the same cluster, in Diagram 5-1, 16 pairs are connected by double lines. Only for these pairs of norms was there consensus among seventeen or more of the thirty subjects.

Although the overall consensus on placing a particular pair of norms in the same pile is not very high, the clustering of connections is fairly impressive, especially for the Good norms. Cluster Diagram 5-1 shows that whenever as many as twelve subjects agree that two norms are similar, these two norms come from the pool of norms that constitute a cluster; that is, there are almost no connections between

[1]The level of consensus may be higher than it appears because the maximum possible consensus may be restricted by variance across subjects in the number of piles into which norms were placed.

clusters.[1] It appears that the boundaries of clusters are much more stable than particular connections within them.

This suggests that the cognitive structure of norms consists of a set of general clusters or dimensions on which there is high consensus. Each of the clusters might be seen as subdivided by several overlapping subdimensions, with relatively low consensus on their relative salience. For example, the Political cluster is subdivided by several dimensions, such as leadership within Zinacantan v. external leadership, or actively settling disputes and helping others v. more passive attributes.

The particular groupings produced by individual subjects are based on these subdimensions, as one can see in the following, randomly selected examples that show how three subjects sorted norm P2, 'he is good at getting people released from jail.' One man grouped this norm with norm P4, 'he speaks wisely,' along with norms about doing people favors (K1) and being good to the poor (E6). Another man grouped norm P2 with three different norms from the Political cluster concerning being respectful and authoritative (P5, P6, and P7), along with three norms from the Kinship cluster about being friendly and good-hearted. A third man placed norm P2 together with all the norms in the Political cluster except the one about becoming a Ladino, which this man grouped with Bad norms. Each of these three men sorted the norm in a different way, stressing different aspects of the role of getting people released from jail. However, each of them grouped the norm with one or more other norms in the Political cluster, a pattern that produced a coherent, bounded cluster in Diagram 5-1, with no consistent connection to other clusters.

The cluster diagrams show that Zinacantecos vary a great deal in the exact way that they categorize particular norms. However, there is considerable consensus on the general categories or dimensions that constitute the norm clusters.

The hierarchy of norms

The previous discussion has shown how Zinacantecos distinguish different categories or clusters of norms. The next issue to be considered in constructing a model of Zinacanteco norms is the hierarchical organization of the clusters. I will show that Zinacantecos perceive some clusters to be very important in determining the respect a man

---

[1] For example, if we examine the Political cluster we see a group of nine norms with sixteen connecting lines among them. Although most of these connections were made by only twelve to sixteen of the subjects, there is no line connecting any of these statements to one from another cluster.

receives in the community, while others are perceived to be relatively unimportant. An elaborate model of Zinacanteco norms might go on to examine whether the boundaries and importance of the norm clusters change in different social contexts. The issue was not systematically explored in my study, although I will present some relevant data in the next chapter.

The data on the hierarchy of norms comes from a survey that was conducted in Zinacantan and that will be described in detail in Chapter 8. The survey questionnaire was given to all adult men in the hamlet of Apas ($n = 114$) and half of the men in the hamlet of Nachih ($n = 108$). The questionnaire included a series of paired comparison questions, in which respondents were presented with two norms, each from a different cluster, and were asked which one was most important. For example, one of the questions was: 'There are two men, the first is good at settling disputes, the other is good at growing beans; which one is more respected'? There were twenty-three such questions comparing Good norms, and twenty-four comparing Bad norms. Each cluster was represented by two or three central norms.[1] (The questionnaire is translated in Appendix 9.)

Table 5-3 presents the percentage of respondents that selected particular norms and norm clusters in the paired comparison questions. These data show that the Good clusters are clearly rank ordered but the Bad clusters are not.

The first two columns of figures in the table give the average percentage of respondents that selected each norm as more important in eliciting respect.[2] For example, the first norm listed on the table is 'he respects God' and the figures show that it was selected by an average of 70% of the Apas respondents, in the four paired comparison questions in which it was included.[3] The second two columns of figures are

[1] The four Good clusters and the Violent and Lazy clusters were represented by three norms, those with the identifying numbers '1,' '2,' and '3.' The Incompetent, Crafty and Irreligious clusters were each represented by two norms, those with the identifying numbers '1' and '2.'

[2] In interpreting these percentages, it should be remembered that all norms from one cluster were not paired with all norms from other clusters, in the interview. Therefore, some of the variance in the average importance of normative statements is the result of what statements happened to be paired. For example, part of the reason for the low average importance of the norm about being a leader of a group of farmers is probably that it happened to be paired with two very popular norms: 'he respects God' and 'he settles disputes.'

[3] The figure of 70% is an average of the percentages for four paired comparison questions. That is, 'he respects God' was selected by 72% of the respondents in the question that paired this norm with 'getting people released from jail,' and was selected by 60%, 67% and 81% in the three other questions in which it appeared; which averages out to 70%.

Table 5-3 Hierarchy of norms and norm clusters

Cluster and norm	Mean % selecting norm		Mean % selecting cluster	
Good clusters	Apas	Nachih	Apas	Nachih
Religious			64	62
Respects God	70	59		
Ritual Advisor	60	60		
Takes religious offices	61	67		
Political			56	54
Settles disputes	75	60		
Speaks Spanish	51	59		
Gets people out of jail	42	44		
Economic			46	42
Grows beans	52	46		
Farm leader	43	48		
Grows corn	44	32		
Kinship			21	23
Good heart	29	27		
Does favors	21	24		
Gifts to mother-in-law	13	17		
Bad clusters				
Crafty			60	60
Changes sides	62	58		
Informs	57	61		
Violent			48	51
Murders	65	62		
Separates from wife	41	45		
Fights when drunk	37	45		
Lazy			47	39
Children hungry	54	43		
Won't help work	42	35		
Lazy	46	38		
Irreligious			46	44
Won't help religious office				
holders	51	54		
Won't take religious offices	42	35		
Incompetent			24	35
Can't talk to bureaucrats	24	40		
Deaf	24	29		

n = 114 for Apas
n = 108 for Nachih

simply the average of the percentages in the first two columns, for norms from the same cluster.

It should be noted that the range of the percentages for individual norms is wide, especially for the Good norms, which range from 13% to 75% in Apas. This shows that there is a considerable consensus among respondents on some of the questions. If there were no consensus, then the percentages would approach 45% (since about 10% of all respondents did not select either normative statements but said that they were both the same). The wide range of percentages also indicates that there is a consistent degree of importance given to a norm over different comparisons. For example, 'doing favors' was consistently judged to have low importance, regardless of whether it was paired with 'being a good ritual advisor' or 'being a good corn farmer.'

The data in Table 5-3 show a clear rank order for the four Good norms clusters. The Religious cluster is the most important. An average of 64% of the respondents from Apas selected the norms from this cluster as more important than the norms from other Good clusters; and each of the three individual norms in this cluster was selected by a high percentage of respondents. The Political cluster is second in importance; the Economic cluster is third,[1] and the Kinship cluster is the least important by far, with a mean of only 21% of the respondents selecting the norms in this cluster as more important than other norms.

It should be noted that the responses from the two hamlets of Apas and Nachih produce the same rank ordering of clusters, and the responses to individual norms are also very similar.[2] This indicates that the rank order of norm clusters obtained from the paired comparison questions is not a random occurrence.

The rank order of the Bad clusters is not so clear. In both hamlets, the Crafty cluster is obviously the most important and the Incompetent

[1]The relative importance of the Political and Economic clusters is less clear in Apas, if one examines the mean percentage of respondents selecting the individual norms in these clusters. The Political cluster is ranked higher than the Economic only because of the extreme importance given to one norm, 'he is good at settling disputes.'

[2]There are also some interesting differences between the two hamlets. In Nachih, respondents are more likely to select norms concerning a person's ability to deal with the Ladino world – for example, speaking Spanish, talking to bureaucrats or being a farm leader. This is consistent with the greater proximity of Nachih to the Pan American highway and to the Ladino city of San Cristobal. It also fits with the apparently higher rates of literacy and bilingualism in Nachih. Respondents from Apas are more likely to favor norms concerning traditional activities, such as respecting God, settling disputes, being a successful farmer and not being lazy and poor. In line with the interpretation presented in Part Two of this chapter, it could be argued that contacts with Ladinos are part of the institutionalized social world of the Nachih, and therefore they place a higher importance on norms like speaking Spanish.

cluster is least important. The other three clusters fall between these two extremes and seem to have a very similar degree of importance.

Several other patterns in the responses to the paired comparison questions suggest that the hierarchy of Good norms is clearer than the hierarchy of Bad norms. First, respondents from both hamlets are slightly more likely to say that two Bad norms are 'the same,' thereby refusing to select one as most important. The mean percentage of the 'the same' responses in Apas is 7% for the Good questions and 11% for the Bad questions. Second, both hamlets show somewhat less consensus in answering the Bad paired comparison questions, as is reflected in the higher range of percentages for Good norms in Table 5-3.[1] Thus, there is less agreement among Zinacantecos on the relative importance of various Bad activities.

Part Two: Social organization and the normative system

The model of Zinacanteco norms presented above describes the content and structure of the normative beliefs of a particular community. The survey data describes the hierarchical order of these beliefs. On the basis of this description, it is possible to raise more general questions about the social causes and correlates of normative systems: Why do Zinacantecos have this set of norms as opposed to some other set? What features of the social organization of Zinacantan explain the particular content and structure of their normative system? The following discussion attempts to answer these questions. It draws on the results of the sorting task and the survey, and on hunches and speculation, in order to formulate some general theoretical guidelines about the relation between normative systems and social organization.

The description of Zinacanteco norms suggests four general principles about the relationship between norms and social structure. First, the content of being good corresponds to successful participation in the major institutions of a community. Second, the relative importance of different good activities depends on the extent to which the activities are incorporated into organized social groups. Third, the content of being bad corresponds to unsuccessful participation in major institutions, e.g., 'he is a poor, unsuccessful farmer.' Bad norms also include participation in deviant roles and failure to meet the minimal requirements of being an adult man, e.g., 'he doesn't want to get married.' The

---

[1]Consensus can be measured by subtracting the percentage of subjects who selected one norm in a paired comparison question from the percentage who selected the other norm, the higher the consensus, the greater the difference. In Apas, the mean difference for the Good questions is 41, and for the Bad questions it is 35.

fourth principle concerns the structure of the normative system. It asserts that clusters of norms will have strong internal connections and will be clearly distinguished from other clusters and clearly rank ordered insofar as they refer to the activities of institutionalized groups or roles. These four principles will now be discussed in more detail.

The content and relative importance of Good norm clusters

The Good norm clusters define ways of being good or positive social identities. The model of Zinacanteco norms indicates that each of the four ways of being good corresponds to the most important social organizations that are differentiated in that community.

The Political, Religious, Economic and Kinship clusters represent the major institutionalized activities in Zinacantan that are carried out by differentiated, supra-household groups or sets of roles. 'Major institutions' can be roughly defined as patterned activities that: (1) are publicly defined as useful to the community and as the legitimate concern and responsibility of the community; and (2) are predictable or are routinely performed according to shared expectations. Institutions are distinguishable or are differentiated from each other insofar as the activities are performed by clearly bounded, organized groups (e.g., a family, a business) or a set of roles (doctor – patient) and are set apart from other activities by such mechanisms as occurring at a special time or place, having a distinctive name, or requiring a special costume.

The Political and Religious clusters are the most clearly defined clusters on the diagrams, i.e., they are the only clusters with no external connections. They focus on the only two activities in Zinacantan that involve all members of the community and are the legitimate concern and responsibility of all Zinacantecos: (1) the system of political offices for settling disputes and organizing community projects, and (2) the system of religious offices for providing ritual protection for Zinacantan and for exchanging individual wealth for community prestige.[1] Furthermore, the political and religious organizations are the only community-wide, formal organizations in Zinacantan, with clearly defined rules for entering and leaving positions, a clear chain of command and definite rights and duties for the occupants of office.

The Economic cluster concerns the major institutionalized activity of adult men: obtaining food and cash, so as to provide for their family

[1]Most religious ritual at the supra-household level is carried out by the formal organization of religious office holders. However, a great deal of political and legal activity occurs outside of the formal political organization, and centers on an informal and fluid network of local leaders.

and obtain respect from the community. The most important economic activity in Zinacantan is corn farming, and it is done by groups of men from different households who rent land together in the lowlands. This is the third most important type of supra-household social group, after the political and religious organizations. The Kinship cluster is the weakest of the four clusters on the diagram and it is the only one that does not refer to a supra-household social group.[1] It is perhaps significant that most of the normative statements in this cluster describe the more public, out-going aspects of kinship such as ritual kinship and affinal relationships; they do not focus on the relationships among the members of a household.

The hierarchical order of the Good clusters also has a clear relationship to the social organization of Zinacantan. As discussed above, the Religious cluster is perceived as most important, and it focuses on the most significant, formally organized, community-wide organization in Zinacantan: the system of religious offices. The Political cluster is ranked second, followed by the Economic and Kinship clusters. This rank order corresponds perfectly to the extent to which these activities are carried out by well organized, supra-household groups.[2]

In sum, the normative system of Zinacantan clearly illustrates the first two principles about norms and social organization that were stated earlier: (1) the content of being good corresponds to successful participation in the major institutions of a community; and (2) the relative importance of different good activities depends on the extent to which the activities are incorporated into organized social groups.

The four Good clusters not only correspond to the major institutions of Zinacantan, they also correspond to the conventional categories that social scientists use to describe the institutions of any society. The list of clusters reads like the chapter titles in a standard ethnography: Political and legal organization, Religion, Economics, and Kinship. These areas of social activity are used for chapter titles because they often correspond to distinct institutions. For each activity, there

[1] Most activities with kinsmen are not carried out by clearly bounded groups such as a lineage. Although Zinacanteco kinship is organized patrilineally in some respects, it operates primarily as a bilateral system. Every household tends to have a unique set of kinsmen, and of course ritual kinsmen, with which it is interdependent. The researchers who have worked in Zinacantan disagree on the importance of patrilineages; see Vogt (1970).

[2] The organization of curers in Zinacantan might also be interpreted as a group with responsibilities for the community as a whole and as a system with considerable formal organization. However, almost all the activities of curers are performed for individual families; Zinacantecos do not know who most of the curers are, outside of their hamlet; and becoming a curer is primarily a process of self-definition through having the appropriate dreams rather than public conferral.

tends to be a special group, physical location, and set of rights and duties.

The importance of the four institutional areas that correspond to the Good clusters has been noted by many sociologists, among them Talcott Parsons. In an early work he identifies four 'empirical cluster-ings of structural components of social systems': (1) Territoriality, force and the integration of the power system, (2) Religion and value-integra-tion, (3) Instrumental achievement structures and stratification and (4) Kinship systems (1951:153-67). In his later work, these structures are interpreted in terms of the idea of four general functions.[1]

These four structural components correspond very closely to the four Good clusters. To Parsons, they represent 'the main line of inter-nal differentiation' (1951:151) of societies, as suggested by the anthropological and sociological literature; my own knowledge of the field confirms his conclusion. For most societies at the same stage of differentiation, there tend to be distinct social organizations focusing on politics and law, religion, economics and kinship.

In sum, the Zinacanteco categories of good action that were iden-tified by the inductive Frame-Sorting Method correspond to the categories developed by social scientists. The four clusters also corres-pond to the activities or institutions that are structurally differentiated in Zinacantan. The process of differentiation seems to be similar in all societies. Therefore, for societies at the same stage of differentiation as Zinacantan, the areas of politics and law, religion, economics and kin-ship will probably be the major clusters of Good norms. The relative importance of these clusters in determining prestige in a particular society will depend on the extent to which they are formally organized on a community-wide basis.

The content of the Bad Clusters

The overall structure of the Bad norms is quite different. As stated in the third general principle about norms and social organization,

[1]Parsons' four functional categories are adaptation, goal attainment, integration, and pattern maintenance. The adaptive function, according to Parsons (1961) is the focus of economic organization, and corresponds to the Economic cluster. The function of goal-attainment is the focus of political organization and corresponds to the Political cluster. Pattern maintenance concerns the maintenance of institutionalized values and of in-dividual commitment to these values; this function is often performed by religious beliefs and rituals and seems to correspond to the Religious cluster. However, the fourth function of integration has little correspondence with the Kinship cluster. Parsons views the legal system as the focus of integration in modern societies but in Zinacantan legal and political organizations are not clearly differentiated. Thus, the match between the four clusters and Parsons' four functional categories is less clear than the match with the four structural components.

some of the Bad clusters correspond to institutionalized activities carried out by well organized groups, but most of them do not. Instead, they focus on partially-institutionalized deviant roles and on membership norms that define the minimal requirements for participating in Zinacanteco social life.

Two Bad norm clusters describe unsuccessful participation in major social institutions. The statements in the Lazy and Irreligious clusters concern failure in farming and in the system of religious offices, e.g., 'his children do not have enough to eat' (L2), 'he does not want to take religious offices' (I1). These clusters are the negative, mirror images of the Economic and Religious clusters, and focus on the absence of the attributes described in the corresponding Good cluster. Twelve of the seventeen statements in these two clusters describe *not* doing something, whereas twenty-seven of the total fifty-eight Bad statements are 'not' statements.[1] (In Tzotzil, 'not' is indicated by the word *'mu'*; see Appendix 8 for a list of the statements in Tzotzil and English.)

It is interesting to note that the two institutions that are most closely related to the stratification system of Zinacantan – the economic and religious systems – also appear as the focus of Bad clusters. The kinship and political systems, which are not an integral part of the stratification system, are not the focus of Bad clusters. The sorting task included many statements about not settling disputes and causing conflict, but they are spread out over different clusters (e.g., N1, O8, C3, V1). There were also many statements about kinship relations but they are dispersed over several clusters (V2, L2, O11).

In sum, one type of activity described by the Bad norms is lack of success in the major institutions of the community. The data further suggest that lack of success will be the focus of a Bad cluster or a negative social identity, only if the institutions are closely related to the stratification system.

The other type of activity described by the Bad norms concerns attributes that are not organized into social institutions and that therefore have been labeled 'personal' attributes. Three of the five Bad clusters focus on personal attributes: Violent, Crafty and Incompetent. The relationship between the norms in these clusters and the social organization of Zinacantan can be interpreted in several ways.

---

[1] Several features of the structure of the Bad norms, as opposed to the Good, suggest the 'marked – unmarked' distinction in Linguistics. Like unmarked elements in languages, Bad norms (as opposed to Good) are larger in number, more varied in structure and show more morphological irregularity. See Greenberg (1966).

One interpretation is based on the assumption that attributes like craftiness and violence are, by their nature, important to every type of activity or social institution. For example, a person who is deceitful or deaf or violently drunk would disrupt any kind of cooperative activity, whether it concerned religion, politics, farming or kinship. Because these attributes are relevant to many institutions, the normative statements that describe them do not form clusters that focus on particular institutions. One difficulty with this interpretation is that some of the norm clusters with an institutional focus incorporate normative statements about personal attributes; for example, statements about being an industrious, fast worker were included in the Economic cluster in the second sorting task, as will be discussed in the next chapter. Furthermore, some societies incorporate attributes like violence into social institutions. For example, in my subculture, drunken violence is part of the social role of being a poor disreputable male, even though it is known that other types of people also get involved in drunken fights.

Another approach is to interpret 'violence' and 'craftiness' in Zinacantan as the focus for partially institutionalized deviant roles. The social organization of Zinacantan does not include well developed deviant roles and institutions as we have in our own society, e.g., 'organized crime,' dope addicts, the Klu Klux Klan, subversives.[1] In our society, these institutions probably organize normative beliefs about being bad in the same way that the political and religious institutions of Zinacantan organize beliefs about being good. Zinacantan lacks such institutions; however, the basic concepts underlying the Violent and Crafty clusters seem to be something like a deviant identity or negative stereotype. One cluster focuses on a type of person who is violent, drunk and irresponsible; the other focuses on a person who is scheming, deceitful and malevolent. These two stereotypes define or structure the major ways of causing conflict in Zinacantan.

This interpretation is supported by the finding that 23 of the 24 statements in these two clusters are positive statements that describe doing something, e.g., 'he murders people,' 'he lies.' In contrast, only 8 of the 34 Bad statements that are not included in the Violent or Crafty clusters describe doing something, as opposed to not doing something. It seems likely that if there is a coherent set of beliefs that describe doing things that are negatively evaluated, then these beliefs define a deviant role.

[1]The closest that Zinacantan comes to a deviant subculture is a group of about ten young men who buy corn from Zinacantecos at the market and then resell it, at the same price, making a profit because they use false measures. These men seem to be held in contempt by other Zinacantecos, yet they view themselves as successful merchants. See Capriata, 1965.

A final interpretation of the content of the Bad norms is based on the distinction between ranking and membership norms. The Good norms are ranking norms and describe ways of participating in major social institutions so as to obtain a high degree of respect and approval. The Bad norms not only describe how to elicit disapproval by failing to succeed in the major institutions or by participating in deviant roles; they also include membership norms. Membership norms have been defined as shared beliefs about what behavior is required of a member of the community in good standing (see Chapter 1). In Zinacantan, they seem to include attributes like feeding one's children, refraining from committing murder and being able to hear and walk. Conforming to these norms does not bring approval and respect, but deviance brings censure or perhaps ostracism. Many of the norms in the Incompetent cluster seem to be membership norms.

Comparing the structure of Good and Bad norms

These alternative interpretations of the Bad norms raise more questions than they answer. However, several important differences between the Good and Bad norms are clear. First, all of the Good norm clusters focus on a major social institution, and describe activities that are performed by organized groups of people. Each of the important supra-household social organizations in Zinacantan is matched by a Good norm cluster. Second, only two of the five Bad clusters describe activities that are carried out in organized groups (Lazy and Irreligious). The Bad norms that do not focus on institutionalized groups seem to describe deviant roles and membership norms.

These different ways in which the Good and Bad norms are related to the social organization of Zinacantan can be used to explain some of the differences in the structure of the two sets of norms. The Frame-Sorting Method and the cluster diagrams revealed several differences. First, the original completions of the substitution frames produced almost twice as many Bad norms as Good. In particular, there were many Bad norms but almost no Good norms concerning central kinship relations. Second, the cluster diagrams show that the boundaries of the Bad clusters are less clear than the Good clusters; that is, there are more cross-cluster connections. The diagrams also show that the Good and Bad clusters are not mirror images of each other. Finally, the survey data on the hierarchy of norm clusters shows that there is less consensus on rank ordering the Bad norms.

These differences can be explained on the grounds that all the Good norms refer to socially organized, institutionalized activities, while most of the Bad norms refer to activities that are not organized. Social institutions consist of shared expectations about what sets of actions and attributes should go together in a particular type of situation. Without such socially organized consensus, it is almost true by definition that there will be less agreement on the boundaries and rank order of the Bad norm clusters. Furthermore, since Bad norms refer to personal, relatively unorganized activities in addition to participation in major institutions, they are more numerous than Good norms. For the same reason, the structure of the Bad norms is not symetrical with the Good norms.

It should be noted that the absence of an institutional focus may also account for why the Bad clusters do not correspond to conventional social science categories. To my knowledge, there is no single set of categories for the domain of personal attributes that is accepted by most social scientists. Compared to institutions, these attributes can be categorized in many more ways within a culture, and the most salient categories probably vary more across cultures. Thus, it is extremely unlikely that an American social scientist with minimal information about Zinacantan would have predicted the distinction between uncontrolled violence and purposeful deceit, or the emergence of the incompetent dimension. On the other hand, the good clusters probably could have been predicted before collecting any data, although many of the details of the clustering would not have been anticipated.[1]

The differences in the structure of Good and Bad norms thus seem to derive from the absence of an institutional focus for the Bad norms. As mentioned before, this absence may be related to a special feature of relatively undifferentiated communities like Zinacantan: the lack of institutionalized deviant roles and subcultures. In societies where deviance is socially organized around deviant roles or despised out-groups, one would expect the structure of Bad norms to reflect these institutions. The social definition of an out-group with a real or imagined deviant subculture would probably produce a great increase in consensus on the structure of Bad norms (see Durkheim, 1933; Erik-

---

[1]Americans probably would not link personal resources and assertiveness with community service, as the Zinacantecos do. For example, in the Political cluster, given the forty-two Good statements, a social scientist would probably have constructed a cluster of norms focusing on political and legal functions and including the kinds of behavior referred to in statements P3, P4, P5 and P7 concerning being a responsible leader and mediator. However, he may well have excluded the norm about respecting the president (P6) from this cluster because it suggests submission rather than dominant leadership, and would probably place the three norms about knowing Spanish (P1, P8 and P9) in a cluster by themselves, or perhaps exclude them altogether from the domain of norms.

son, 1966). The increased consensus would remove one of the differences in the structure of the Good and Bad norms. Furthermore, insofar as Good clusters emerged that focused on the absence of participation in the deviant culture, there would tend to be the same number of Good and Bad norms and the two sets of norm clusters would tend to be symmetrical.

The extent and the consequences of institutionalizing Bad attributes is an empirical question that merits substantial comparative research. In the meantime, it seems possible but unlikely that deviance from all membership norms (e.g., murder, deceit, insanity) could be linked to particular deviant roles or institutions. For this to occur, a society would have to be so polarized that all bad attributes were assigned to out-groups like the Jews, the blacks, or the Communists. In the absence of such total institutionalization, I would expect the structure of Good and Bad normative beliefs to show the same differences in other societies that they show in Zinacantan.

This discussion has attempted to explain the relation between the social organization of Zinacantan and the structure of norms. Insofar as these explanations are adequate, specific predictions can be made for the normative systems of all societies. Perceptions of Good action will be organized into clusters that correspond to the major institutions of the society and will be similar for all societies at the same level of differentiation. Perceptions of Bad actions will not all be organized around institutions and therefore will show less consensus; consensus will be low insofar as membership norms cross-cut institutions and there is an absence of real or imagined deviant subcultures. These predications will hopefully be amended and refined as the result of future comparative research on normative systems.

6

VERIFYING THE MODEL OF ZINACANTECO NORMS

THIS BOOK BEGAN by posing a problem. I argued, in Chapter 2, that studies of norms should begin with a careful description of the categories of actions and attributes that are important to the members of the community; and I pointed out that there were no available methods for producing such a description. My solution to this problem has been presented in the last two chapters. I have presented the Frame-Sorting Method for describing normative systems and discussed the model of Zinacanteco norms that resulted from applying this method.

In this chapter, I will consider whether or not my solution is a good one. In particular, is the model produced by the Frame-Sorting Method a valid representation of the normative beliefs of Zinacantecos? I will test three aspects of the validity of the model, which can be labeled reliability, generality and accuracy.[1] Each aspect will now be stated as a testable proposition. The model is valid insofar as the data support these propositions.

First, if the Frame-Sorting Method is *reliable,* then the norm clusters defined by the sorting task are the major categories of norms, and the same clusters will emerge if different statements are included in the sorting task. Second, if the model is *general,* then the norm clusters represent the cognitive categories that Zinacantecos use to evaluate and understand each other, and these categories will be used in many situations besides sorting statements into piles. Finally, if my interpretations of the underlying dimensions of the norm clusters are

---

[1]The concepts 'reliability' and 'validity' have been defined in many different and overlapping ways in methodological discussions. See Campbell and Stanley (1966, chapter 1) for a discussion of the meanings of validity.

accurate, then these interpretations can be used to predict how other normative statements will be grouped.

This chapter presents three sets of data that make it possible to test these propositions. In the first test, the sorting task was repeated with a new set of normative statements. The results of the second sorting task are very similar to the first, and this confirms both the reliability of the sorting method and the accuracy of the interpretations of the norm clusters.

The second test was an interview in which respondents rated particular individuals on some of the traits described by the norms. The results show that individuals tend to be given similar ratings on norms drawn from the same cluster. This indicates that the clusters are general categories that are used in perceiving individuals, not only in placing slips of paper into piles. The interview also examined some of the differences between norms that are central to a particular cluster and norms that are peripheral. In the final test, the results of the survey were analyzed to determine whether norms from the same cluster elicit the same responses on a questionnaire. These results also confirm the generality of the norm clusters. They show that norms from the same cluster tend to be given the same relative importance and tend to be associated with the same actions.

The three tests will now be presented, in order. The discussion will be of most interest to readers who are concerned with the methodology of describing belief systems, or are interested in the details of the normative system of Zinacantan. Other readers may want to move on to the concluding section of this chapter.

Repeating the sorting task

The second sorting task confirms the reliability of the Frame-Sorting Method in identifying norm clusters. It supports most of the original interpretations of the underlying dimensions of the norm clusters, and suggests some new ones, as will be shown below.

The second sorting task was conducted in the same manner as the first, except that about half of the normative statements were changed. The 80 statements[1] that were used in the second sorting task included 37 'old' statements, from the original 100.[2] These statements consist of several key norms from each cluster, and they are marked with an

[1] Although 80 norms were originally used in the second sorting task, one was later excluded because it had an ambiguous meaning to most subjects.

[2] Three old norms were slightly altered for the second sort by omitting the words indicating that the behavior was good or bad (statements E1, K9 and V3).

asterisk on the lists in Tables 5-1 and 5-2, in the previous chapter. The 43 new norms are listed in Table 6-1, below. They are given a double identifying letter, to distinguish them from the old norms (e.g., PP for Political cluster).

The new norms include eighteen that were selected to test my interpretations of the clusters. These 'test norms' are marked by a plus (+) on the list below and are given the identifying letters of the cluster with which I expected them to be grouped.[1] For example, the original norms in the Incompetent cluster seemed to share a common element referring to physical deformities or an inability to learn valued activities. To verify this interpretation, new test norms about being cross-eyed and illiterate were included in the second sorting task (NN2 and NN3) and I expected that they would be grouped with the old norms that were retained from the Incompetent cluster (N1, N2 and N4).

The placement of the test norms in the second sorting task can be seen as testing the accuracy of my translation of the underlying dimension of each cluster. These norms were designed to represent my (English) interpretation of the clusters. In some interviews with three American tourists, I found that each test norm was in fact perceived as belonging to the American concept described in the interpretation.[2] If Zinacantecos, working in Tzotzil, also place the test norms in the appropriate clusters, then my translation of the underlying dimensions of the clusters is supported.

The other new norms were selected for several different reasons. Some of them were chosen to provide information about areas of behavior that seemed important but were not included in the 100 normative statements, although they were elicited by the substitution frames. Examples are: being stingy, being well-dressed, and being physically strong. Other norms were selected to give greater symmetry to the Good and Bad norms. For example, since 'informing on others' and 'getting drunk' turned out to be crucial Bad norms in the first sorting task, norms about not getting drunk and not informing on others were included in the second sorting task.[3] Finally, some of the new norms were labels that subjects had used in explaining the way they had grouped the norms in the first sorting task. All of these norms are

[1] Test norms that did *not* confirm my expectations are followed by a parenthetical note on the lists, indicating the cluster with which they were actually grouped.

[2] The informal interviews consisted of showing each person a randomly ordered list of the eighteen test norms (translated into English) and a list of the nine cluster labels with brief interpretations. The Americans were then asked to match each norm with one of the labels. All of the test norms were properly placed, with two exceptions.

[3] There was a bias against symmetry in the first sorting task because of the method of eliminating redundant statements. See the discussion in Chapter 4.

given the identifying letters of the cluster with which they were grouped in the second sorting task, in the lists below.

Table 6-1   New Good norms for second sorting task

Political cluster

PP1 he is an intelligent leader, good at giving orders and settling disputes

+PP2 he settles disputes well, without getting mad or changing sides

+PP3 he serves well on the *ejido* land committee

Religious cluster

+RR1 he celebrates the May fiesta well

+RR2 he respects the rituals and taboos of Good Friday

Economic cluster

EE1 he is good at selling things at the market

EE2 he is well dressed, clean, has well made clothes

EE3 he knows well how to grow flowers (for sale)

EE4 he is good at looking for work, making money

+EE5 he finishes his portion of farm work very quickly

EE6 he is strong and fearless

+EE7 he is an industrious worker

Kinship cluster

+KK1 he is good at buying candy for his children

KK2 he is good in giving food to visitors

+KK3 he is friendly with his neighbors

Not in a cluster

001 he doesn't inform on people

002 he doesn't drag people off to jail, he doesn't have people put in jail

003 he doesn't get drunk much

004 he doesn't do bad things (steal, lie, get mad)

The selection of a new set of norms for this sorting task also made it possible to assess the amount of bias introduced by depending so heavily on one informant in selecting the first set of 100 norms. In a few cases the particular concerns of this informant, Palas, had clearly determined which statement he chose to represent a group of norms.[1] I selected the new norms that were used in the second sorting task myself; therefore, insofar as the same clusters emerge in the two sorting tasks they cannot be attributed to Palas's idiosyncratic concerns.[2]

The second sorting task was done by twenty subjects. All but two of them were the same men who had done the first sorting task,

[1]For example, his skill in riding horses at fiestas probably influenced him to select the norm about riding horses to represent a large pile of norms about different ritual activities at fiestas.

[2]However, they might be attributed to a peculiar common culture that Palas and I built up, since I worked with him in selecting the first set of 100 representative statements.

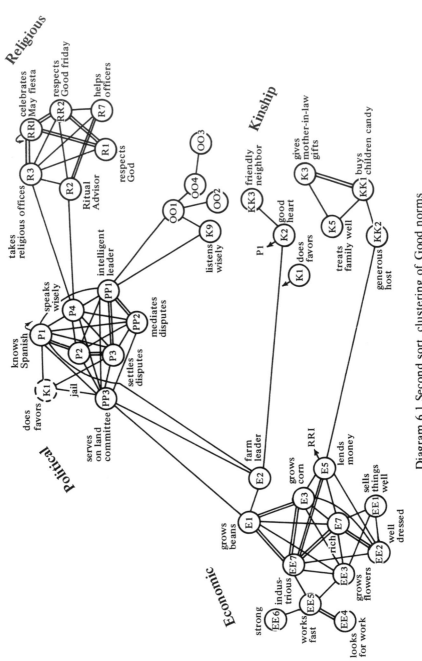

Diagram 6.1 Second sort, clustering of Good norms

because it was difficult to locate quickly other literate men. The time interval between the two tasks varied from two weeks to four months.

Verification of the Good norm clusters by the second sorting task

The results of the second sorting task are presented in the two cluster diagrams below. The diagrams were constructed somewhat differently from the diagrams in the previous chapter. Old norms are given the *same location* that they had on the first diagram, in Chapter 5, to make it easier to compare the two sets. New norms are located on the diagram according to the results of the second sorting task, using the same procedures that were described in the last chapter.[1]

The diagram of the Good clusters clearly shows that the Political, Religious and Economic clusters remain very much the same, even though half of the norms are different from those used in the first sorting task. All of the six test norms were placed in the predicted clusters (PP2, PP3, RR1, RR2, EE5, EE7). And the other new norms that are attached to the cluster generally fit in well with the original interpretations of the clusters. No systematic procedure was used to measure the degree of similarity between the results of the two sorting tasks. However, on the basis of inspection and the placement of the test norms, the two diagrams for the Good clusters appear to be quite similar.

In some cases, the placement of the new norms clarifies the original interpretation of the cluster. The Religious cluster picks up two test norms that refer to relatively private religious activity, while the original norms in the Religious cluster concerned participation in the community-wide system of fiestas and religious offices.[2] This result indicates that the Religious cluster includes private as well as public activities. The Economic cluster picks up five new norms concerning economic success: the capacity to work hard and make money (EE1, 3, 4 and 6) and the ability to dress well (EE2). None of these statements directly concerns farming, which confirms the interpretation that the cluster focuses on economic activities in general, not only on farming.

---

[1] The formula for calculating cut-off points for single and double lines between norms is the same as in the previous diagrams: two and a half and three and a half times the random rate. With twenty subjects and an average of 6.1 piles of Good norms, eight subjects must agree on placing two slips in the same pile to produce a single line on the diagram, and twelve must agree to produce a double line. For the Bad norms, the corresponding numbers of subjects are seven and ten.

[2] For example, the statement 'he respects Good Friday' (RR2) refers to religious observances on the individual or household level, such as eating white beans instead of black.

One of the major differences between the two diagrams of Good norms concerns the Kinship cluster, which is quite fragmented in the second sorting task. The old norms from this cluster that concern general helpfulness are not linked to each other but are connected to other clusters, primarily the Political cluster. In fact, the norm about doing favors for others (K1) moves entirely out of the Kinship cluster, into the Political cluster.[1] This fragmentation can be explained by my incorrect original interpretation of the cluster. I first thought that the underlying dimension of this cluster was general helpfulness, not kinship. Therefore, the second sorting task included only two old norms and one new norm about kinship, and none at all about ritual kinship. These few norms about kinship form a coherent cluster in Diagram 6-1 and are not linked to other clusters. If more of them had been included, the Kinship cluster would probably have emerged more clearly in the second sorting task.

Another major difference between the two diagrams is that the second diagram shows many more lines connecting norms, indicating a higher degree of consensus among subjects in the second sorting task.[2] Diagram 6-1 shows many more connections *within* each cluster, than Diagram 5-1. For example, in the first sorting task, the nine norms in the Political cluster show sixteen internal connections. In the second sorting task, the seven norms in the cluster (excluding K1) show twenty-one such interconnections, the highest possible number. There are also more connections *across* clusters; Diagram 6-1 shows six cross-cluster connections,[3] as opposed to none in Diagram 5-1. (Note that two of these connections are indicated by short arrows and a note in the legend of Diagram 6-1, to avoid confusion.)

The most obvious explanation for the rise in consensus is that the subjects were more experienced with the task on the second trial since

[1] For that reason it is drawn twice on the diagram, once where it originally was located on the first diagram, and once, in broken lines, up in the Political cluster.

[2] To make precise statements about relative consensus, it would be necessary to state mathematically how the number of subjects placing two statements together depends on the number of piles used by each subject. My approach only takes account of the mean number of piles used by all subjects.

[3] Some of the connections between these three clusters seem fairly easy to interpret. The new statement about serving on the land commission (PP3) was grouped with the Political cluster, as predicted, but it is also connected with two statements from the Economic cluster about growing beans (E1), and about being a leader of farmers (E2). The latter statement is also connected to the statement about speaking Spanish (P1) in the Political cluster. The only surprise in this is that such connection did not also show up in the first sorting task, since speaking Spanish is one of the crucial skills necessary for leading a farming group and dealing with Ladino landowners. In the first sorting task, 9 out of 30 subjects placed these norms together, which is less than twice the random rate, while in the second sorting, 10 out of 20 subjects placed them together.

the same men were used for both sorting tasks. Therefore, each subject was able to group the norms according to a more consistent set of categories, and make fewer mistakes. Each individual used similar categories, resulting in higher consensus.

The final new element in the second diagram is the appearance of a new group of five norms. Four of the norms are new ones (001, 2, 3 and 4). They were included to explore the symmetry of Good and Bad clusters, with the idea that, for example, craftiness seemed to be the opposite of many norms in the Political cluster, and, therefore, a norm about the absence of craftiness would be placed in the Political cluster. Instead, these norms formed a new 'absence of bad traits' cluster.[1] This 'cluster' merits little attention in itself; it is weak and also somewhat artificial, since two of the four new norms were not from the original list of 775 norms elicited by the substitution frames. However, it does provide additional evidence on the asymmetry of Good and Bad norms.

The new norms that were included in the second sorting task because they were the opposite of important Bad norms were not grouped with any of the four Good clusters. This suggests that these new norms are not important, since the four clusters are the major categories of Good norms. In other words, the major components of being Good are not the negative mirror image of the major components of being Bad. Therefore, researchers should not assume that a particular belief is a meaningful part of the normative system simply because it is the negation of an important norm.[2]

In conclusion, both sorting tasks show the same three major clusters of Good norms. They focus on leadership in politics and law, participation in religious activities at both the community and private level, and success in economic endeavors. Relations with kinsmen are the focus of a weaker fourth cluster. The model indicates that Zinacantecos believe that a man gains respect and prestige in the community by successful participation in these institutions; and according to all the information available about Zinacantan, their beliefs are correct.

Verification of the Bad clusters by the second sorting task

The results of the second sorting task for the Bad norms are shown in Diagram 6-2. They support the model based on the first sorting task,

[1] It is possible that three of these norms (001, 2 and 4) were grouped together because they are the only Good norms that are negative sentences; each one starts with the Tzotzil phrase meaning 'he is not capable at ...' (*mu sna*).

[2] This apparently incorrect assumption was made by William A. Scott in his study of community values (1959). Good norms were inferred to exist on the groups that they were the opposite of Bad norms that had been elicited from subjects (1959: 302, footnote 13).

with two major changes. First, the Irreligious cluster is fragmented; the three original norms that were retained have no links between them (norms I1, I2 and I4), although they were all interconnected in the first sorting task. One of the new test norms that was expected to be included in the Irreligious cluster was included (II1), but the other was grouped with the Violent cluster (II2: 'he is arrogant and uncooperative when he has the position of musician at rituals'). The collapse of the Irreligious cluster leaves only one stable Bad cluster focusing on institutions. The three Bad clusters focusing on personal attributes (Violent, Crafty and Incompetent) retained their clear boundaries in both sorting tasks.

Table 6-2   New Bad norms for second sorting task

Violent cluster
   VV1 he is grumpy and annoyed when he's spoken to, irritable
   VV2 he watches people from a distance with evil intentions, without speaking
   VV3 he calls other people stupid
   VV4 he is too angry and envious
   VV5 he spends all his money at bars
+VV6 he hits people too much, beats them up
+VV7 he threatens people too much that he's going to shoot them
   VV8 he scolds, reprimands his wife too much

Lazy cluster
   LL1 he doesn't know how to grow flowers
+LL2 he ran off to work on the plantations because he is lazy
+LL3 his hair is wild, he never has it cut (actually placed in Incompetent cluster)

Incompetent cluster
   NN1 he is dumb, stupid, wild-haired
+NN2 he is cross-eyed
+NN3 he doesn't know how to read or write

Crafty cluster
+CC1 he is always spreading gossip
+CC2 he intensifies disputes

Irreligious cluster
   +II1 he is no good as a Ritual Advisor
   +II2 he is arrogant and uncooperative when he has the position of musician at rituals (actually placed in Violent cluster)

Not in a cluster
   005 he doesn't have big curing ceremonies for his wife
   006 he is too stingy
   007 he doesn't want to buy bananas for his children
   008 he doesn't obey orders and do his duty
   009 he doesn't want his family to accompany him to fiestas

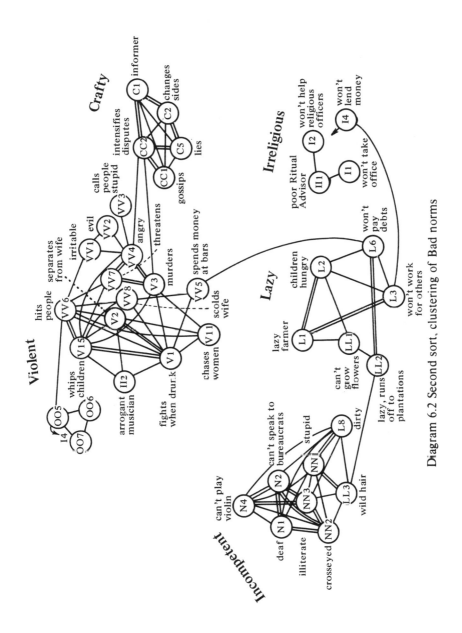

Diagram 6.2 Second sort, clustering of Bad norms

The second major difference in the results of the two sorting tasks is the shift of norms about sloppy, poor appearance. They move out of the Lazy cluster and into the Incompetent cluster. Thus, 'being dirty' (L8) was a central norm in the Lazy cluster in the first sorting task, but it is just as central to the Incompetent cluster in the second sorting task. Similarly, the test norm about being unkempt (LL3), which was expected to be included in the Lazy cluster, was in fact grouped in the Incompetent cluster.

Another new element is the suggestion of an additional cluster, focusing on stinginess, that is connected to the top of the Violence cluster. The three norms in this quasi-cluster (005, 6 and 7) are all new ones, specifically included to investigate the meaning of stinginess, since generosity was referred to in many of the Good norms. Once again, when new norms were included to test the meaning of the opposite of a behavior found to be important in the first sorting task, the new norms cluster together and do not closely attach themselves to any of the original clusters.

Outside of these changes, the results of the two sorting tasks are very similar. Violent, Crafty, Lazy and Incompetent are clearly defined clusters with many internal connections. Old norms that were linked in the first sorting task are also linked in the second, and the links between clusters remain the same.[1]

In sum, the second sorting task tends to confirm the original model of how Zinacantecos categorize ways of being good and being bad. Although the structure does change somewhat when different norms are used and the task is done at a different time, the overall pattern remains stable. The results indicate that the sorting task is a fairly reliable method for constructing a model of a normative system, and they confirm the accuracy of most of my interpretations of the dimensions underlying the norm clusters.

Verification of the clusters from the Person Perception Interview

The Person Perception Interview examined whether the norm clusters are general cognitive categories that are used in other situations besides doing a sorting task. In the interview, subjects were asked to rate particular people on the attributes referred to in the normative statements. The main purpose of this interview was to see if norm *clusters* define categories of similar attributes that are used in interper-

---

[1]That is, the connection of Crafty with Violent, Violent with Lazy, and Lazy with Incompetent and Irreligious.

sonal perception. If they do, then all the attributes from the same cluster should be treated as similar in rating individuals. For example, if a subject rates a person as high on one attribute from the Political cluster – such as settling disputes – he should also rate that person high on the other attributes – such as speaking Spanish and getting people released from jail. The validity of this method for testing the similarity of the norms within a cluster is supported by a study done by D'Andrade. In a re-analysis of several experiments, he found that 'traits which the observer considers similar will be recalled as applying to the same person ...' (1970:5).

The second purpose of the interview was to see whether norms that were central to a cluster on the cluster diagrams would be more powerful than peripheral norms in discriminating between respected and unrespected people. Subjects were asked to rate the two persons they most respected and the person they least respected. I anticipated that respected and disrespected people would be given very different ratings on central attributes like settling disputes, and less different (or more random) ratings on peripheral attributes that were not connected to any cluster.

The interview was given to twenty Zinacanteco men,[1] eleven of whom had done one or both of the sorting tasks. At the beginning of the interview, I asked each subject to name the person he most respected.[2] Then the subject rated the person on a three-point scale, for twenty attributes. For example, the first question, in translation, was 'Does [name of person] know how to settle disputes well? Does he know how to settle disputes a little? Does he not know how to settle disputes'? There was also a 'don't know' option. After rating the person on all twenty attributes, the subject rated a second person that he highly respected, and finally, he rated the person he *least* respected.

The 20 attributes included three central norms from the Political cluster, three from the Religious cluster and three from the Economic cluster. These attributes were used to test whether norms from the

[1]The interviews were done in a short period of time, just before we left Mexico, and the subjects were the first twenty men who appeared at our house.

[2]I told the subjects that I just needed to know the person's first name. This was done to ensure that the subject kept the same person in mind through all the rating questions, without necessarily divulging the identity of this person, since many people in Zinacantan have the same first name. After naming the person, the subject was asked an open-ended question: 'What is it about this person that you like and respect'? Most of the subjects responded by stating some of the more general norms used in the sorting task. The most frequently mentioned attributes for the respected men were: being reasonable, talking well, and having a good heart; for the disrespected men the most frequent attributes were: reprimanding others and talking angrily, and being drunk.

same cluster would elicit similar ratings. There was also one central norm from the Kinship, the Violent and the Crafty cluster.[1]

In addition, the attributes included eight norms of varying degrees of peripherality to the norm clusters, in order to compare central and peripheral norms. Two norms were weakly attached to a cluster (C7, K10); three were not attached to any cluster (02, 04, 010); and the three most peripheral norms were not even on the list of 100 representative norms.[2]

The results of the Person Perception Interview are presented in Table 6-3, which shows whether subjects gave a person the same ratings on attributes from the same cluster. For example, when rating the person they most respect, do subjects tend to give the person the same rating on two attributes from the Political cluster: (P3) 'he knows how to settle disputes' and (P1) 'he speaks Spanish well.' Two-by-two tables were constructed for every pair of norms from the same cluster that showed sufficient variance,[3] and for six randomly selected pairs of norms from different clusters. The data is presented separately for the three persons that were rated: the first, most respected man, the second respected man, and the third disrespected man. The table shows the direction of the association (+ or −) and its statistical significance or probability; the lower the number, the stronger the association.

The data in Table 6-3 give some support for the assumption that the norm clusters define general categories of similar attributes. The three pairs of norms that are significantly associated at the .05 level are pairs from the same cluster, and none of the six pairs from different clusters is associated this strongly. Moreover, all thirteen associations for pairs of attributes from the Political cluster and from the Religious cluster are positive.

[1] Another norm from this cluster was originally used: K1, does favors. But the manner in which it was restated in order to fit into the format of rating people, turned out to change its meaning. Therefore, the ratings on this attribute were not used.

[2] The three most peripheral norms were selected from a group of 33 norms that had no relation to any of the other original 775 norms, according to two informants. The three that were selected for the interview are: (1) 'he eats a lot of hot chili peppers'; (2) 'he sells salt'; and (3) 'he flees' (runs away from Zinacantan when in trouble). The distribution of ratings for each norm that was included in the interview is shown in Appendix 2.

[3] For some norms, all persons were given the same rating, e.g., respected people were all rated high on the attribute. Therefore, the degree of association between these norms could not be analyzed. This is indicated by the phrase 'no variance' in Table 6-3. For the other norms, the middle response category, 'he does it a little,' was combined with either the high or low category, so as to produce a more even distribution. The exception is the attribute 'rich,' for which the middle category was always combined with the high category.

Table 6-3   Association of ratings on two attributes from the same cluster

Cluster and pair of norms	Direction and significance of association		
	Man 1 Respected	Man 2 Respected	Man 3 Disrespected
1. Political			
(P3) Disputes and (P1) Spanish	+.12*	+	+
(P3) Disputes and (P2) Jail	+.02	+.02	+.02
(P1) Spanish and (P2) Jail	+	+.12	+.12
2. Religious			
(R7) Help and (R3) Take offices	No variance	+.005	+
(R7) Help and (R1) Respect God	No variance	No variance	+.12
(R3) Take offices and (R1)			
Respect God	No variance	No variance	+.12
3. Economic			
(E3) Corn and (E2) Leader	No variance	+.02	+
(E3) Corn and (E7) Rich	No variance	−	−
(E2) Leader and (E7) Rich	No variance	−	+
Six randomly selected pairs of norms	No variance	+	+.12
from different clusters**		−	−
		+	+

*Fisher Exact Test: Significance level indicated if p @ .125.
**Pairs for Man 2, in order: P3 and R3, P1 and R3, P2 and E3.
  For Man 3: R1 and E2, R7 and P1, E3 and P3.

However, the data for the Economic cluster do not support the assumption that attributes from the same cluster have a similar meaning. Three of the six associations are negative, and all three involve norm E7, 'he is rich.' During the interviews I noticed that the meaning of this attribute seemed to be different in the situation of rating another person than in the situation of doing the sorting task. Many subjects preferred to rate the people they respected as 'a little rich' even if they were obviously very rich, since it is immodest for Zinacantecos to admit to being wealthy. This suggests that in the situation of describing a particular person, 'being rich' has a negative meaning referring to immodesty as well as a positive meaning referring to economic success.[1]

The Person Perception Interview also examined some of the implications of the centrality of a normative statement in the cluster diagrams. The concept of the centrality of normative beliefs has been given considerable attention by other researchers, especially Rokeach.

[1]The alternative responses on this attribute were 'rich,' 'a little rich,' and 'poor.' See Appendix 2 for the distribution of responses on each attribute.

He defines centrality as the extent to which 'a given belief is functionally connected or in communication with other beliefs' (1968:5); and he has hypothesized that the more central a belief, the greater its resistance to change. Rokeach's efforts to test this hypothesis were hampered by the absence of an adequate measure of centrality (1968:58-61).

The cluster diagrams seem to be a useful way of measuring centrality. The findings reported below suggest that centrality can be measured simply by counting the number of connections between one normative statement and the other statements in a cluster.

The ratings obtained in the Person Perception Interview were analyzed to determine whether the centrality of a norm was related to its ability to discriminate between respected and disrespected people. For each norm that was included in the interview, I computed a number that represents its discrimination power. This number is the sum of differences between the ratings given to the respected and the disrespected men: the higher the number, the greater the discrimination power.[1]

Table 6-4 shows that central norms tend to be more powerful in discriminating between respected and disrespected people, although several norms do not conform to this pattern.[2] The norms are arranged

[1]For example, the data for calculating the discrimination power of the norm about settling disputes is given below. The discrimination power of the norm is equal to the difference between the number of subjects who rated the first respected man 'high' on settling disputes and the number who rated the *dis*respected man 'high,' or the difference between 13 and 2; plus the difference between the number who rated the first man 'medium' and the number who rated the disrespected man 'medium,' or the difference between 6 and 2, etc. The data for calculating all the discrimination power scores is presented in Appendix 2.

Method of calculating the discrimination power of 'settling disputes'

	1. Respected man	2. Respected man	3. Disrespected man	1-3	2-3	Sum of differences
High	13	13	2	11	11	22
Medium	6	4	2	4	2	6
Low	1	3	15	14	12	26

54 = Discrimination power

[2]One of the twelve central norms has a very low discrimination power: speaking Spanish. This can be explained after the fact on the grounds that speaking Spanish is an amoral type of ability, that can be used to help others or to harm them. The centrality of this norm to the Political cluster can be explained on the grounds that speaking Spanish is a necessary but not sufficient condition for settling disputes with the outside world. This suggests that there are different types of logical relations among the norms that

Table 6-4 Power of norms to discriminate between respected and disrespected people

Type of norm		Norm	Discrimination power of norm	Mean Discrimination power
Central to clusters	P1	knows Spanish	14	
	P2	helps out of jail	48	
	P3	settles disputes	54	
	R1	respects God	46	
	R3	takes offices	34	
	R7	helps officers	52	
	E2	farm leader	41	45
	E3	grows corn	50	
	E7	rich	42	
	K2	good heart	54	
	V1	fights if drunk	56	
	C2	changes sides	46	
Peripheral to clusters	K10	chases suitors	46	
	C7	mocks	50	38
Outside of clusters	02	curer	10	
	04	pays debts	43	36
	011	cares for sick	56	
Outside of 100		eats chili	9	
representative norms		sells salt	5	19
		flees	44	

on the table in order of decreasing centrality, and most of the low levels of discrimination power occur at the bottom of the table. The effect of centrality emerges more clearly in examining the mean discrimination power of different types of norms: the mean decreases from 45 to 19 with decreasing centrality.

The comparison of the mean scores for discrimination power suggests that the structural centrality of a norm is related to its social significance, as Rokeach has suggested (1968). The more connections a norm has with other norms on the cluster diagrams, the more likely that the attribute will discriminate between types of people or will be used as a basis for allocating prestige. This relationship between cognitive structure and social evaluation provides an intriguing lead for future research.

were judged to be similar in the sorting task, and that a norm may be central without in itself being an important social discriminator. More exceptions to the overall pattern occur among the eight peripheral norms, three of which have a discrimination power that is above the mean for the central norms.

Verification of the clusters from the survey

The final set of data for testing the generality of the norm clusters comes from a survey of all the adult men in two hamlets of Zinacantan. The survey contained many questions based on the normative statements that were used in the sorting task. If the clusters define general categories that are applied in many situations, then questions that include norms from the same cluster should elicit the same responses in the survey.

There are two sets of questions in the survey that are relevant to testing the generality of the norm clusters: the paired comparison questions and the association questions. In the paired comparison questions, as described earlier, respondents were presented with two norms from different clusters and were asked which one was most important. For example, one of the questions was: 'There are two men, the first is good at settling disputes, the other is good at growing beans; which one is more respected'? There were twenty-three such questions comparing Good norms, and twenty-four comparing Bad norms.[1]

If norms from the same cluster are similar in meaning, then an individual who selects cluster X over cluster Y in one question should do the same in another question; and when all the individuals are combined, there should be a positive correlation between the responses for the two questions.

This hypothesis was tested with the data from the hamlet of Apas ($n = 114$).[2] Two-by-two tables were constructed for pairs of paired comparison questions that contrasted the same norm clusters, and that had an adequate amount of variation in response, i.e., no more than 75% of the respondents selecting the same norm. For example, Table 6-5 below shows the results of cross-tabulating the responses of individuals to the question comparing 'lazy' and 'informs on others' with their responses to the question comparing 'won't help others' and 'changes sides.' Both questions compare the Lazy and Crafty clusters, and the table shows that 73% of the subjects selected the same cluster in both questions. Twenty-five such tables were constructed, and almost all of them confirmed the generality of the norm clusters. All but two tables

---

[1]Each cluster was represented by two or three central norms from the first sorting task. The norms from the Good clusters and the Violent and Lazy clusters are identified by the number 1, 2 or 3 on the lists in Chapter 5. The representative norms for the other clusters are identified by the number 1 or 2.

[2]The data from Nachih were not used because of the problems with the Nachih data discussed in Chapter 8.

Table 6-5 Similarity of responses to two questions comparing the same clusters*

		Lazy cluster v. crafty cluster		
		'won't help others'	'changes sides'	
Lazy cluster v. Crafty cluster	lazy'	17	11	28
	'informs'	14	51	65
		31	62	

Kendall's Tau B = 0.38
Chi Square** = 11.81

*Apas adult population, excluding people who responded 'the same.'
**Corrected for continuity.

showed positive correlations; seventeen of them were 0.20 or greater, and eight reached a correlation of 0.30 or greater.[1]

Table 6-6 below summarizes the findings on the tendency to consistently select one cluster over another, even though the clusters are represented by different particular norms. The table shows that there was a substantial correlation between pairs of questions that compared the same norm from cluster X with two different norms from cluster Y. For example, the responses to a question comparing 'respects God' with 'speaks Spanish' were correlated with the responses to a question comparing 'respects God' with 'settles disputes.' This correlation could be explained on the grounds that the same norm was included in both questions. However, the table shows almost the same correlation for questions in which two different norms from cluster X were compared with two norms from cluster Y. In contrast, there is almost no correlation between pairs of questions that compared the same norm from cluster X with one norm from cluster Y and one from cluster Z.

These findings, based on the questionnaire responses of the total population of a hamlet, strongly confirm the generality of the norm clusters. When norms from the same two clusters are compared, individuals consistently favor one cluster. But when questions do not

[1]The two negative correlations were almost zero: −.08 and −.04. Given a sample size of about 100, a Kendall Tau of .20 is significant at the .001 level.

Table 6-6   Correlations between pairs of paired-comparison questions

Types of pairs of questions	Mean correlation (Kendall Tau B)
A. Comparing same clusters	
1. Same norm in cluster X v. two norms in cluster Y (13 pairs)	.26
2. Two norms in cluster X v. two norms in cluster Y (12 pairs)	.22
B. Comparing different clusters	
1. Same norm in cluster X v. one norm from cluster Y and one from cluster Z (7 pairs)	.02

compare the same clusters, there is no consistency of response, even when the same norm appears in both questions. The correlations among paired comparison questions also support the previous finding of greater consistency for the Good clusters than the Bad, since the correlations are considerably higher for pairs of Good paired comparison questions.[1]

The responses to the paired comparison questions also show the hierarchical ordering of norms in Zinacantan, as was discussed in the last chapter; and this data provides another test of the generality of the norm clusters. The previous analysis showed that individuals respond to the paired comparison questions in terms of the cognitive categories defined by the norm clusters. The following analysis examines whether Zinacantecos shared a common rank ordering of these clusters. Insofar as they do, a clear hierarchy of norm clusters will emerge when the responses of individuals are aggregated.

The data presented in Table 5-3, in the last chapter, indicate that norms from the same cluster tend to be seen as equally important. The first two columns of the table show, for example, that each of the three norms from the Kinship cluster are perceived to be relatively unimportant.

A more appropriate method for assessing consensus on the hierarchy of norm clusters is to focus on the clusters that are being

[1] The correlations also provide additional information on the norm about 'being a leader of a group of farmers' (E2), which is not treated as similar to the other norms in the Economic cluster. Correlations that include this norm were usually very low; out of six, only one is higher than .10. This norm has a complex meaning, and is connected to the Economic cluster in the first sorting task and to the Political cluster in the second sorting task. The only other norm that was included in the survey and shifts its location in the two sorting tasks is 'doing favors.' There should also be low correlations between questions that include this norm, but this is impossible to test, because questions that include the norm do not have enough variance.

compared in a particular question.[1] If Zinacantecos rank clusters of norms rather than individual norms, and if they agree on the rank order of the norm clusters, then the response to any paired comparison question can be predicted from the rank order of the clusters represented in the question. Most respondents will select the norm from the highest ranking cluster, regardless of which particular norm it is.

The data show just this pattern. For the Good norms, the average of all paired comparison questions shows that the Religious cluster is ranked highest by most respondents, followed by the Political, Economic, and Kinship clusters, in that order. In any particular paired comparison question, when a norm from the Religious cluster is compared with a norm from the Political, Economic or Kinship cluster, most respondents select the Religious norm. When a Political norm is compared with an Economic or Kinship norm, most respondents select the Political norm; and when Economic and Kinship norms are compared, most respondents select the Economic norm. This pattern holds for all but two or three questions on Good and Bad norms in both Apas and Nachih.[2] Clearly, the norm clusters are a set of rank ordered categories that Zinacantecos use in deciding which of two norms is more important.

The final set of survey results that supports the generality of the norm clusters comes from the responses to the association questions. In these questions, respondents were asked to associate a norm with one of two behavior alternatives, e.g., 'who is better at settling disputes, the man who farms far away or the man who farms nearby'? The behavior alternatives were: farming nearby or far, going to the doctor or not, sending children to school or not. Since the questions included several norms from the same cluster, it is possible to test whether norms from the same cluster are associated with the same behavioral alternative. For example, if an individual associates 'settling disputes' with farming far, will he also associate 'speaking Spanish' with farming far?

The data presented in Table 6-7 below show that there is a clear tendency for individuals to associate all the norms from a cluster with

[1]The percentages in Table 5-3 are not very appropriate for examining equal importance within a cluster because they represent averages over all the questions in which a particular norm was included. Each norm was *not* compared with each of the other norms, in the paired comparison questions; therefore the average popularity of a norm depends in part on the popularity of the other norms or clusters that it happened to be paired with.

[2]I use the Nachih data here, even though it has problems, because I am using the hamlet as the level of analysis. Previous discussions in this chapter considered only the Apas data because I was using individuals as the level of analysis and the superior Apas data was sufficient to test propositions about individuals.

the same behavioral alternative. Correlations were tabulated for every pair of association questions containing norms from the same cluster, if less than 75% of the respondents associated a norm with the same behavioral alternative. The absence of a correlation in the table because of inadequate variance is indicated by dashes in the appropriate cell.

Twenty correlations were calculated and not one is negative, except for the near-zero correlation of −0.02 for two norms from the Economic cluster. All but three of the correlations reach the value of 0.20 or greater, and four reach the level of 0.30 or greater.

The distribution of very low correlations in this table also supports the interpretation that the norm clusters, as defined by the sorting task, are the categories that Zinacantecos use in a wide variety of settings. The three correlations that are close to zero all involve the norms 'does favors' (K1) and 'farm leader' (E2). These are the only two norms included in the survey that moved from one cluster to another in the two

Table 6-7   Norms from same cluster associated with same behavior: correlations between pairs of association questions*

| | Behavioral alternative | | |
Pairs of norms	Farming	School	Doctor
Political cluster*			
1. Settles disputes & Talks with officials	.47**	—***	.32
Religious cluster			
2. Takes religious offices & Respects God	—	.37	.25
3. Takes religious offices & Helps religious officers			
4. Respects God & Helps religious officers	.21	.23	—
Economic cluster			
5. Corn farmer & Farm leader	—	.00	.22
6. Corn farmer & Helps others work	—	.24	.21
7. Helps others work & Farm leader	—	—	.02
Kinship cluster			
8. Good heart & Does favors	.25	.04	.21
Violent cluster			
9. Picks fights & Separates from wife	.20	.29	.23
Crafty cluster			
10. Changes sides & Informs	.23	.24	.29

*'Talks with officials' is not formally from the Political cluster, nor is 'Helps others work' from the Economic cluster. See discussion of Association questions in Chapter 8 for the rationale for including the statements in these clusters.

**Numbers show the Kendall Tau B for a pair of questions; individuals answering 'the same' on either question omitted; therefore n varies from 78 to 105, Apas adult population.

***Correlation not calculated because of insufficient variation in responses to question(s).

sorting tasks. The data from the survey, collected from different subjects in a very different manner, also suggest that these two norms do not clearly belong to the clusters into which they were placed in the first sorting task.

Summary of the data confirming the model of Zinacanteco norms

The data presented in this chapter confirm the validity of the model generated by the Frame-Sorting Method. When the sorting task was repeated, the same norm clusters tended to emerge, in spite of the fact that half the norms were different. In addition, it was possible to predict the placement of new norms on the basis of the underlying dimension of each cluster. These findings confirm the reliability of the Frame-Sorting Method and the accuracy of my interpretations of the dimensions underlying the norm clusters.

The results of the Person Perception Interview gave some support for the generality of the norm clusters. In the interview, individuals were given similar ratings on attributes from the same cluster, indicating that the categories defined by the norm clusters are general categories that are used in perceiving and evaluating others. The findings on the differential salience of central and peripheral norms suggest the additional, intriguing possibility that the social significance of an attribute can be measured by its structural properties in a cluster diagram.

The survey provides confirming evidence on the generality of the norm clusters from a large and unbiased population of Zinacantecos. Questions that contained normative statements from the same cluster elicited the same response. In the paired comparison questions respondents tended to select norms from the same cluster, although the particular norms varied. In the association questions, individuals tended to associate all the norms from a cluster with the same behavior alternative.

In sum, these results indicate that the Frame-Sorting Method produces a valid model of the actor's normative beliefs. Each of the findings can be questioned on methodological grounds; however, the series of confirming results from independent tests is impressive.

Conclusion

The first part of this book has focused on describing a particular normative system. I have presented a new method for constructing a model of the actor's normative beliefs, and have discussed the model of Zinacanteco norms that was produced by this method. Finally, I have presented several independent tests that confirm the validity of the model and show that the norm clusters are important cognitive categories that Zinacantecos use to organize their responses in a variety of situations.

The description of Zinacanteco norms supports the usefulness of the Frame-Sorting Method. It shows that this methodological approach produces a valid model of the domain and structure of norms from the actor's point of view, thereby helping to resolve a major obstacle to the scientific study of norms and values.

The description of Zinacanteco norms also suggests some of the ways in which normative systems are related to social action and social organization. This issue is the focus of the second part of the book. The previous chapters have systematically analyzed the norms of Zinacantan, but how does this analysis help explain social action in Zinacantan? What do you know when you know what the norms are?

7

THE THEORY OF THE SOCIALIZED ACTOR V. THE EVIDENCE

How DO NORMS shape the actions of individuals and the organization of social systems? Most social scientists assume that norms are a crucial element in understanding the consistency of behavior patterns within a culture and the differences between cultures. But the nature of the relation between norms and social action is far from clear. The remaining chapters of this book explore two theoretical approaches to this issue: the theory of the socialized actor and the social identity approach.

The theory of the socialized actor, as formulated by Talcott Parsons, is the most influential conception of norms and social action in contemporary sociology. This theory views action as a process in which individuals choose between alternatives so as to satisfy their goals and needs. Through socialization, individuals internalize norms and values that shape their needs. For example, the needs of Zinacanteco men are shaped so that they want to take religious offices. Norms and action are consistent because individuals are motivated to conform.

This viewpoint is taken for granted by many social scientists,[1] and vigorously attacked by others.[2] But it is the major point of reference for contemporary discussions of norms (for example, see Blake and Davis, 1964; Williams, 1968; Scott, 1971).

[1]The pervasiveness of this point of view can be seen by examining introductory textbooks in Sociology, such as Broom and Selznick (1963). It was also evident in the sessions of the 1971 A.S.A. Meetings that I informally observed; most participants attempted to explain part of their results by referring to the (unmeasured) norms and values of their subjects.

[2]Many critics have strongly attacked Parsons' theory of values, but none of them seem to reject the idea that norms are sometimes an important determinant of behavior. These critics are reviewed in Blake and Davis (1964).

105

The controversy about the theory of the socialized actor has not been very productive because it has been divorced from research. With a few exceptions,[1] the concepts of norms and values have been ambiguously defined and their relation to social action has been unclearly stated. As a result, the relation between norms and action is rarely the explicit focus of sociological research, and the relevance of existing data is not perceived. Instead, the theory of the socialized actor tends to be accepted or rejected as an article of faith.

The social identity approach is a loosely formulated theoretical orientation that is closely related to the ideas of 'symbolic interaction,' 'social construction of reality,' and 'reference group.'[2] This approach starts with the conception of the collective definition and maintenance of social identities. Norms specify what identities or roles exist and what actions define a person as a member-in-good-standing with a particular rank. For example, the normative system of Zinacantan specifies 'being a religious office holder' as the most respected public identity in the community and defines how a person goes about being a good office holder. A Zinacanteco takes a religious office because he and the other members of the community agree that taking offices is what respected men do. Conformity to norms primarily depends on perceived consensus about the identity implications of actions, and not on the individual's motives or needs.

The remainder of this book shows how these two approaches lead to different conceptions of norms and different testable propositions about how norms change and how norms relate to action and social structure. The next two chapters focus on the relation between norms and action that is implied by the theory of the socialized actor. This chapter restates the Parsonian theory of the socialized actor so as to clarify its empirical implications, and reviews some findings from past research. Chapter 8 discusses the results of a survey of Zinacantan that was designed to test the Parsonian theory of norms and action. Finally, Chapter 9 presents the social identity approach to norms and action and considers some of the other implications of these two ways of thinking about norms.

The Parsonian theory of the socialized actor

Many aspects of the theory of the socialized actor were anticipated in the works of Sigmund Freud, Emile Durkheim, and others.

[1]In particular, Blake and Davis (1964).
[2]See references and discussion at the beginning of Chapter 9.

However, it was Talcott Parsons who developed a comprehensive sociological theory of how individual actors are integrated into a social system through internalizing shared norms, and his early works still constitute the most convincing presentation of the theory of the socialized actor. Therefore, I will refer to the theory as the 'Parsonian theory of norms,' even though Parsons himself has criticized some aspects of the simplified version presented below.[1]

The cornerstone of Parsons' early work is his explanation of how shared values account for social integration. The theory grows out of Parsons' conception of social action, whereby actors are viewed as orienting themselves to a situation and selecting among alternative actions. A value is 'an element of a shared symbolic system which serves as a criterion or standard for selection among the alternatives of orientation which are intrinsically open in a situation' (1951:12). In specific situations, values are embodied in norms or moral standards, which define the mutual rights and obligations, or role expectations, of the relevant actors (1951:14 and 251).

According to Parsons, a person learns these evaluative standards by interacting with significant others and internalizing the common values of their interaction into his own personality (1951:211). As a result of internalization, people develop a need or motive to conform to shared normative standards. Conformity is also maintained by sanctions, or the reactions of others. That is, a person is dependent on the other's response, and getting what he wants from the other usually depends on conforming to the shared standards. However, the 'basic type of integration of motivation with a normative pattern-structure of values' results from internalization, whereby acting in conformity with the standard 'becomes a need-disposition in the actor's own personality structure, relatively independently of any instrumentally significant consequences of that conformity' (1951:37). In this way, 'the "deeper" layers of motivation become harnessed to the fulfillment of role expectations' (1951:42).

The process of learning shared standards of evaluation continues throughout a person's life and the standards are maintained by the mechanisms of social control that are a part of everyday interaction (1951: chapters 6 and 7). However, the major value patterns tend to be

[1]Parsons has pointed out the necessity of specifying how norms and values influence action in a particular situation, since 'values cannot control action by mere "emanation"' (1961:55). He makes a more fundamental criticism of the theory of the socialized actor when he points out the problem of explaining social regularities by childhood socialization, given the great variance in the socialization experience of individuals (1951:229).

established in childhood and 'are not on a large scale subject to drastic alteration during adult life' (1951:208). This is because 'these patterns can only be acquired through the mechanism of identification, and because the basic identification patterns are developed in childhood' (1951:228).

In order to clarify the empirical implications of this theory, two elements need to be specified further: the definition of norms, and the proposition relating norms to action. Readers who are interested in more detailed expositions of Parsons' theory are referred to his own works (1951, 1961) and the critical comments of Devereux (1961), Scott (1971) and Williams (1961).

In the theory of the socialized actor, as developed by Parsons and others, norms are defined as standards of evaluation, or ranking norms. They are rarely defined as reality assumptions or membership norms. Parsons defines norms or value orientations as shared standards for selecting among alternatives, varying from general to specific.[1] In his most explicit definition, he states that 'a norm is a verbal description of a concrete course of action, ... regarded as desirable, combined with an injunction to make certain future actions conform to this course. An instance of a norm is the statement "Soldiers should obey the orders of their commanding officers" ' (1937:75). Most definitions of norms are similar, as was discussed in Chapter 1.

Norms influence behavior, in Parsonian theory, because they are part of an individual's motives. The theory states, in summary, that in an integrated system, norms become part of the actor's personality through socialization, that many crucial norms are learned in early childhood, and that early learning is difficult to change. After a person is socialized, conformity with the norms becomes part of 'the actor's own personality structure, relatively independently of any instrumentally significant consequences of that conformity' (Parsons, 1951:32).

This position implies that the norms and actions of individuals will be consistent. In other words, variation in the norms of individual members of a community will correlate with variation in behavior. Furthermore, Parsons' definition of norms suggests that the theory of the socialized actor should be able to explain the results of previous research on the relation between behavior and normative beliefs, opinions or attitudes. To qualify as a norm, the belief should be an 'ought' or 'should' statement, and imply an evaluation of action. Most

---

[1]See Scott (1971:67-79) for a discussion of Parsons' definitions of norms and for other definitions of norms and references.

sociologists would add that the belief should be shared[1] and be enforced by some type of sanction. The most relevant data for examining the theory would consider beliefs that are stressed in early socialization.[2]

This restatement of the theory of the socialized actor suggests that the theory can be tested with the vast body of data on individual variation in norms (or attitudes) and behavior. These data are reviewed below. The reader will note that in the review, the term 'behavior' is often used in preference to 'action.' This is because most of the studies were done by psychologists, who tend to prefer the former term. I have used the word 'action' throughout this book simply because it is more congenial with my theoretical point of view.[3]

Before turning to the data, it should be acknowledged that the idea of directly testing Parsons' general assumption about norms and social action may seem somewhat strange. Parsons' conception of norms is usually interpreted as the guiding assumption underlying a grand theoretical scheme, and not as a proposition about empirical events. However, in actual practice, social scientists often treat the assumption as if it were an empirical assertion; they explain the behavior patterns that they find in their research as the result of childhood socialization, which produced in their subjects a motive or disposition to act in that particular way.[4] More important, if we are to advance our understanding of social norms, it will be necessary to draw out the empirical implications of alternative theoretical orientations, and create a closer relationship between theory and research.

For these reasons, the general theory of the socialized actor has been restated in a simplified form. It will now be confronted with the results of previous studies on attitudes and behavior, and with the findings of the Zinacantan survey. The following discussion shows that these data do not support the theory.

Previous research on norms or attitudes, and behavior

Most of the research on the co-variation of norms and behavior among individuals has been done by social psychologists investigating

[1]This raises a difficulty that will be discussed in Chapter 9. If norms are shared, by definition, then how is it possible to talk about *individual* variation in norms?

[2]It is not clear whether the theory of the socialized actor (1) asserts, as a testable proposition, that important norms will be stressed in early socialization, or (2) defines important norms as those that are stressed in early socialization.

[3]The term 'behavior' suggests that what people do is not difficult to describe and can be measured independently from their cognitive categories or world view. Both of these ideas are questionable, as will be discussed in Chapter 9.

[4]For example, see Maccoby (1966:43-51).

attitudes, not norms. According to most theoretical definitions, the concept of 'attitude' is broader than 'norms'; however, the operational definitions of the two concepts are often the same. Allport's definition is still accepted by many psychologists (McGuire, 1969). He defines an attitude as 'a mental and neural state of readiness, organized through experience, exerting a directive or dynamic influence upon the individual's response to all objects and situations with which it is related' (1935). 'Attitudes' include 'norms,' or shared beliefs about how people should behave or about what behavior deserves respect and approval. However, 'attitudes' also include individual opinions, beliefs and preferences.

Some theoretical definitions of 'attitude' are very close to a definition of 'norms.' For example, Harding, *et al.* define the conative or behavioral component of ethnic attitudes as 'a pattern of beliefs about the way in which members of that group should be treated in specific contexts' (1954:1027). In general, the concept of attitudes is similar to 'norms' conceived as attributes of individuals, and much less similar to 'norms' conceived as attributes of groups.

In some cases the operational definitions of the two concepts are identical; and then the findings about 'attitudes' obviously can be generalized to 'norms.' For example, one of the questions in *The American Soldier* study was: 'On the whole, do you think it is a good idea or a poor idea to have colored soldiers used as infantry troops'? (Star *et al.,* 1958). This question could be used to measure norms or attitudes; in this study it was interpreted as measuring attitudes. Many attitude scales contain normative items, such as 'Fascists and Communists are entitled to preach their beliefs in this country' (Cook and Selltiz, 1964:42) or 'I believe the Negro deserves the same social privileges as the white man' (Deri *et al.,* 1948:262).

The main finding of more than four decades of research on attitudes and behavior is that there is no clear relation between them. Many studies have found virtually no relation between what an individual says he does, or likes to do, or should do, and what he actually does (La Piere, 1934; Kutner *et al.,* 1952). Some studies report a positive relation between attitudes and behavior (De Fleur and Westie, 1958), and others suggest that the relation may be negative (Deutscher, 1966:250).

The most famous finding of no relation between verbal statements and behavior is La Piere's early research on 'Attitudes and Actions' (1934). He traveled through the United States with a Chinese couple and stopped at 251 hotels, motels and restaurants, and was refused service only once. Six months later, questionnaires were mailed to these establishments, and one of the questions was: 'Will you accept members of the Chinese race as guests in your establishment'? Over 90% of the respondents answered 'no.' Inconsistency between attitudes and behavior has also been found in studies in which the measure of attitudes is closer to normative beliefs. Thus, Saenger and Gilbert (1950) found virtually no relationship between attitudes toward Negro store clerks and actually making a purchase from a Negro clerk, using an attitude scale that included items like 'What would you think if all New York department stores hired Negro sales personnel'?

Research in other areas besides 'attitudes' has also failed to find a consistent relationship between an individual's stated attitudes and his actions. A review of psychological research on moral values reports that no one has been able to construct a test of moral attitudes or values that successfully predicts moral behavior (Pittel and Mendelsohn, 1966:26). Recent research on altruistic norms and behavior suggests that children's normative behavior is determined only by what others do (Bryan, 1970). And a recent study of power in the family has found no relationship between the way family members say they behave and their observed interaction (Olson, 1969; also, Weller and Luchterhand, 1969).

These findings have been interpreted in various ways. A review by Deutscher (1966) suggests that the relationship between 'Words and deeds' tends to be positive in laboratory research but not in field studies. On the other hand, a recent review of research on ethnic attitudes and behavior concludes that attitudes are most likely to determine behavior in intimate, long-lasting relationships and least likely to determine behavior in the specific and transitory situations that are usually measured in experimental studies (Harding *et al.,* 1969:43; also Tittle and Hill, 1967).

Some researchers believe that we now have sufficient evidence to conclude that attitudes, or verbal statements about behavior, usually have very little relationship with actual behavior (Deutscher, 1966), while others remain convinced that attitudes and behavior are positively related, and that the findings of the contrary can be explained by inadequate methods and poor theoretical distinctions (Campell, 1961; Ehrlich, 1969). According to the most detailed recent review (Wicker, 1969), the only empirical generalization that can be drawn from scores of studies is that attitudes and behavior are unrelated, or have a slight positive correlation. Other reviewers conclude that we still know very little about the relationship between attitudes and behavior (McGuire, 1969; Fishbein, 1967).

There have been a few studies by sociologists that explicitly focus on norms; these studies also have failed to demonstrate a positive correlation between norms and behavior on the individual level. Kenkel (1963) observed married couples as they made a series of decisions, and measured their norms or attitudes on family roles. His results showed no consistent relation between norms and behavior. An early series of studies by Hartshorne and May on norms and behavior concerning honesty among school children also failed to find any consistent relationship (1928).

Rationale for the Zinacantan survey

The review of previous research has shown that there is little empirical support for the theory of the socialized actor. Most studies find little or no correlation between an individual's attitudes or normative beliefs and his behavior.

Unfortunately, these negative findings are almost always ignored in sociological discussions of norms and social action. The most influential recent review article on 'Norms, values and sanctions' (Blake and Davis, 1964) does not refer to any of these studies in its extensive bibliography, even though one of the major points of the paper is to question the Parsonian theory of normative determinism. Sociologists do not usually see the similarity between the concepts of 'attitudes' and 'norms'; therefore they do not consider the research on ethnic attitudes to be relevant.

The apparent dismissial of previous research by sociological theorists is not entirely unjustified. Almost all the studies that have been reviewed focus on individual attitudes or opinions, not shared norms. They concern beliefs that may not be very important to the respondent or to his community, and may not be stressed in early socialization. Ranking norms have been defined as 'shared beliefs about what behavior brings respect from oneself and others,' and it can be convincingly argued that these studies have not measured the important ranking norms of the respondents.[1]

The Zinacantan survey was designed to test the theory of the socialized actor with data that would be more convincing to sociologists. The questions in the survey are based on the carefully constructed model of Zinacanteco norms that was presented in the first part of this book. The Frame-Sorting Method identified nine norm clusters as the major categories that Zinacantecos use in evaluating

[1]The major exceptions probably are the studies of beliefs and behavior concerning marital roles; see Kenkel (1963) and Olson (1969).

each other, and several tests confirmed the validity of this model. Therefore, unlike previous studies of norms and action, the questions in the Zinacantan survey cannot easily be challenged on the grounds that they do not represent the major ranking norms of the community. Furthermore, most of the measures of behavior in the survey are accurate and concern activities that are of vital importance to Zinacantecos.

The results of the survey thus constitute an important test of the theory of the socialized actor. If these results are consistent with the negative findings of previous studies, then there will be more evidence that is relevant to the theory but cannot be explained by it. There will be more reason to revise or abandon the Parsonian approach to norms and social action.

8

DISCONFIRMING EVIDENCE FROM THE ZINACANTAN SURVEY

THE SURVEY OF Zinacantan was designed to test the theory of the socialized actor. According to this theory, norms are internalized standards for selecting among alternatives, and an individual's norms will affect his actions in situations where several alternative actions are possible and acceptable, and one alternative is more consistent with his norms than the others. The survey examined whether or not norms tend to be correlated with behavior in this type of situation. If norms are a major determinant of an individual's actions, then, at the least, there should be a moderate positive correlation between the two variables.

Three specific hypotheses on the relation between norms and social action were tested. Each one predicts that norms will be correlated with actions that are consistent with the norms, but uses a different method for defining 'consistency' (see Chein *et al.*, 1949). The first hypothesis is: 'Individuals who believe that a norm is important will tend to engage in actions that *the community believes* is consistent with the norm.' The survey included a set of 'association questions' that measured the respondents' beliefs about which norm clusters are consistent with particular behavior alternatives. Hypothesis One predicts that individuals who select the norms from a particular norm cluster will engage in actions that are associated with this cluster by most respondents. In the second hypothesis, consistency is defined by the individual's own responses to the association questions. The hypothesis is: 'An individual who believes that a norm is important will tend to engage in actions that *he believes* are consistent with the norm.' Finally, the third hypothesis is: 'Individuals who believe that a norm is important will tend to engage in actions that are *specifically referred to*

114

by the norm.' For example, taking religious offices is specifically referred to by the norms in the Religious cluster; therefore, individuals who select norms from this cluster in the paired comparison questions will take religious offices more than individuals who do not select these norms.

The three hypotheses are not confirmed by the survey data. The evidence is presented below, following a discussion of the measures of norms and behavior, the population of respondents and the interviewing situation.

Measuring the norms of individuals

The norms and actions of Zinacantecos were measured by a survey of the adult men of two hamlets. Variation in norms was measured by determining the relative importance of the norm clusters to each individual. This method was used because there is almost no disagreement among Zinacantecos on what is good and what is bad. Therefore, variation in norms was conceptualized in terms of differences in the importance assigned to particular norm clusters.

The relative importance of the norm clusters for each individual was measured by the paired comparison questions.[1] In these questions, the respondent was presented with two norms from different clusters, and was asked to judge which one was more important. For pairs of Good norms, they were asked which one brings most respect (see questionnaire in Appendix 9). For example, one of the questions for the Good norms was the following (with the Tzotzil translated into English): 'There are two men, one is good at settling disputes, the other is a good Ritual Advisor; which one is more respected'? The final phrase in the question, '(he) is more respected,' means 'he is more respected by people in general.' It also means 'I respect him more' and 'he is more of a good person.' The results of pretesting different wordings of this question showed that these specific meanings of the phrase, which can be separately expressed in Tzotzil, elicit the same responses as the more general phrase.[2]

---

[1] Paired comparison questions have been used to measure the relative importance of norms in several previous studies, e.g., Sherif (1965), Wallace (1966), Rokeach (1968).

[2] In the pretest, seven Zinacantecos responded to two sets of paired comparison questions, each set having a different final phrase. In the first set, the final phrase was 'who do *you* respect more'; in the second set, the final phrase was 'who is respected more *by other people* in your village.' Four of these subjects would not answer the second set of questions, insisting that the two final phrases were not different; those that did answer both sets of questions produced nearly identical responses. Finally, the response to the two sets of substitution frames indicates that 'who is respected' means virtually the same thing as 'who is good' (see Chapter 4).

The model of Zinacanteco norm clusters made it possible to construct paired comparison questions that represent the major normative categories of Zinacantecos. From each cluster, I selected two or three norms that had the highest number of links to other norms in the cluster, and had the lowest overlap in meaning.[1] These norms include the norms from each cluster that are labeled number 1, 2 or 3 in the lists in Chapter 5, except for norms N3, C3 and I3. Pairs of these norms, from different clusters, were randomly chosen, to arrive at a workable number of twenty-three Good paired comparison questions and twenty-four Bad questions.

Each individual's responses to the paired comparison questions are summarized by his norm scores, which consist of the number of questions in which the respondent selected a norm from a particular cluster. For example, if an individual selected a norm from the Political cluster in nine paired comparison questions, he would receive a Political norm score of 9. There were 12 paired comparison questions containing a norm from the Political cluster; therefore, a person could attain a maximum Political norm score of 12. There were 11 or 12 questions representing each of the Good clusters, and 8 to 12 questions for each of the Bad clusters.[2]

The validity of the paired comparison questions is supported by the data reported in Chapter 6: individuals tend to give the same response to questions with norms from the same clusters, and the mean response of all the individuals shows a fairly clear hierarchy of norms. These findings indicate that the responses to the paired comparison questions were determined by the particular norms included in each question. The reliability or stability of the responses was checked by repeating one of the questions. The data show that 156 respondents gave the same answer both times, while 52 changed.[3] This indicates that the reliability is considerably better than one would expect by

---

[1] The norms to be used for the paired comparison questions were selected on the basis of preliminary results from the first twenty subjects who did the first sorting task, because of time pressure.

[2] The 24 Bad paired comparison questions included 12 questions containing a statement from the Violent cluster, 12 for the Lazy cluster, 9 for the Incompetent cluster, 7 for the Crafty cluster, and 8 for the Irreligious cluster. The smaller number of questions for some clusters was necessary given the decision to limit the number of paired comparison questions, and the larger number of Bad clusters.

[3] Question 13, comparing giving soda to mother-in-law and respecting God was repeated, as Question 24. Each time the respondents could select the first statement, or the second, or say that both were 'the same.' The results are from the adult population of Apas and Nachih, which totals 222 men. Fourteen of them responded that the statements were 'the same,' in answering one of the two identical questions.

chance, but a large amount of error remains. Therefore, one should not expect very strong correlations involving the norm scores.

Measuring the actions of individuals

The survey focused on three sets of action alternatives that were selected because they seemed most appropriate for testing the theory of the socialized actor. In the first place, each one represents a series of decisions that is important to Zinacantecos. Decisions that are trivial or are made at one point in time may be determined in large part by the particular situation, but over a series of important decisions, the effect of an individual's norms should be more apparent. Secondly, none of the action alternatives requires a large investment of money, or special skills, so that the selection of a particular alternative will not be strongly influenced by these instrumental, non-normative considerations. Finally, there appeared to be adequate variance in each area to permit an examination of the correlation between an individual's norms and his actions.[1]

The three sets of alternative actions were: (1) whether an individual farmed nearby or took advantage of the new roads and farmed far away; (2) whether he sent his children to school; and (3) whether he used Western doctors in addition to native curers. Information was also obtained on the respondent's age and relative wealth, and on the religious offices that he had taken.[2] The social context of each alternative and the questions used to measure an individual's actions will now be outlined.

The alternative of renting farmland far away from Zinacantan is a new activity made possible by the developing road system.[3] Ten years ago, men walked between the mountains and the lowland cornfields and brought corn home by mule. With the construction of the Pan

[1]In addition, each set of action alternatives is relevant to modernity. This is because I was originally interested in examining the relation between norms and modernization. However, the survey data show no correlation between the three modern activities, which suggests that the unifying concept of 'modern' is misleading.

[2]An additional measure of behavior was the selection of one of eight gifts by each respondent after his interview was over. Each gift represented one of the four Good norm clusters. For example, the Religious cluster was represented by two pictures of saints. The idea of having respondents choose a gift was prompted by interest in investigating the direction of causation, if there was a strong positive correlation between norms and behavior. However, such correlations were not found. Moreover, the extent to which the gifts actually 'represent' the clusters is unclear. Therefore, this measure will not be described further.

[3]The changing economics of lowland corn farming has been intensively studied by Frank Cancian (1972).

American Highway and a network of secondary roads, most Zinacantecos now use trucks. This has made it possible to rent farmland far from Zinacantan, where the land has lain fallow for many years and will yield a much larger harvest. Every year, more men farm further away.

In the interview, each respondent named the ranches where he had rented land for three previous years. The ranches were then classified into regions of increasing distance from Zinacantan, with distance defined in terms of the time necessary to reach the location (see Frank Cancian, 1972). The region scores for the three years were combined in a single index of farming distance that took into account the shift over the last three years towards farming farther away. The index represents a respondent's tendency to farm near or far, compared to the other men in his hamlet.[1]

Sending children to school has been possible for Zinacantecos for several decades. There has been a school in Zinacantan Center for at least 100 years, and in the 1930s the Mexican government began constructing public schools in several hamlets of Zinacantan, including those where the survey was conducted. These schools provide three years of education that focus on learning Spanish, but many Zinacantecos who have been to school for several years remain illiterate and know very little Spanish.

The implications of going to school vary a great deal with the child's sex and age. Zinacanteco boys have been going to school for several generations. Since boys do not regularly accompany their fathers to the lowlands until they are about ten or twelve, school and farming can be combined.[2] Sending girls to school is much more controversial in Zinacantan because parents fear they will lose control of courtship and because girls have little need to learn Spanish in school since they have few contacts with Ladinos.[3] Virtually no girls went to

---

[1]To calculate the farming index, all the region scores of all respondents from a particular hamlet in a given year were rank ordered. Then the rank orders for the three years were added together. Nine respondents had not farmed in the lowlands in 1966. Eleven had not farmed in 1965 *and* 1964. These twenty men were excluded in calculating rank orders and in all data analysis involving farming distance. Three men had not farmed in hot country in one of the two years, 1965 and 1964; their 'region score' for the years in which they did farm was also used as their region score for the year they did not farm. The rank orders were done separately for the two hamlets included in the survey because some ranches are far from one hamlet but close to the other one.

[2] However, many Zinacantecos see a conflict between corn farming and going to school (see data on association questions in Appendix 4), perhaps because they fear that school will acculturate their sons and make them less interested in being hard-working peasants.

[3] In most families, girls do little economically useful work before they are about ten or twelve, and most of the work they do could be done before or after school.

school until a year or two preceding the interviewing, when the political officials of Zinacantan, acting under pressure from the National government, told parents that they must send their daughters to school, or face fines and jail.[1]

In the interview, the respondents were asked about the school attendance of each of their children, and indices were constructed to represent the education of sons and daughters. The index of boys' education was based on the school history of sons who were between fifteen and twenty-four at the time of the interview. Younger sons were excluded because there was no variance in their school attendance; in Apas, 94% of the sons between ten and fourteen at the time of the interview (1967) had gone to school.[2]

Fifty-one respondents had at least one son between fifteen and twenty-four. They were assigned to one of two groups: (1) high score on boys' education – all sons went to school for four years or more; and (2) low score – some sons went to school for less than four years. The cut-off point of four years was selected because it was the lowest point that yielded sufficient cases with a low score.[3]

The index of girls' education is less problematic, since there is a considerable variance in this behavior. The seventy-one respondents who had daughters between eight and fourteen were divided into two groups: (1) low score – no daughters went to school; and (2) high score–some or all daughters went to school.[4]

[1]This produced a great deal of dissension, especially in the wooded, sparsely populated hamlet of Nachih, where there was one alleged case of a girl being raped on the way to the schoolhouse.

[2]59% of the Apas respondents said they went to school as children, and 28% of the Nachih respondents. Of the children aged ten to fourteen, 82% of the Nachih boys, 37% of the Apas girls, and 34% of the Nachih girls had some schooling.

[3]Unfortunately, the distinction between going to school for three v. four years has no significance to Zinacantecos, as far as I know. Also, this measure might bias the boys' education index against men with many sons between 10 and 24, since the greater the number of sons, the higher the probability that one of them would have gone to school less than four years, resulting in a low boys' education score. The possibility was checked, and in Apas there is no relation between the index and number of sons between 15 and 24. However, in Nachih, there is an inverse relationship between the index and number of sons.

[4]Note that the indices of boys' and girls' education refer to behavior that occurred at quite different times. The girls' index measures behavior that is current or occurred within the last six years, since a daughter that was fourteen at the time of the interview could not have been sent to school more than about six years before, when she was eight years old. The boys' education index measures behavior that could have occurred up to sixteen years ago since it refers to the schooling of boys that were fifteen to twenty-four years old at the time of the interview. The appropriateness of relating current norms to past behavior depends on how fast an individual's norms change. See the discussion in Chapter 9.

The third set of action alternatives was whether a man and his family went to Western doctors, in addition to using curers. Modern medical service became available to Zinacantecos in the early 1950s when the National Indian Institute came to San Cristobal and opened a clinic specifically organized to treat monolingual Indians. At the time of the survey, doctors were available to Zinacantecos at two government clinics. They charged about 5 pesos for an examination, which is cheaper than most traditional curing ceremonies; however, going to a clinic entails extra social costs. It is difficult to communicate with the nurses and doctors in Tzotzil, although there is usually someone around to translate. Moreover, the Ladinos at the clinic, including the professional staff, often show their contempt for the 'dirty, ignorant Indians and their foolish superstitions.' The index of the tendency to go to the doctor, as opposed to just the curer, is simply based on the 'yes' or 'no' response to the question 'Do you ever go to the doctor'? Other indices of the use of doctors were explored, which were based on the relative frequency of going to doctors as against curers. However, this simple measure was the most adequate, and was highly correlated with the more complex measures.[1]

In addition to these three areas of activity, the survey also measured each respondent's participation in the system of religious offices. As explained in Chapter 3, the religious offices are hierarchically arranged into four levels, and only the wealthiest and most respected men take the most prestigious and expensive first-level offices and go on to complete all four levels. Participation in the religious system was not a major focus of the survey because taking an office depends largely on a man's wealth, not on his normative beliefs. However, taking religious offices is very important to Zinacantecos and it is closely related to the Religious norm cluster; therefore, it was used to test some of the hypotheses, with an effort to control the effect of wealth. Respondents were classified as low on taking offices if they had taken no office or one of the lowest status first offices (see Frank Cancian, 1965); otherwise, they were classified as high. All men younger than

---

[1]An index was constructed that measures the relative frequency of going to the doctor v. the curer in the last eight months (since the fiesta of San Lorenzo), and the Appendices show how this doctor/curer index is correlated with other measures. This measure cannot be used for all respondents because it excludes respondents who went to neither doctors nor curers in this time period. It shows the same patterns of intercorrelations as the simpler doctor index; therefore, only the simpler index is referred to in this chapter.

Questions on the use of pharmacies were included in the interview, in the expectation that using pharmacies meant moderate participation in Western medicine and going to doctors meant high participation. In fact, the data show that these behaviors do not form a scale; just as many people go to the pharmacy and not the doctor as go to the doctor and not the pharmacy. Therefore, these questions were not used.

fifty were excluded, since many men do not begin to participate until that age; this leaves thirty men from Apas, and twenty-two from Nachih for analyses involving taking religious offices.

All the measures of an individual's actions were checked, where possible, and were found to be highly accurate. The responses to the questions on farming distance, education, and religious offices were checked by informants who knew the respondents, and in the few cases where errors were discovered, they were corrected.[1] The accuracy of the responses about going to the doctor could not be checked directly, since my informants did not have the necessary information. An indirect check was made by examining the correlation between responses and the known opinion of the interviewer, on the assumption that if the respondents were lying, their lies would tend to conform to the beliefs of the interviewer. The results were reassuring and showed that the interviewer who mistrusted doctors and was generally conservative was slightly *more* likely to elicit reports of going to the doctor.[2]

The population of respondents

The respondents for the interview consist of all the married men from the hamlet of Apas and about half the men from Nachih. The sample was restricted to these hamlets because some of the information that was needed – such as age – could only be obtained from a complete census of the hamlet,[3] and doing a census is a very time-consuming job. It was also necessary to have a list of all members of the hamlet in order to select a sample or keep track of who had been interviewed.

[1]The accuracy of responses on education could not be checked for the more dispersed hamlet of Nachih.

[2]In Apas, of the 66 respondents interviewed by conservative Manvel, who opposed modern medicine, 51% said they had been to the doctor. Of the 69 respondents interviewed by modern Chep, who supported modern clinics, 36% said they had been to the doctor. Somewhat different results are produced by the doctor/curer index, which measures the relative frequency of going to the doctor and the curer in the previous eight months, for respondents who had sickness in their family during that time. 36% of Manvel's respondents received a high score, indicating a relatively high frequency of going to the doctor, and 48% of Chep's respondents received a high score.

[3]Many Zinacantecos do not know their absolute age, but they all know their relative age within their circle of relatives and neighbors, because of the rituals of bowing and drinking according to relative age. Therefore, the best way to measure age is to find out the absolute age of a few men in a hamlet, and then interview some knowledgeable informants about the relative age of the other men in the hamlet.

The hamlet of Apas was selected because a careful census had already been done.[1] Apas is an isolated hamlet of about 600 people. There is no road leading to it and it takes almost an hour to walk to the Pan American highway. From there it is still a 45-minute drive to San Cristobal, and about the same distance to Zinacantan Center. On the other hand, Apas is close to the lowlands and the men can walk to the nearest cornfields in about six hours.

Nachih provides a good contrast to Apas.[2] It is much larger, and contains about 1,000 people widely dispersed over a wooded area, while the people of Apas are packed into one small valley. Nachih is located on both sides of the Pan American highway, and is about two hours' walk from Zinacantan Center and fifteen minutes' drive from San Cristobal. However, Nachih is relatively far from the lowland farmlands and fewer men walk to their cornfields. The people of Nachih seem more worldly than those of Apas, probably because of their central location, and many of them speak Spanish and are literate.

The interview was originally given to all but 18 of the 392 married men of Apas and Nachih.[3] Unmarried men were excluded because their behavior is largely controlled by their fathers and hence could not be expected to relate to the young men's norms. All the married men were interviewed, instead of a sample, because of the many advantages of obtaining data from a total population.[4] However, about half of the Nachih interviews had to be discarded because the interviewer failed to follow the proper procedures.[5] Therefore, most of the discussion of

[1] The census was done by Frank Cancian and George Collier, on the basis of intensive interviews of a few residents of Apas.

[2] The Nachih census was initiated by George Collier and completed by Frank Cancian.

[3] Nine additional residents of Nachih were discovered after the survey was over.

[4] The first advantage in obtaining data from the entire adult male population of two hamlets is that this controls for all the variables associated with living in a particular community, e.g., the distance of the respondents' hamlet from the city, or the friendliness of the teachers available to the community. Another advantage is suggested by the theoretical assumptions that most social positions exist in any bounded social system and that a person's position can best be defined relative to other members of his social system. If the hamlet is a bounded social system, then obtaining data from all its members is the best method of ensuring that most social positions will be represented. A final advantage is that the results of the data analysis can be directly attributed to the population without considering the relationship between the sample and the population. There is no need for significance tests. The values obtained are those of the actual population, except for measurement error.

[5] The problem with some of the Nachih interviews became evident when I coded the forty-seven paired comparison questions. The respondents from Apas and some of those from Nachih exhibited the expected pattern of selecting the first statement in a pair for a few questions and then selecting the second statement, resulting in a series of responses like: first, first, second, first, etc. However, many of the Nachih respondents

survey results is based on the Apas interviews, where there were no such difficulties. In particular, the discussion of results focuses on the adult population of married men, excluding those younger than twenty-five, because a large proportion of these young men still live with their fathers and guide their actions by their father's decisions. The adult population of respondents is 114 men from Apas, and 108 from Nachih.

The interviewing situation and interviewer bias

The interviews were done in Tzotzil by four Zinacanteco assistants, except for a few that I did to meet emergencies. The interviews were conducted in a large rented house near the main market in San Cristobal. Following the traditions built up by the Harvard–Chiapas Project, all the respondents were paid.[1]

Five Zinacantecos were selected to be interviewers: two from Apas, two from Nachih, and one from Zinacantan Center. They were chosen on the basis of residence, literacy, and having a personality that would not antagonize or overpower the respondents. Most of the interviewers had to be respected men from Nachih and Apas, so that they could persuade the respondents to come to be interviewed. The interviewers usually knew the men they were interviewing, which made it difficult for the respondents to lie on the questions about their behavior.

The five interviewers were trained for about a month by myself and Frank Cancian. One man could not successfully complete the training, and one could not work because his son was very sick and he was occupied with curing ceremonies. Thus, almost all of the respondents were interviewed by three men. The responses that they elicited are compared below for evidence of interviewer bias.

---

[1]In exchange for the half hour of being interviewed and several hours of waiting, they received 8 pesos (almost the equivalent of the daily wages of a farm laborer) plus the cost of round trip transportation by truck to San Cristobal. A farm laborer also receives a daily meal, in addition to 8 pesos (or 64 cents).

---

consistently selected the first statement in each pair or consistently selected the second resulting in response patterns like: second, second, second, second, etc. The 112 Nachih interviews that showed this repetitious responses pattern were discarded. A cut-off point of five identical responses in a row, on the paired comparison questions, was used to differentiate unacceptable interviews. Not one respondent from Apas reaches this cut-off point.

I have not been able to explain definitely what went wrong with the Nachih interviews. All the unacceptable Nachih interviews were done by one man who was highly motivated to complete more interviews than my other assistants, and this may have led to the difficulty. Appendix 3 discusses some alternative explanations.

Half of the respondents from Apas were interviewed by Chep, a wealthy, self-confident man in his thirties, who is fluent and literate in Spanish, has worked closely with anthropologists for several years, and is already a leader in his community. The other half of the Apas interviews were done by Manvel, who also did some of the Nachih interviews. Manvel is a relatively poor and shy man in his thirties. He is not politically prominent in Apas, speaks a very halting Spanish and had never cooperated with American social scientists before this job. His general orientation is much more traditional than Chep's; for example, he is very suspicious of Western doctors.

Despite these marked and publicly known differences between the interviewers, Table 8-1 shows that there are very small differences in the responses they elicited. The first two columns of the table give the mean norm scores for the respondents from Apas who were interviewed by Chep and by Manvel. The four Good norm scores are virtually identical for the two groups of respondents, and only one of the five Bad norm clusters shows a significant difference (shown by asterisks between the scores elicited by different interviewers). A further check on interviewer bias in Apas was made by comparing the responses of these two groups of subjects to the questions about going to the doctor, and no significant differences between the groups were found (see footnote on page 121).

Table 8-1 Differences in mean norm scores* by interviewer

Norm scores	Apas men interviewed by:		Nachih men interviewed by:	
	Chep $n = 69**$	Manvel $n = 66$	Manvel $n = 17$	Marian $n = 77$
Good clusters				
Political	7.1	7.1	7.1	7.2
Religious	7.7	7.4	7.5	7.5
Economic	5.7	5.9	5.9	5.5
Kinship	2.4	2.6	2.6	2.8
Bad clusters				
Violent	5.9	6.6	6.8	6.5
Lazy	6.3	6.7	6.1 **	** 5.2
Incompetent	2.5	2.1	1.6 **	** 3.6
Crafty	4.7	4.7	5.3 **	** 4.3
Irreligious	4.5 **	** 4.0	4.1	4.3

*Scores not adjusted for differences in maximum possible score, which varies from 7 to 12 for different norm clusters.

**Total population including married men under twenty-five.

** **Indicates a critical ratio of 2.0 or greater. Standard deviations range from 1.2 to 2.0.

In Nachih it is more difficult to check on interviewer bias because almost all the interviewing was done by Marian, a wealthy and fairly influential man in his forties who had taken the most expensive first religious office, and could speak Spanish fairly well.[1] However, a few interviews had been done by Manvel. The mean norm scores elicited by these two interviewers are displayed in the last two columns of Table 8-1. These data show no substantial differences for the four Good norm scores; but significant differences for three of the five Bad clusters.

In sum, both Apas and Nachih show no significant interviewer bias in the responses to questions about the Good norm clusters, and a moderate degree of bias in responses about the Bad norms clusters. This finding, together with the previously reported evidence on the greater stability of the Good clusters, indicates that the data on Good norms should be given more weight in testing the hypotheses about norms and behavior.

Testing the hypotheses

The survey data were used to test three hypotheses about the relation between norms and action. All the hypotheses predict that an individual's actions will be consistent with the norms that he thinks are most important. However, each one uses a different criterion for defining what actions are consistent or inconsistent with a particular norm cluster: the judgment of the community, the judgment of the individual and the specific content of the norm cluster.

For example, consider the Zinacantecos who selected the norms from the Religious cluster as the most important. Hypothesis One predicts that these men will avoid going to the doctor *if* most members of the community think that religious norms are consistent with avoiding doctors. Hypothesis Two predicts that the men will avoid going to the doctor *if* they themselves think that religious norms imply avoiding doctors. Finally, Hypothesis Three predicts that religious norms will not be related to going to doctors since these norms do not specifically refer to this activity; instead, men who select religious norms as most important will take religious offices and engage in the other actions that are described by the normative statements in the Religious cluster.

---

[1]In the current political fight about sending girls to school, Marian was a prominent leader of the faction that supported the schools.

*Testing Hypothesis One: Individuals who believe that a norm is
important will tend to engage in actions that the community believes are
consistent with the norm*

Testing this hypothesis requires a measure of community beliefs
about what actions are consistent with particular norms. These beliefs
were measured in the survey by the association questions, which asked
respondents to associate norms with one of two behavior alternatives.
The questions took the following form: 'Who is better at settling disputes, people who go to school or people who don't go'? There were
three sets of behavior alternatives: going to school v. not going, farming far away v. farming near, and going to the doctor v. not going.[1] In
order to shorten the questionnaire, three norm clusters were omitted
from the association questions (Lazy, Irreligious, Incompetent).

Table 8-2 lists the average association scores in Apas, between the
norm clusters and the three action alternatives; the scores from
Nachih are very similar and are shown in Appendix 4.[2] The scores can
vary from +3 to −3. A high positive score indicates that most respondents associate the norms from a cluster with the more 'modern'
behavior alternative, i.e., farming far away, going to school, and going
to the doctor. A high negative score means that most respondents associate the norm cluster with the traditional behavior alternatives.

Table 8-2 shows four strong associations between norm clusters
and behavior alternatives (1.32 or greater). The Political cluster, represented by norms like 'he speaks Spanish,' is associated with going to

[1]In order to hold down the length of the interview, the association questions used
sixteen of the twenty-four norms that were used in the paired comparison questions.
Each Good cluster, and the Violent and Crafty clusters, were represented by two or three
norms. The other clusters were not included in order to shorten the questionnaire. All
the clusters were originally represented by at least one norm. But some of the Bad norms
were interpreted to represent other Good clusters for two reasons: (1) these norms were
originally negative statements that had to be restated positively in order to be com-
prehensible to the respondents; the restatement made these norms very similar to
norms in the respective Good cluster, and the responses to these added norms were
highly correlated with the responses to the original ones; (2) shifting these norms increased the number of questions going into the association scores for the Political, Economic and Religious clusters, thereby stabilizing these scores. 'Works for others' originally represented the Lazy cluster, and was interpreted as representing the Economic
cluster; 'speaks to officials' from the Incompetent cluster was used to represent Political
norms, and 'helps cargo holders' from the Irreligious cluster was used to represent
Religious norms. These reinterpretations left the Lazy cluster with one norm and the Incompetent and Irreligious clusters without any representative norms: therefore, no association scores were calculated for them. Three questions were available for the Kinship,
Violent, and Crafty clusters.

[2]The major difference between the two hamlets is that the mean association between the Religious cluster and farming far away is fairly large in Nachih (.92) and small
in Apas (.21).

Table 8-2 Mean association scores between norm clusters and action alternatives in Apas*

	Mean association score with		
Cluster	farming far away	going to school	going to doctor
Political	.99	2.63	1.36
Religious	.21	.24	−1.66
Economic	1.32	.00	.50
Kinship	1.11**	1.08	.40
Violent	− .49	− .67	− .60
Crafty	− .69	− .85	− .03

*Adult population

**The new association scores for the Kinship, Violent and Crafty clusters had a maximum value of 2 because they were based on two questions. Therefore, they were multiplied by 1.5 to make them comparable with the association score for the other three clusters, which had a maximum value of 3.

school and going to the doctor, both of which involve contact with Ladinos. The Religious cluster is negatively associated with going to the doctor, which reflects the tension between Western medicine and the religious aspects of the Zinacanteco curing system. Finally, the Economic cluster is associated with the profitable practice of farming far away.[1]

Given these community beliefs about what actions are consistent with particular norms, Hypothesis One implies the following four predictions:

1. Individuals with high Political norm scores are more likely to send their children to school than individuals with low Political norm scores.
2. Individuals with high Political norm scores are more likely to go to the doctor.
3. Individuals with high Economic norm scores are more likely to farm far away.
4. Individuals with high Religious norm scores are less likely to go to the doctor.

A fifth prediction is suggested by the obvious association between the Religious cluster and the behavior of taking a religious office. Tak-

[1]It is interesting to note that the most important norm clusters tend to have the strongest associations with behavior, and that the Bad clusters show weaker associations than the Good clusters.

ing a religious office was not one of the three central activities considered in the survey (because this behavior is heavily influenced by a man's wealth), and therefore taking offices was not included in the association questions. Nonetheless, it seems safe to assume that Zinacantecos would make this association. This leads to the last prediction for testing Hypothesis One:

   5. Individuals with high Religious norm scores are more likely to take religious offices.

Table 8-3 presents the results of testing these five predictions in Apas and Nachih. Each prediction was tested by constructing a two-by-two table in which individuals were categorized according to whether their norm score and behavior was high or low;[1] the correlation (Kendall's Tau B) between norms and action was then computed. According to the predictions, the correlation between religion and going to the doctor should be negative and all other correlations should be positive.

Table 8-3   The correlation between norm scores and action*

	Norm score	Action	Correlation	
			Apas	Nachih
1a	Political	Son's education	−.25	−.30
1b	Political	Daughter's education	.06	.33
2	Political	Going to doctor	.00	−.07
3	Economic	Farming far away	.05	.01
4	Religious	Going to doctor	.15	.06
5	Religious	Taking religious offices	.41	−.01

*Kendall's Tau B. Adult population. *n* varies with different behavior.

The data clearly do not support the hypothesis. In Apas, only the prediction of a positive correlation between the Religious cluster and taking religious offices is confirmed. The Nachih data only confirm the prediction about Political norms and daughter's education. The other ten correlations are either close to zero or are in the opposite direction from what was predicted.

> *Testing Hypothesis Two: An individual who believes that a norm is important will tend to engage in action that he believes is consistent with the norm*

Each respondent's beliefs about which norms are consistent with particular action alternatives were measured by the association ques-

[1]The median for all adult subjects from Apas and Nachih, considered as one group, was used as the dividing point for all scores.

tions. For some of these questions, almost all respondents agreed on which norms were associated with which alternative; this consensus was the basis of the predictions used to test Hypothesis One. However, there is sufficient variance to test the effects of an individual's particular associations on the relation between norms and action. Of the fifty-one association questions, there is consensus among more than 75% of the adult men in Apas on only nine questions.

According to Hypothesis Two, there should be a positive relation between associating a Good cluster with an action and engaging in the action, for individuals with a high norm score on that cluster. For example, the hypothesis predicts that individuals who have a high Religious norm score *and* associate religion with going to the doctor will

Table 8-4 Correlation between association score and action, for respondents with high norm scores

	Association of norm with action		Correlation of association and action*	
	Norm	*Action*	*Apas*	*Nachih*
Political		Farm	−.06	−.12
		Ed.	.16	**
		Doc.	−.10	−.05
Religious		Farm	−.04	−.07
		Ed.	.04	
		Doc.	.27	.25
Economic		Farm	.18	.06
		Ed.	.31	
		Doc.	.56	−.15
Kinship		Farm	.12	.04
		Ed.	.17	
		Doc.	.12	.10
Violent		Farm	−.14	.13
		Ed.	.19	
		Doc.	.23	.29
Crafty		Farm	.12	.02
		Ed.	−.27	
		Doc.	.12	.23

*For correlations involving daughter's education, n is between 17 and 30. For all other correlations, n is greater than 34.

**Cells are left blank where n is less than 17.

go to the doctor more than individuals who have a high Religious norm score and associate religion with not going to the doctor. For the Bad clusters, it seems reasonable that the more people associate Bad norms with an action, the less they would engage in the action.

The data for testing Hypothesis Two are presented in Table 8-4, which shows the correlation between associating a norm cluster with an action and performing that action, in Apas and Nachih. For example, the first number in the Apas column(−.06) is the correlation between farming far away and associating farming far away with Political norms, for respondents with high Political norm scores. The second number (+.16) is the correlation between daughter's education and associating education with Political norms, for this group of respondents;[1] and the third number (−.10) is the correlation between going to the doctor and associating it with Political norms.

The data do not confirm the hypothesis. According to the hypothesis, there should be positive correlations between associating a Good norm cluster with an action and performing that action. In fact, most of the correlations are negative or near zero, except for the data from Apas concerning the Economic and Kinship clusters. The hypothesis also predicts negative correlations between associating a Bad norm cluster with an action and performing that action, but most of these correlations are positive.[2]

The correlations between norm scores, association scores and action do not support the theory of the socialized actor. In addition to the correlations shown in Table 8-4, I also examined the correlations for respondents with low norm scores.[3] The only discernible pattern in the total set of correlations is that there is a weak tendency for Apas men to associate Good norms with the actions that they engage in, *regardless* of

[1] Daughter's education was used instead of son's because there were too few cases of men with sons of the appropriate age to permit a three-way cross-tabulation.

[2] The only explanation that accounts for these positive correlations involving the Bad clusters, as well as the positive correlations for the Good clusters, does not use the concept of norms at all. It could be argued that there is a tendency to associate any attribute with action that one has engaged in; people may tend to have a richer and more varied set of cognitions about familiar events. Accordingly, Zinacantecos who go to doctors, for example, are more likely to associate this activity with any norm – Good or Bad – than people who are unfamiliar with going to the doctor. Individuals who go to the doctor would then have high association scores for Bad clusters.

[3] According to Hypothesis Two, there should be fewer positive correlations between associations and actions for respondents with low norm scores, i.e., if a norm cluster is less important to an individual, then his actions will be less affected by his judgments about what actions are consistent with those norms. In fact, for respondents with low norm scores, there were slightly more positive correlations, as opposed to zero or negative correlations. The predicted differences between high and low norm score respondents showed up only in the Apas data on the Economic norm cluster.

whether they personally judge the norm cluster to be important. In other words, the normative beliefs of individuals are not related to their actions. However, there is a slight tendency for individuals to perceive their actions as consistent with the general norms of their community.

Testing Hypothesis Three: Individuals who believe that a norm is important will tend to engage in actions that are specifically referred to by the norm

It could be argued that Hypotheses One and Two are not fair tests of the consistency between an individual's norms and actions because the norm clusters are not clearly relevant to the actions that were measured. For example, one could argue that the Political norm cluster is not clearly related to going to the doctor, even though the responses to the association questions indicate that most Zinacantecos think that Political norms are consistent with going to the doctor.

Hypothesis Three deals with this argument by examining whether an individual's actions are related to those norms that specifically refer to the action. The hypothesis was tested by examining two norms that were included in the paired comparison questions and that specifically refer to an activity that was measured in the survey.

One of the norms from the Religious cluster that was included in the paired comparison questions is: 'he takes religious offices.' There is an obvious connection between this norm and the behavior of taking religious offices. Thus, according to the hypothesis, the more often a respondent selects this specific norm in the paired comparison questions, the more likely that he will in fact take religious offices. The hypothesis also suggests that taking offices will be correlated more strongly with this specific norm than with the general Religious norm score, which is based on responses to all three statements from the Religious cluster: 'he takes religious offices,' 'he is a good ritual advisor,' and 'he respects God.'

The second norm that was used to test Hypothesis Three is 'he knows Spanish,' which is one of the three norms from the Political cluster that was included in the paired comparison questions. Knowing Spanish has a fairly direct connection to the behavior of going to school, since the explicit purpose of the schools is to teach Spanish. According to the hypothesis, respondents who select this norm will tend to send their children to school. In addition, sending children to school should be more strongly correlated with this specific norm than with the general Political norm score, which also includes responses to the other two statements from the Political cluster: 'he is good at settling disputes,' and 'he is good at getting others released from jail.'

The norm about taking religious offices provides an excellent test of Hypothesis Three, but the norm about knowing Spanish is not as appropriate because of the somewhat unclear connection between knowing Spanish and going to school. Many Zinacantecos learn Spanish outside of school or go to school without learning Spanish. On the other hand, as shown above, Zinacantecos are virtually unanimous in associating this norm with going to school.

Table 8-5 presents the relevant correlations for testing Hypothesis Three, and these data clearly do not support the hypothesis. In Nachih, all three correlations between behavior and norms that specifically refer to that behavior, are negative or near zero. In Apas, two of the three correlations are near zero. Apas does show a positive correlation between the behavior of taking religious offices and the norm that refers to this activity. However, the behavior is more strongly correlated with the general religious norm score.[1] The table shows that norms that specifically refer to an action do not have stronger positive correlations with the action than more general norms.

Hypothesis Three is not supported. Individuals who believe that a normative statement is important do not tend to perform the action that is clearly implied by the norm.

Table 8-5 Correlations between actions and specific v. general norms

| *Action* | *Type of Norm* | *Correlation** | |
		Apas	Nachih
Sending son to school	Specific (knows Spanish)	.07	−.48
	General (Political norm score)	−.25	−.30
Sending daughter to school	Specific (knows Spanish)	.07	.09
	General (Political norm score)	.06	.33
Taking religious offices	Specific (takes offices)	.20	−.09
	General (Religious norm score)	.41	−.01

*Kendall's Tau B. Adult population.

[1]In both hamlets the pattern of correlations involving taking religious offices is not substantially changed by controlling for wealth.

Further analyses of the relation between individuals' norms and actions

In addition to testing the three hypotheses discussed above, the survey results were analyzed in several other ways, to determine whether there were any indications of a positive correlation between an individual's norms and his actions. I explored the effects of wealth and age, and inspected the matrices of correlations between norm scores, actions, and association scores.

The relationship between norms and actions is not clarified by controlling for wealth.[1] One might expect that norms and behavior would be more consistent among the rich since the poor may not have adequate resources to act as they wish. However, the results of retesting the hypotheses, holding wealth constant, show that the consistency of norms and action is no greater among the rich than among the poor, in both hamlets. Controlling for age[2] also fails to produce a striking shift in the relation between norms and action. There is a slight tendency, in both Apas and Nachih, for norms and actions to be more consistent among the young than among the old.[3] However, these differences according to age were not strong, and even among the younger respondents, most of the correlations did not confirm the hypothesis that an individual's norms are consistent with his actions. In addition, a careful inspection of the matrices of correlations between actions, norm scores, measures of social position, and association scores failed to uncover any consistent relationship between norms and actions. (Some of these correlations are presented in the Appendix.)

Conclusions

The careful survey of the norms and actions of Zinacantecos failed to support the theory of the socialized actor. Individuals with a particu-

---

[1]Wealth was measured by asking informants to place the men in categories of wealth, ranked from high to low. In Apas, one informant ranked the men once, another ranked them twice, and the three rankings were then averaged. In Nachih, two informants ranked the men separately and then the two cooperatively ranked them, and the three rankings were averaged. On the basis of these average rankings, the men in each hamlet were divided into four wealth groups, each containing about the same number of people. This data was collected by Frank Cancian.

[2]The age of each respondent was established in the census of the hamlets, using the method of interviewing informants. After establishing the absolute age of a few individuals, the relative ages of other individuals was carefully elicited and cross-checked.

[3]For example, in Apas, among the younger half of the respondents, not one of the four correlations that were used to test Hypothesis Two and could be controlled for age (correlations 1b, 2, 3 and 4 on Table 8-3) were in the wrong direction. The older respondents also tended to have a higher frequency of deviant association scores. For example, more older men than younger associated Political norms with *not* going to school.

lar normative orientation do not behave as the community in general would expect them to. An individual's actions do not follow his own definition of what would be consistent with his norms. Finally, norms that specifically refer to an action alternative are not correlated with the individual's actions any more than general norms.

These negative findings, together with the results of previous research reported in Chapter 7, strongly suggest that the theory of the socialized actor must be revised. The large number of studies that have failed to find a substantial positive correlation between an individual's norms, or attitudes, and his behavior, may be questioned on the grounds that superficial beliefs and behaviors were measured, or that the questionnaire items were not meaningful to respondents. The results from the Zinacantan survey cannot be dismissed on these grounds. The measures of norms were based on a careful study of how Zinacantecos view their normative system, and the actions and the norms that were considered in the survey are extremely important to Zinacantecos. In addition, most of the measures are reasonably reliable and valid.[1]

Moreover, three alternative interpretations of 'a consistent relation between norms and action' were tested. If the theory of the socialized actor were adequate, then the correlations between an individual's norms and his actions should have been consistently positive for at least one of the hypotheses, although they might have been small because of measurement error or the influence of other variables. However, as we have seen, the survey data show no pattern of positive correlations.

The next chapter develops an alternative to the theory of the socialized actor. It presents the social identity approach to norms and social action, and shows how this approach explains many of the findings of previous research.

[1]Evidence supporting the reliability and validity of the measures includes stability of response to one paired comparison question that appeared twice in the survey; similarity of response to questions using norms from the same cluster, for both paired comparison and association questions; the low level of interviewer bias for the Good paired comparison questions; the confirmation of the responses on behavior by knowledgeable and trusted informants; and the high correlation between two independent measures of the behavior of going to the doctor. On the other hand, the stability of response to the paired comparison question that was repeated in the survey was not very high. This evidence has been discussed in Chapter 6 and in the early parts of this chapter.

9

SOCIAL IDENTITY: AN ALTERNATIVE THEORETICAL APPROACH[1]

HOW ARE NORMS related to the structure of social action and the organization of society? The theory of the socialized actor has been the most widely accepted approach to answering this question. However, it fails to account for much of what we know about the functioning of norms. It does not explain why the relation between an individual's normative beliefs and his actions is often very weak, as has been shown in the last two chapters. Nor does it explain why norms and action often seem to be strongly related when groups or cultures are compared, or why norms sometimes change very rapidly.

The social identity approach suggests how to explain many of these relationships. First, it accounts for why norms and action tend to be strongly related across groups but not across individuals. This approach assumes that norms affect behavior by specifying what action will cause others to validate a particular identity. Therefore, beliefs that are perceived to be shared by a group will be related to action, while the personal beliefs of an individual may not be.

Second, the social identity approach suggests that norms can be learned and can change rapidly. In contrast to the theory of the socialized actor, this approach assumes that norms do not need to be internalized into the individual's personality in order to affect action. Therefore, new norms can be adopted in a short period of time and without intensive interaction.

[1]Many of my ideas on the social identity approach developed out of discussions with John Meyer. I have also learned a lot from the comments of Frank Cancian, Albert Bergeson and Stephen Olsen.

The following discussion focuses on these two issues where the differences between the theories are clearest: individual v. group norms, and normative change and the concept of internalization. The first part of the chapter considers some of the basic assumptions and implications of the social identity approach, and presents some general propositions about norms. In particular, I will discuss: (1) the relation between norms and action; (2) normative change and the relation between the individual and identities; (3) types of normative beliefs; and (4) the concept of action or behavior. The second part of this chapter reviews some findings from previous studies that support the propositions suggested by the social identity perspective, and do not support the theory of the socialized actor.

Part One: The social identity approach – assumptions and implications·

The social identity approach has a long history in the social sciences. It is part of the 'symbolic interaction' and 'social construction of reality' perspectives, formulated by Emile Durkheim, G. H. Mead and Alfred Schutz, and developed in the contemporary work of Goffman, Becker, Berger, Garfinkel and many others.[1] It is also related to reference group theory.[2]

A few social scientists have moved towards developing a social identity theory of norms and action, or have urged others to do so. Thus, Sherif et al. argue that the study of attitudes or norms should be linked to 'group contexts and the reference groups of individuals' (1965:212). Similarly, John Finley Scott (1971) states that conformity to norms should be explained in terms of on-going (and past) interaction with others, and not in terms of an internal state of the individual.[3] But there has been little progress in constructing a coherent alternative to the theory of the socialized actor, and there is, as yet, no systematic social identity theory of norms and action.

The following discussion clarifies the basic ideas and implications of the social identity perspective, but it leaves many theoretical problems unresolved. In particular, the direction of causation between

[1]For a representative sampling, consult Becker (1963), Goffman (1967), Berger and Luckmann (1966), Douglas (1970), Blum and McHugh (1971).

[2]On reference group theory, see Merton (1957).

[3]Much of the following discussion is similar to J. F. Scott's analysis of how norms are changed by changing a person's status or withholding symbolic validations of identity. The difference is that this chapter is stated in a phenomenological, actor-oriented terminology instead of in behaviorist, learning-theory terms. Learning-theory concepts seem less useful, for reasons that are presented later.

norms and action is usually unspecified, and some crucial concepts such as 'group' and 'important identity' are not clearly defined. However, first steps are often uncertain and I believe that this clarification of the differences between the two theoretical approaches identifies some critical problems for future research.

1. Norms and action

The social identity approach begins with the concept of a social identity, or a collectively defined kind of person. An identity is a 'role' that covers a relatively broad range of actions and that includes assumptions about the probable motives or reasons that explain the actions of that kind of person.[1] Norms are treated as perceived rules – rules that inform persons and groups[2] that if an individual does certain things or has certain attributes then he or she is a particular kind of person. More precisely, norms are collective perceptions or beliefs about what actions or attributes will cause others to validate a particular identity. Individuals conform to norms in order to validate an identity.

This concept of norms and action differs from the theory of the socialized actor in several important respects. First, in the social identity approach, norms affect action because they are perceptions of what others will do or what others know is proper; norms are not personal beliefs. For example, a woman who wants to become a graduate student conforms to the norms about working for high grades because she expects that the relevant others will not accept her as a graduate student unless she does. Her personal beliefs about whether these actions are good or appropriate are unimportant.

Second, norms are collective or shared in a double sense. A rule is a norm insofar as members collectively perceive that those who validate the identity agree on the rule. For example, in a graduate department, the rule that graduate students should read Marx would be a norm if the students agreed that the faculty agreed that reading Marx was an attribute of a good graduate student. In the social identity ap-

---

[1]The concept of 'social identity' is difficult to define precisely. It is particularly difficult to state criteria for deciding what to exclude. What is the minimum amount of perceived consensus necessary for *collective* definition of a kind of person? How many kinds of actions constitute a *broad* range and how general or powerful do the motivational assumptions have to be?

[2]I am using the work 'group' very loosely in this chapter, to include any collectivity or social category of which a person can be a member or incumbent (e.g., a club, a nation, an ethnic category, or an age category).

proach, norms are shared in this sense, but in contrast to the Parsonian approach, a rule can be a norm without any person being personally committed to it. For instance, in the department described above, there might be a state of pluralistic ignorance, in which each faculty member privately believed that reading Marx was a waste of time.[1] In such a situation, members would conform to the norm unless their misperception of other people's beliefs was exposed, as suggested by the fable 'The Emperor's New Clothes.'[2]

Third, the social identity approach implies that norms are located within the groups that have the right to validate the relevant identity.[3] Norms are not located in individuals. However, individuals must agree that a particular group has the right to define an identity; otherwise the group will lose this right and individuals will not conform to the rules promulgated by the group, at least not for normative reasons.[4]

Thus, the norms that define being a professor are located within departments, universities and national associations of scholars. The norms that define a person as sane v. insane are located primarily in the profession of psychiatry. In a secondary way these norms are located in the society as a whole, since every competent adult has some right to define a person as sane or insane.

These three ideas are the basis of the social identity approach to norms and action. They suggest the following general proposition: *norms* (or collective perceptions of what will cause others to validate an identity) *will be consistent with action.*

The social identity approach makes no predictions about personal beliefs; they are outside the scope of the theory.[5] For example, accord-

[1]The state of pluralistic ignorance recalls one of Laing's comments on alienation: 'When we have installed them in our hearts, we are only a plurality of solitudes in which what each person has in common is his allocation to the other of the necessity for his own actions' (1968:84).

[2]My own experience as a Harvard graduate student provides another illustration. When I first arrived at Harvard, I expected that Harvard students would be the kind of people who dressed formally, and I observed that my fellow students in fact did so. Therefore, I concluded that my fellow students believed that it was important to dress well, and I quickly abandoned my casual dressing habits. About a year later, I discussed my perceptions with some fellow students and discovered that they had gone through the same process. Almost all of them perceived that everyone else cared about good clothes and almost none of them personally believed that formal clothes were a good thing. As I recall, most of us eventually went back to our sloppy clothes.

[3]The authority to define an identity may be contested by several groups, as shown in the study of school superintendents by Gross *et al.* (1958).

[4]However, they may conform because of the resources and coercive sanctions that are controlled by the group.

[5]A correlation between beliefs and action might be found for a variety of reasons besides either socialization or the identity implications of the action. For example, the statement of belief may be a description of a recurrent behavior pattern, e.g., 'I like

ing to this perspective, if a man believes that it is a good thing to live in a racially integrated neighborhood, this belief may or may not be consistent with his actions. However, if he perceives that his circle of friends will not define him as a member of their group unless he lives in an integrated neighborhood, then his perceptions are likely to be consistent with his actions. Some of the evidence that supports this proposition will be reviewed later on.

2. Normative change and the relation between individuals and identities

In the Parsonian approach, individuals conform to situationally specific norms primarily because they want to conform, and feel frustrated or guilty if they do not. The degree of conformity is explained in part by the degree of internalization, or the extent to which social norms have become identical with personal desires. Since the personality is assumed to be a stable structure that is largely formed in early childhood through intensive interaction, this theory implies that norms change slowly and through intensive face-to-face relationships.

The social identity approach to norms is more cognitive and less motivational. It assumes that individuals conform to norms because that is the way to validate identities. Norms, in effect, are the rules for being a particular kind of person, and the rules often change. Being a 'patriotic American' may mean killing Japanese one year and entertaining them the next. Beliefs about what behavior validates an identity may change very rapidly and without intensive interaction.

However, there is an important motivational assumption in the social identity perspective. The approach assumes that individuals are motivated to maintain particular identities for themselves and to cast others in the appropriate reciprocal identities. It assumes that some identities are more important than others. This means that the concept of motivation or commitment is 'pushed back' from particular norms to identities. That is, the concept of personal motivation is not relevant to explaining why, for example, a 'good woman' does not initiate sexual intercourse, or why 'important politicians' drive big, expensive cars. These norms can and have changed rapidly and without intensive interaction. But it does seem necessary to invoke a concept like personal motivation to explain how people come to be so highly committed to

chocolate ice cream better than vanilla' meaning 'I always buy chocolate ice cream.' Or the statement of belief may mean an intention to perform a particular act, e.g., 'I like presidential candidate McGovern better than Nixon' meaning 'I intend to vote for McGovern.'

identities like being a woman, being high status, or being sane. One problem with this argument is that it is often difficult to distinguish an identity from the norms that define it. However, the distinction seems useful in accounting for the differential resistance to change of identities and norms.[1]

Changing a person's identity often requires intensive face-to-face interaction and creates considerable emotional stress. The evidence on total institutions, on brainwashing and various rites of passage shows that the process of changing an individual's status or identity often involves total isolation from previous social contacts, intensive interaction with the others who validate the new identity and total dependence on these others (see review in Scott, 1971, chapter 5). There are clear similarities between these situations and childhood socialization, and the entire process looks like what is meant by reconstructing the personality.[2] On the other hand, some changes in identity seem to occur without intense emotions and social rituals, e.g., the change from being a student at a working-class high school to being a Harvard freshman.

Explaining the differential commitment of individuals to identities is a key problem in the social identity approach, and there are several theoretical strategies for dealing with it. A social structural approach is suggested by the analysis of Zinacanteco norms. It showed that the perceived importance of different 'good' identities depends on the extent to which the identity is located in formally organized, community-wide activities. According to this interpretation, one would expect that in the United States, the most important identity for an adult male would be his occupational role, since the economy is the only institutional sector that is formally organized on a society-wide basis and in which virtually all adult men actively participate, i.e., any two strangers can begin to relate to each other by first locating themselves in the occupational system.[3]

[1]The distinction was first suggested to me by John Meyer. He found it useful for explaining his surprising finding that adults do not respond differently to the actions of a small child when they are told that the child is a boy as opposed to a girl (Meyer and Sobieszek, 1972). Meyer reasoned that if sexual identity is not learned through the differential response of others, perhaps what is learned is the 'simple' social fact that 'I am a girl (and will become a woman)' or 'I am a boy.' The norms specifying the appropriate actions for these identities may be learned later and may be much easier to change.

[2]Dramatic changes in identity or personality can also occur on the society or community level, not only on the individual level. Revolutions, revitalization movements and events like the Cambodia crisis on American campuses seem to involve a redefinition of the basic identities that constitute the community.

[3]This approach also suggests that women will not have an identity in the community or society insofar as they are not expected to participate in any society-wide or community-wide organization.

There are several other approaches to explaining commitment to identities without using the concept of personality. Differential commitment can be explained in terms of shared beliefs about the relative importance of different identities. Alternatively, a behaviorist might consider the valued resources that are associated with different identities. Another possibility is to focus on certain ascribed statuses, such as sex role, which seem to function as 'master identities' that determine the importance of other identities.

None of these approaches seems totally satisfactory because they fail to explain why individuals and groups sometimes withdraw commitment from institutionalized identities, or experience alienation of their 'selves' from certain identities. The relation of an individual to an identity seems to vary from a mechanical, minimal performance of a stereotype of a role to an active, passionate creation of an identity that combines social definitions with personal interpretations. In order to explain these occurrences, it may be necessary to use the Freudian – Parsonian theory of personality or to develop a concept of the self. But this issue is too complex to resolve here.

The important point, for this preliminary consideration of an alternative theory of norms and action, is the following: *given* commitment to an identity, conforming to norms does not involve internalization. Contrary to the implications of the theory of the socialized actor, norms may change very rapidly and without resocialization.

In sum, the social identity approach suggests the following general proposition: (1) *norms* (or collective definitions of an identity) *can change rapidly and without intensive interaction.* In addition, this approach suggests that (2) *change in identity or status produces an immediate change in the norms that are relevant to an individual.* For example, when a person changes from being single to being married, the norms that define 'being a good husband or wife' suddenly become relevant. The evidence that supports these propositions will be presented shortly, following a discussion of the types of normative beliefs and the concept of action.

3. Types of normative beliefs

The previous discussion has shown how the social identity approach and the theory of the socialized actor suggest different propositions about norms and action, and normative change. The two approaches also lead to a different definition of the domain of normative beliefs. The assumptions of the theory of the socialized actor imply a narrower definition that minimizes the importance of beliefs about ascribed attributes and ignores membership norms and reality assumptions.

The theory of the socialized actor assumes that action is a process in which individuals choose between alternatives so as to satisfy their wants. Norms affect action by being internalized and shaping the wants of the individual. In this perspective, norms are 'should' statements that guide the actor's choice among alternatives, e.g., 'a young child should obey his parents.' Norms are not 'is' statements that define the social world, e.g., 'a young child is dependent on his parents.' In contrast, the social identity approach views norms as 'is' statements that define what identities exist and what actions and attributes validate them.[1]

The emphasis on choosing among alternatives in the theory of the socialized actor implies that the domain of norms is limited to statements about actions over which the actor has some control and therefore can make a choice. Statements describing attributes over which the actor has no control are not norms, e.g., 'he is not respected because he is deaf,' or 'men are not good at being nurses.' In the social identity approach, these statements are norms that define identities.

The analysis of Zinacanteco norms showed that the domain of norms in that community includes attributes over which the actor has no control, or ascribed as opposed to achieved attributes. In most communities, being a respected, high-ranking person depends in part on ascribed attributes like age, sex, race, physical appearance, kinship, etc.

The importance of ascribed attributes in ranking systems is probably recognized to some extent by all sociologists, including those who think in terms of the theory of the socialized actor. However, these norms tend to be ignored or misinterpreted because they do not fit the basic assumptions of the theory.[2] Insofar as beliefs about ascribed attributes are an important part of the normative order, the social identity approach is a more productive way of thinking about norms.

A related difference between the two theories concerns the importance of ranking norms v. other normative beliefs. Since the theory of the socialized actor stresses choice and decision making, it leads to a

---

[1] Most 'should' statements can be phrased as 'is' statements that define how to be a high ranking member, e.g., the 'should' statement presented above can be restated as 'a child that obeys his parents is a good child.' However, many 'is' statements cannot be phrased as 'should' statements. All the statements in the model of Zinacanteco norms can be phrased either way, except for those in the Incompetent cluster.

[2] I believe that the books of Berger (1967) and Berger and Luckmann (1966) made a great impact on American sociologists because they focused on norms as 'is' statements, not 'ought' statements. Their ideas provided a new perspective for the many sociologists, including myself, who had come to take the theory of the socialized action for granted.

focus on ranking norms or standards for evaluating alternatives. The theory tends to ignore those normative conceptions that have nothing to do with making choices or evaluations, i.e., membership norms and reality assumptions.

In contrast, the social identity approach provides a framework for thinking about these beliefs. The three types of beliefs defined in Chapter 1 can be seen as three components of social reality that are critical to claiming or attributing identities.

Reality assumptions are collective definitions of what identities, roles or corporate institutions exist or are possible.[1] For example, the members of a community must agree that individuals and groups can be divided into the aristocracy, the bourgeoisie and the people, before anyone can claim or be assigned the identity of 'bourgeois traitor' or 'defender of the people.' Membership norms are shared beliefs about what actions or attributes identify bona fide incumbents of particular roles or members of social groups or categories. For example, these norms specify how a defender of the people can be distinguished from a bourgeois traitor. Finally, ranking norms are beliefs that identify the rank of an individual within a particular group or category, e.g., the belief that a good defender of the people is successful in prosecuting traitors.

The importance of reality assumptions and membership norms has been recognized by many social scientists, but they have rarely been studied.[2] The social identity perspective focuses attention on these normative beliefs and suggests some possible ideas for research.[3]

One of the most interesting implications of the concept of reality assumptions is that rapid social changes may occur if these assumptions can be changed; and conversely, if they are not changed then many social patterns will remain stable. This suggests that rapid changes might occur if a few prominent people publicly performed and gave meaning to an act that was previously impossible or meaningless. Thus, the rate of breaking windows at universities in the 1960s proba-

---

[1]Reality assumptions also include conceptions that have nothing to do with kinds of people, e.g., the idea that the time of year when the days are shortest is December and Christmas time. See discussion of the limited aspect of norms considered in this book in Chapter 1.

[2]See Homans (1950:127), Berger and Luckmann (1966), Garfinkel (1967). Parsons also seems to be commenting on the significance of reality assumptions when he states that, in addition to shared norms and values, social order requires 'order in the symbolic systems which make communication possible' (1951:36). Finally, most anthropologists include reality assumptions within the concept of culture, e.g., Kluckhohn (1958).

[3]See Cancian (n.d.) for a more detailed discussion of reality assumptions that was written before this chapter, from a somewhat different theoretical perspective.

bly increased rapidly after the first students threw rocks at windows and announced, on television news, that 'trashing' was part of a political protest. Before this event, 'trashing' did not exist for American students as a meaningful political act.

The effects of reality assumptions can also be investigated in situations of social stability. For example, Meyer argues that the reality assumptions about the products of different kinds of schools influences the degree to which these schools affect their students. 'For example, a school whose graduates are generally understood to become members of an elite with broadly-defined powers will have much greater impact on the values of its students than will a school whose graduates are defined as eligible for more limited technical roles' (1970:565).

This discussion of different types of normative beliefs may raise some methodological questions. In particular, how useful is the Frame-Sorting Method that was presented in the first part of this book for describing different types of norms? The Frame-Sorting Method seems to be a useful way of describing ranking norms, whether they are defined as 'should' statements or 'is' statements.[1] The particular frames that were used to describe Zinacanteco norms elicited primarily norms about actions that the actor can control, although one of the nine norm clusters focused on ascribed attributes (the Incompetent cluster). The Frame-Sorting Method can also be used to describe membership norms, using frames like 'Doctors are . . .' or 'Doctors are . . . but nurses are . . .' However, reality assumptions, since they are taken for granted, probably require a different methodological strategy, as was discussed in Chapter 1.

In sum, the social identity approach interprets norms as 'is' statements that define the social world, and it provides a framework for understanding many types of normative beliefs. In contrast, the theory of the socialized actor views norms as 'should' statements and leads to a more limited conception of norms.

This concludes the discussion of how the two theoretical approaches interpret the concept of norms. I will now consider the fourth and final topic in this presentation of the social identity approach: the concept of action.

---

[1]A study of American norms might show that these two types of norms are separate domains that can be elicited by different frames. For example, 'should' statements might be elicited by a frame like 'a good professor should . . .' while 'is' statements might be elicited by a frame like 'the professors that are respected around here are . . .'

4. The concept of action or behavior

Most studies of norms and action assume that what a person does is 'out there' as an objective event that can be categorized and measured by any competent scientist. But the social identity approach suggests that the perception and performance of meaningful action is limited by the reality assumptions and norms that define possible acts. For example, in the United States, it is not possible for one person to be a president and a transvestite. If the president began to wear women's dresses and makeup, then either he would be impeached or labelled as crazy and be redefined as a non-president, or his new appearance would be defined as appropriate for men. Similarly, my impressions of the traditional South suggest that it would not have been possible for a male Negro member of a predominantly white group to be both (1) responsible and trustworthy and (2) angry and aggressive.

The beliefs and assumptions of a community may also limit action in a less absolute way and simply make certain acts or combinations of attributes less likely. Thus it is possible but unlikely that an American woman will be both (1) warm and feminine and (2) assertive and aggressive. A social scientist who records her interaction and operates within a different set of reality assumptions may find that she emits a high rate of both aggressive and affectionate acts. However, the woman and the other members of the group probably will not perceive this and will not respond to both types of behavior as meaningful. That is, she will not elicit both the responses that validate an action as aggressive and the responses that validate an action as warm and feminine.

There is some empirical evidence that supports this argument. D'Andrade (1970) examined how group members rate each other on attributes like agreeing with others or making suggestions. He found that members tend to give each other the same rating on attributes that are culturally defined as similar; they do not give each other the same ratings on attributes that are shown to be highly intercorrelated when social scientists record the group's behavior. In other words, the ratings reflect the group's beliefs about correlated attributes, not the behavioral correlations observed by social scientists. D'Andrade reanalyzed the results of several small group experiments. He examined the correlations among categories of behavior (e.g., 'agrees,' 'suggests') in four sets of data: (1) group members' ratings of each other's behavior, (2) observers' ratings of the group members' behavior, (3) an on-going record of behavior using a modified version of the Bales category system, and (4) judgments of semantic similarity among the behavior categories. He found that the correlations based on semantic similarity were very similar to those based on the ratings of members and observers. But the correlations based on the on-going record of behavior were unrelated to the members' rating and to the judgments of semantic similarity.[1] In other words, the group members were perceiving (and probably responding to) each other as performing sets of actions that have similar social meaning.

Additional supporting evidence is reported by Hall (1972), who found that women who are highly active in a discussion rate themselves as very low on cordiality, although a record of their behavior shows that they have an extremely high rate of initiating positive reactions and a low rate of initiating negative reactions.[2]

The preceding discussion implies that the perception and performance of meaningful action will *necessarily* conform to the reality assumptions of the actors. Moreover, within the context of those acts defined as meaningful by the reality assumptions, the norms of a group will tend to be consistent with action as defined by the norms for the reasons discussed in section one of this chapter.[3] However, the norms may well be inconsistent with action as defined by an outside observer. The social identity approach starts with the assumption that people conform to norms in order to obtain validation for particular identities from certain others. Norms concern action-as-responded-to-by-those-others, or meaningful action insofar as it confirms a particular membership or rank. Norms do not concern behavior that is measured 'objectively' without reference to its meaning to the group. Therefore, if a researcher measures behavior in terms of a category system that is not shared by the group, we should not be surprised if the data show a low correlation between norms and behavior.

[1]D'Andrade interprets his results as showing that the long range memory of observers and members (i.e., their ratings of members at the end of group meetings) is not a good measure of behavior. The relations among the four sets of correlations discussed above, for a series of task-oriented groups were: 1 and 2 $r_s = .52$; 1 and 3 $r_s = .07$; 1 and 4 $r_s .50$; 2 and 3 $r_s = .20$; 2 and 4 $r_s = .64$; 3 and 4 $r_s = -.05$.

[2]All of the active women in Hall's study were extremely supportive and positive and seemed to be trying to soften and obscure their leadership role. Other group members rated these women as higher than active men on cordiality.

[3]This argument raises the following question: Do the membership norms of a group function like reality assumptions? For example, if an American professor says he is illiterate, will this be responded to as a meaningful act because the statement makes sense in other settings in the United States, or will it be treated as a statement that is crazy or 'really means something else' because it contradicts the membership norms that define 'being a professor'? There is a problem of system reference here, and of the relations among society-wide definitions of possible actions and the definitions that are limited to particular settings or groups.

This conception of action raises many difficult theoretical and methodological issues, none of which will be considered here. This book has focused on the concept of norms, not action, but it would be misleading to ignore completely the implications of the social identity approach for the concepts of action and behavior.

Part Two: Evidence in support of the social identity approach

The remainder of this chapter reviews some research findings on two issues where the Parsonian and social identity approaches have different empirical implications: (1) individual beliefs v. group norms, and (2) normative change. This presentation should not be taken as a systematic test of specific hypotheses. The propositions suggested by the social identity approach are much too general to be tested and the review of the literature is neither exhaustive nor systematic. My purpose is rather to show that the Parsonian and social identity approaches have different empirical implications and are not merely two languages for saying the same thing.[1] I will demonstrate this by describing examples of research that support the social identity perspective but do not support the theory of the socialized actor.

1. Evidence on the consequences of individual beliefs v. group norms

The social identity approach suggests the following proposition on the relation between norms and action: *Norms* (or collective perceptions of what will cause others to validate an identity) *will be consistent with action.*[2] This approach makes no predictions about individual beliefs. However, the theory of the socialized actor implies that individual beliefs will be consistent with action, as discussed in Chapter 7.

This proposition is supported by three types of evidence. First, there are many studies that show that the beliefs of individuals are consistent with action only if the beliefs are group norms. Second, there are several studies that have found that variation in beliefs across groups is consistent with action, and beliefs that are shared by a group are probably norms. Finally, the most relevant evidence comes from a few studies that have found that norms in particular, as opposed to

---

[1]It is true that both theoretical approaches could be modified so that both have the same empirical implications, but this is a trivial point that denies the usefulness of theories.

[2]This proposition does not refer to reality assumptions. They are consistent with meaningful action, but this is true by definition, as discussed above.

other shared beliefs, are strongly correlated with action. These three types of studies will now be described, in order.

The first type of evidence comes from studies of the beliefs and actions of individuals. The results of many of these studies can be interpreted as confirming the proposition, and as not confirming the Parsonian approach. Many studies of attitudes and behavior have found that an individual's beliefs about race relations or honesty are not strongly related to the individual's actions, as discussed in Chapter 7. In most of these studies, the attitudes or beliefs that were measured probably did not define an important social identity. Therefore they are outside the scope of the proposition, but they are relevant to the Parsonian approach and they fail to confirm it.

Some other studies do seem to have measured beliefs that define important identities, though they still found no relationship between beliefs and action. For example, the Zinacantan survey found no relationship between the perceived importance of different norm clusters and action, even though the norm clusters defined the important identity of being a respected man in the community (see also Kenkel, 1963). These results seem to contradict my proposition. However, they can be explained by the social identity approach on the grounds that, in these studies, the variance in beliefs among individuals did not represent a significant difference in norms.

The social identity approach suggests that two norms are significantly different if they imply that an action will have different effects on membership or rank. For example, among Zinacantecos, believing that the Religious norm cluster is more important than the Economic cluster, or vice versa, may not be significantly different because the difference is not related to any social identity in Zinacantan. This explanation could be tested by finding out whether Zinacantecos associate a particular rank ordering of the norm clusters with a particular kind of person.

A particular rank ordering could become part of a social identity. For example, a set of Zinacantecos could emerge that was publicly defined as kinds of people who both make a lot of money by using advanced farming techniques *and* refuse to participate in the system of religious offices. Two mutually recognized subgroups might then develop, each defined by a different rank ordering of Economics and Religion. Under such conditions, one would expect to find a strong relationship between variation in ordering these norms and the relevant actions.

Some of the findings of a positive relationship between individual beliefs and behavior seem to come from studies that did measure significant variance in norms. In a study of college students, Rokeach found that individuals who gave a high rank order to the value of 'salvation' were much more likely to attend church regularly than individuals who gave this value a low rank (1969). It is likely that among these students, beliefs about salvation functioned as membership norms that distinguished religious, church-going types of students from other socially defined types. In another study of college students, Walter L. Wallace (1966) found that if freshmen changed their beliefs about the importance of grades, this affected their subsequent academic achievement. Once again, it is likely that beliefs about grades defined different subgroups on campus.

In sum, the available data tend to confirm the proposition that an individual's beliefs will be consistent with his actions insofar as the beliefs define an important identity, and are shared with others who validate the identity. In Sherif's language, norms affect behavior insofar as they are anchored in a reference group (1965).

The second source of evidence in support of my proposition comes from studies that have compared groups or cultures and have found a consistent relationship between beliefs and action.[1] These findings support the proposition that group norms are consistent with behavior insofar as group consensus indicates that a belief is a norm. Consensus usually corresponds to social institutions; if the members of a group agree on a belief about appropriate action, the belief is probably a membership or ranking norm that defines the identities included in the group.

Many comparative studies have found a consistent relationship between normative beliefs and action. Kohn (1969) found that the values and socialization behavior of parents from different social classes were positively correlated. Strodtbeck (1951) observed decision making in married couples from three cultures, and found that the observed authority structure corresponded to the norms of the culture, as measured by Florence Kluckhohn's value-orientation questionnaire. Her questionnaire has been used in a large number of societies (Kluckhohn and Strodtbeck, 1961), and it would be easy to draw up long lists of actions that varied across these societies consistently with the variation in values or norms.[2]

---

[1] The importance of beliefs shared with a group v. individual beliefs is indirectly supported by studies showing that individual perceptual judgments are more stable if they are supported by others. See Sherif's description (1965) of Pollis's study.

[2] Many comparative studies in anthropology are also relevant, although the methods of measuring norms and action usually make the results difficult to interpret.

A comparison of the two hamlets that were included in the Zinacantan survey also provides some supporting evidence. There is one consistent difference in norms that can be related to an action that was measured in the survey: speaking Spanish and dealing with Ladino bureaucrats is judged to be more important in Nachih than in Apas (see Table 5-3). If group norms are consistent with the rates of activity within a group, then more people in Nachih than in Apas should speak Spanish. Several bits of data confirm this expectation. All respondents were asked whether or not they knew Spanish, and 16% of the Nachih respondents said they knew Spanish well, compared to 10% of the Apas respondents.[1] My own impression is that the difference is much larger, since it was easy to find men from Nachih who were literate enough to do the sorting task, but almost impossible to find such men from Apas.[2]

The third type of evidence that supports my proposition comes from studies that have explicitly set out to measure variation in group norms. This evidence is the most relevant, since the proposition refers to group norms, not other shared beliefs.

A strong relationship between norms and action has been found in many case studies of the normative basis of stratification, such as Homans' analysis of the Bank Wiring Room (1950) or Whyte's description of the Norton Street gang (1955). However, there is no appropriate data from studies of a large sample of groups.

The results of an exploratory study by Schoonhoven and Gross (n.d.) illustrate the type of research that is needed to confirm clearly the importance of norms that define group identities. Schoonhoven and Gross investigated norms and actions in two groups involved in the Women's Liberation movement; one was a consciousness-raising, encounter-type group and the other was an action group organized to create a day care center. The members of both groups unanimously endorsed the normative beliefs of the movement, such as sharing household tasks with men, and entering traditionally male occupations. However, the members of the encounter group conformed to these norms to a much greater extent than the members of the action group.

Both groups were interviewed about the attributes of the most respected group members and 'the activities that are most approved of'

[1] The validity of the responses elicited by this type of linguistic-ability question has been confirmed by Fishman and Cooper (1971).

[2] Apas appears to give much greater importance to the Economic norms; however, the hamlets cannot be compared on farming far away, since different measures of distance are used for each hamlet and there is no data on other behavioral alternatives that might be related to the Economic norms. Nachih appears to value taking religious offices more than Apas, but the Bad norm of not taking religious offices is given more importance in Apas than in Nachih. In Nachih 40% of the respondents over fifty years old had taken a low-prestige cargo, or no cargo, compared to 50% of the Apas respondents.

by the group. The responses showed that in the encounter group, the Women's Liberation beliefs were the ranking norms and defined how to be a respected member of the group. In the action groups these beliefs were not the ranking norms; instead, being a valuable member was defined in terms of contributing to the task of creating the day care center.[1] These results support the idea that beliefs that define important identities will be consistent with action, while other shared beliefs may not be. However, the data are merely suggestive since only two groups were studied.

The results of Alexander's research on 'situated identity' also show a relationship between beliefs that define group identities and action. Alexander and his associates have found that the actions of participants in experiments can be predicted by the normative attributes that define 'being a good participant.' Most participants behave so as to maximize their evaluation in terms of the attributes that are culturally defined as relevant to that experiment (Alexander and Knight, 1971).[2] The subjects in Alexander's studies are asked to take the role of a participant in some social psychological experiment. The setting and the behavioral alternatives in the experiment are described and then the subjects are asked to check the personal attributes that are most relevant for evaluating the participants in the experiment (e.g., friendly, intelligent, rational). They also rate participants who behave in different ways, using the relevant attributes; for example, they rate the friendliness of participants who changed their minds in some experiment, and the friendliness of participants who did not change. Other subjects estimate how most participants will act. The typical findings in these studies are (1) subjects estimate that most participants will select the behavior that brings the highest evaluation, in terms of the relevant attributes; (2) when the experiments are actually conducted and not simulated, most participants do in fact select this behavior alternative. In a related study Alexander and Lauderdale (n.d.) found that if there was no consensus on the evaluation of different behaviors, then actual and estimated behavior was widely distributed over the different behavior alternatives.

[1]The interview also showed that the members of the action group were more likely to give 'don't know' responses when asked about the conformity of fellow members to the Women's Liberation beliefs.

[2]Alexander stresses the situational specificity of normative beliefs and has found that the attributes judged to be relevant change considerably when the experimental situation is slightly altered. The specificity v. generality of norms clearly is an important issue. I tend to agree with Rokeach's argument that if norms or attitudes are different for every particular situation, then the concepts are of little use in constructing general explanations of behavior (1968: 128-9).

In other words, ranking norms are consistent with action. If the members of a society share the belief that acting in a particular way in an experiment will elicit a high evaluation or will validate their identity as 'a good participant,' then they will perform that action, and will expect others to do the same. If there is no agreement on the identity implications of different actions, then there will be a high degree of variance in action and in expectations.

The preceding analysis of research on individual and group norms illustrates the type of evidence that supports the social identity perspective on the relation between beliefs and action. These studies do not support the theory of the socialized actor. That theory cannot easily account for the lack of relationship between individual beliefs and action; nor does it explain why beliefs that define identities are most important in shaping action. The main implication of the Parsonian approach is that the behavioral consequences of beliefs depends on prior socialization and the extent to which the belief is internalized.

These results also fail to confirm other theoretical approaches to norms and action. One theory that has been suggested by a few investigators on the basis of their research findings is that beliefs and behavior are independent.[1] However, this approach cannot account for the existence of a relationship between group norms and action. The behaviorist theory that normative assertions and other behaviors are simply the result of sanctions can explain the findings on individual and group norms. However, this can only be done by adding assumptions about the greater rewarding power of group membership and rank, as opposed to other possible rewards or sanctions (see Scott's behaviorist formulation, 1971). All social science theories can probably be restated in behaviorist language, because of the infinite flexibility of the concepts of punishment and reward and the tautological nature of behaviorist explanations;[2] any recurrent action of individuals or groups that is caused by some previous event is 'explained' by calling that event a reward. The usefulness of the social identity approach is that it indicates what types of rewards or sanctions will affect action.

[1]Bryan's studies of how children learn altruism (1970) showed that children's altruistic behavior was influenced only by the behavior of a model and not by the model's statements, and children's altruistic statements were influenced only by the statements of the model. However, since the model's statements do not seem to be an instance of group norms, this finding does not challenge the social identity perspective.

[2]See Campbell (1961) for a convincing demonstration of how the theoretical statements in cognitive, phenomenological psychology can be translated into behaviorist, learning-theory statements, and vice versa.

2. Evidence on normative change

According to the social identity perspective, the commitment to a particular identity may be internalized and very resistant to change, but the norms that specify how to validate that identity are not internalized. Therefore, they may change rapidly and without face-to-face interaction or resocialization. For example, a person's commitment to being a man or a woman is probably very strong and stable, but the norms defining the appropriate physical appearance, sexual behavior, occupational activities, etc., for each sex may change in a short period of time.

Norms specify what actions will cause others to validate membership and rank in a particular identity. If each member of a group believes that the others have changed their beliefs about membership and rank, then the group norms will have changed.

This theoretical perspective on normative change is roughly summarized in a second proposition: *Norms* (or collective definitions of an identity) *can change rapidly and without intensive interaction.*

There is considerable evidence that confirms this proposition, but much of it can also be interpreted as supporting the Parsonian internalization hypothesis. For example, Newcomb and others have found substantial normative change among college students, from their freshman to senior year (Newcomb, 1943). However, these changes could be explained as resulting from intensive interaction among students, identification with upperclassmen and subsequent internalization of the new norms.

There is clearer support for the social identity approach in several studies that have found that the greatest amount of normative change among students occurs in the first few months of the freshman year. Thus Walter L. Wallace (1966) unexpectedly found that the percentage of freshmen who reported that getting high grades in college was 'highly important' to them changed from 75% to 40% between September and November. It then dropped to 31% by April (the percentage of all non-freshmen was 35%). This finding can easily be explained by the social identity theory: learning the norms for a new identity is largely a process of obtaining information about the membership and ranking norms of others. A person who enters a status like 'college student' has a great deal to learn in the first days and weeks, and a declining amount of information to learn after that. In other words, learning norms is often very similar to learning other things, like how to build a house or how to travel by bus in a new city. In contrast, the theory of the socialized actor implies that there would be more normative change after the freshman had been in college long enough to form close relationships, contrary to Wallace's results.

A few other studies of normative change also tend to support the social identity perspective. Two studies of Stanford seniors in 1965 and 1972 found a massive change in the occupational plans and aspirations of women (Katz, 1969; Cancian and Jones, 1972). For example, in 1965, 36% planned to teach in primary or secondary schools, compared to only 10% in 1972. It is hard to believe that all the women who changed experienced close interpersonal relationships that resulted in internalizing new norms. It seems much more likely that the change was caused by the proclamation of new norms for evaluating women by the Women's Liberation movement, and the widespread support for this movement.

A study of the changing norms of college professors shows how a dramatic public action can cause a rapid change in norms, or collective perceptions of the beliefs of others. Wilson and Otto (n.d.) studied the beliefs of fifty Stanford professors about legitimate grounds for firing a tenured professor. Their beliefs were measured before and after a famous radical professor was fired by the joint action of a faculty committee and the university president.[1] There was an interval of six weeks between the measures. After the decision, the percentage of professors who personally supported the firing increased from 30% to 56%. However, there was a greater and more important change in the professors' perceptions of the beliefs of others. Before the decision, 54% of the professors said that most members of their respective departments believed that the radical professor should be fired, compared to 88% after the decision. Thus the public decision seemed to produce a consensus among the faculty that their colleagues supported the firing, although, in fact, the faculty was almost evenly split on the issue. These findings suggest that within a few months a new norm was established that redefined the basic rights of professors, and the norm was based on pluralistic ignorance.

These studies provide some support for the idea that group norms are shared perceptions about the beliefs of others, and that these perceptions can change very rapidly. The issue of how quickly norms change and how soon the new norms begin to affect action has important implications for the research design of studies on norms and ac-

---

[1]Fifty professors were interviewed in October and again in January. The sample included all the members of one department in the School of Humanities and Sciences, and a random sample of several departments in the Schools of Engineering and Medicine.

tion. It is possible that the existence of a time lag may partially explain the negative findings of studies made at one point in time, such as the Zinacanteco survey. If normative beliefs change rapidly, but take time to affect action, then longitudinal research will be necessary to document the relation between norms and action.

Finally, the social identity perspective suggests a third proposition that contrasts with the theory of the socialized actor: *A change in identity or status produces an immediate and major change in the norms that are relevant to an individual.* Norms have been defined as beliefs about what action will cause others to validate membership and rank in important identities. If there are changes in the identities that are important to an individual, and in the kinds of others who validate these identities, then the individual's norms will change. For example, when a person is admitted to a college, the identity of being a college student suddenly becomes much more important. Cultural beliefs about what college students are like quickly become part of the individual's self-concept, even though he or she probably had shared these beliefs for many years. The significant others also change, and the beliefs of fellow college students become more important than the beliefs of parents or high school students.

The ideal study that is suggested by this proposition would measure norms at two points in time: first, prior to the identity change, and, second, after the identity change but before the individual had the opportunity to observe or interact with new role models. However, to my knowledge no such research has been carried out. The closest approximation is a study done by Jose Benitez (1971).

Benitez attempted to test the general hypothesis that students would be changed simply by being admitted to an elite high school, and that the nature of the change would be determined by the high school's 'charter,' or the common assumptions about the products of the school. He investigated the effects of being admitted to a new Philippine high school, whose charter was to produce the scientists, scholars and leaders that would form the new elite of the nation. The students' self-esteem and their beliefs about modernity were measured at two points in time. First, all students who applied for admission were given the questionnaire; then the students who were admitted were given the questionnaire again, nine months later, after the students had been in the high school for four months. At both times, data was also obtained from non-freshman students at the school. For our purposes, the most important findings of the study are: (1) the students who were accepted showed a considerable increase in self-esteem and modernity in this nine-month period, and (2) although students showed increasing self-esteem and modernity with each additional year of attendance at the school, the changes after this initial admission period occurred at a slower rate. As Benitez points out, these results would support the hypotheses more clearly if the second questionnaire had been administered after the students were admitted, but before they arrived at the high school. As it stands, this study suggests that receiving a new identity causes important changes in a person's self-concept and normative beliefs, and that the content of these changes is determined by cultural beliefs about that identity.

This review of previous research has shown that the social identity approach and the theory of the socialized actor lead to different empirical predictions. It is possible to do research, like Benitez' study, that supports one approach and not the other.

The studies that have been described all concern normative change or norms and action – areas where the difference between the two approaches is clearest. However, the social identity approach does more than offer an alternative to the theory of the socialized actor. It also opens up some new lines of research on norms in society, and I would like to mention briefly some of them in closing. First, the idea that there are particular groups with the authority to validate an identity and formulate norms provides a way to think about the structural location of norms, or where norms come from. It also links the concepts of 'norms' and 'authority.' Second, defining norms as perceptions of what other people do and think focuses attention on the concept of pluralistic ignorance. In addition, the idea that norms are conceptions of what actions define an identity suggests how normative change is linked to social structure; for example, a new technology may produce new patterns of activity for women, and hence new conceptions of what actions define being a woman. These ideas are being explored in some current studies.[1] I mention them here only to indicate the rich research potential of the social identity perspective.

General implications of the study

This book has examined the concept of norms from three perspectives: (1) the methodology of measuring or describing norms, (2) the rela-

[1] I am beginning some small group laboratory experiments that will examine the types of norms produced by a highly rational technology v. a less rational technology. Reeves (1973) is testing the hypothesis that formal organizations will have the same structure if the members of the organizations accept the same agency as having the authority to validate identities and formulate norms. Bergesen (1973) has shown that in one-party states, where the Party has the authority to define many identities, deviance in a wide variety of spheres is interpreted as political deviance that redefines a person's political identity.

tion between norms and social organization in a particular community, and (3) alternative theoretical approaches to norms. Each perspective has produced some clarification and defined new issues for future research.

The concept of norms is important to sociologists because most of us assume that in some way norms are a critical component of social action. That is, we assume that common meaning and evaluation is necessary to social order. However, norms and action must first be separated, if we are to put them back together again on the basis of their observed interrelationships. Therefore, in constructing a method for describing norms, the social meaning and evaluation of action was treated as independent from what people do. Norms were initially defined as beliefs about action, particularly beliefs about the allocation of respect, approval, and disapproval.

Normative beliefs are an aspect of culture or a community's particular world view. Therefore, a valid description of norms must represent the domain and structure of normative beliefs as perceived by the members of the community. To this end, the Frame-Sorting Method was developed and was used to construct a model of the normative beliefs of Zinacantecos. The model appears to be a valid representation of how Zinacantecos conceptualize types of good and bad action. This methodological approach removes a major obstacle to investigating normative beliefs and it demonstrates that it is possible to scientifically study complex systems of meaning. The Frame-Sorting Method also points to some of the problems that will have to be resolved in order to describe the norms of large, differentiated societies.

The description of Zinacanteco norms was guided by the assumption that beliefs or meaning can be separated from action. However, the total independence of norms and action is theoretically unacceptable, both because it portrays the social world as chaotic and because it contradicts the idea of social action as opposed to behavior. The interpretation of Zinacanteco norms and the consideration of alternative theoretical approaches were two ways of re-establishing the relation between norms and action.

The analysis of Zinacanteco norms and social organization in Chapter 5 clarifies the relation between norms and organized action in two ways. First, the norm clusters produced by the Frame-Sorting Method correspond to institutions that are found in most societies. In other words, the particular cognitive categories that Zinacantecos have constructed to evaluate each other correspond to general patterns of social organization as they are usually viewed by outsiders. Second, the analysis of Zinacanteco norms showed important differences between the structure of the Good norms that focus on well-defined, society-wide institutions and the structure of the Bad norms that do not have this focus. The analysis suggests that positive and negative evaluations have different relations to social structure; the two types of evaluation are different processes and not two poles of the same dimension. In sum, the normative beliefs of this particular Maya community seem to be structured in terms of general principles of social organization and of positive v. negative evaluation. Extensive comparative research will be necessary in order to clarify the underlying structure of different normative systems and determine whether the norms of all communities show the same structure.

The analysis of norms in Zinacantan raises the general theoretical issue of how to relate the concepts of norms and action, and the concepts of the individual and society. The predominant approach to this question in American sociology is the theory of the socialized actor. It focuses on norms as standards for choosing appropriate action that become established in individuals through internalization and then motivate the recurrent actions that constitute social order. This approach suggests that the norms held by individuals will be relatively stable and will be reflected in their actions.

Both the review of the literature in Chapter 7 and the results of the survey of Zinacanteco norms and action in Chapter 8 show that this Parsonian view of the problem leads to predictions that resist confirmation. The differences in the normative beliefs of the individual members of a community are not consistently reflected in behavioral difference. Thus it seems that we must reject either the assumption that norms are related to action, or the assumption that the individual actor is the basic unit of society, if we are to integrate theory with the results of empirical research.

The social identity approach which was developed in this chapter attempts to maintain the first assumption at the expense of the second. In the social identity approach, norms are defined in terms of the ongoing validation of identities by particular others. Norms define identities that are located in groups or institutions; norms are not located in individuals. This approach suggests that norms, or the collective perceptions of identities, will be reflected in action and that norms may change rapidly.

The general implications of the social identity perspective are different from the theory of the socialized actor and they are supported by some previous research, as this chapter has shown. However, this perspective leads to some unresolved problems, in particular, the relation of the individual to the identities that constitute society.

Hopefully, the methods, findings and theoretical interpretations of this study will help to resolve these problems and further our understanding of norms in society.

APPENDIX 1

Classification of statements elicited by substitution frames, by informant

THE STATEMENTS ELICITED by the four substitution frames were first sorted into twenty-one *ad hoc* categories, such as aggression, drunkenness, and farming, so that it would be possible to locate identical phrases. The table below shows the number of statements in each category produced by each of the three informants, and also rank orders the categories in terms of these frequencies.

The table shows some striking contrasts among the three informants. Chep's unique concern with personal appearance fits in with the fact that he is the most careful dresser of the three. Romin lived alone with his mother for much of his life, without a father or siblings, therefore, his preoccupation with kinship is understandable. Shun is the oldest and least literate of the three. He is a controversial political leader in Zinacantan, and, according to gossip, he and the leader of the opposing faction have been involved in some lurid political murders. This might account for his concern with agression, politics and law. His lack of concern with drunkenness may be related to the fact that he is the only one of the three men who refuses to drink hard liquor.

This variation among the three informants indicates that a more representative definition of the domain of norms would have been obtained by using more informants and selecting them randomly. On the other hand, in some ways the distribution of phrases over categories is very similar for the three men. For each of them, the seven most frequent categories include filling religious offices, private religious ritual, and politics and law. For two of the three men, the seven most frequent categories include being strong and rich, kinship, drunkenness and aggression.

160

APPENDIX TABLE 1   Types of normative statements produced by three informants

Category of norm	Number* of norms in each category and rank order for each informant separately					
	Romin		Shun		Chep	
	Rank	Number**	Rank	Number	Rank	Number
1. Kinship	1	385	8	320	4	240
2. Aggression	4	230	1	600	10.5	150
3. Filling religious offices	2	270	3.5	390	3	265
4. Private religious ritual	12	150	3.5	390	5	225
5. Politics and law	3	250	2	415	6.5	200
6. Personal appearance	15	90	7	355	1	360
7. Rich and strong	10.5	170	9.5	300	2	305
8. Talks well	8.5	175	6	365	8	195
9. Stealing, witchcraft	10.5	170	5	380	17	100
10. Drunkeness	5.5	210	16.5	135	6.5	200
11. Obedient and miscellaneous	8.5	175	11	245	15	110
12. Friendly	13.5	110	9.5	300	17	100
13. Curing sickness	5.5	210	13.5	150	12.5	125
14. Sexual offenses	7	190	15	145	19	90
15. Borrowing and lending	13.5	110	12	185	17	100
16. Farming	16	80	13.5	150	10.5	150
17. Non-agric. occupational skills	21	20	20	75	14	115
18. Other skills (inc. musician)	17.5	75	18	125	9	175
19. Kind, generous	17.5	75	16.5	135	20	70
20. Becoming Ladino (inc. Spanish)	20	35	21	65	12.5	125
21. Buying and selling	19	60	19	80	21	60
Total		3240		5305		3460

*Listed in rank order of the frequency of normative statements in that category, all three informants combined.

**Number estimated by measuring height of piles of slips, after eliminating norms about women and children and repetitions by the same informant.

APPENDIX 2

Distribution of ratings on person perception interview: number of subjects who gave each rating for each of 3 types of people rated

Type of norm:		Political cluster			Religious cluster			Economic cluster		
Particular norm:		disputes	Spanish	helps out of jail	helps officers	takes office	respects God	grows corn	farm leader	rich
Label on cluster diagram		P3	P1	P2	R7	R3	R1	E3	E2	E7
Man 1. Respected n = 20	high	13	7	11	18	20	20	19	17	7
	medium	6	7	5	1	0	0	1	1	13
	low	1	6	4	1	0	0	0	1	0
	don't know	0	0	0	0	0	0	0	1	0
Man 2. Respected n = 20	high	13	11	11	15	12	18	14	12	5
	medium	4	5	6	1	1	1	3	2	11
	low	3	4	3	4	7	1	3	6	4
	don't know	0	0	0	0	0	0	0	0	0
Man 3. Disrespected n = 19*	high	2	5	3	3	7	7	4	3	1
	medium	2	8	1	6	1	11	13	3	6
	low	15	6	15	10	11	1	2	11	12
	don't know	0	0	0	0	0	0	0	0	0

*One of the 20 subjects said there was no one he disrespected.

Kin-ship cluster	Bad cluster		Peripheral to cluster		Outside of cluster			Outside of 100 norms		
good heart	fights if drunk	changes sides	mocks	chases suitors	curer	cares for sick	pays debts	eats chili	sells salt	flees
K2	V1	C2	C7	K10	02	011	04			
16	0	3	0	1	3	20	19	12	0	0
3	10	5	4	2	1	0	0	8	0	0
1	10	12	16	12	16	0	0	0	20	20
0	0	0	0	5	0	0	1	0	0	0
16	1	1	1	0	5	16	16	10	1	1
3	4	6	5	3	1	4	2	7	1	2
1	15	13	14	10	14	0	0	2	17	17
0	0	0	0	7	0	0	2	1	1	0
2	14	13	11	12	1	4	7	11	1	9
3	3	3	6	0	2	3	2	5	1	3
14	2	2	2	3	16	12	10	2	17	7
0	0	0	0	4	0	0	0	1	0	0

APPENDIX 3

Explanations and attempted remedies for the failure of some of the Nachih interviews

THERE ARE SEVERAL credible explanations of what went wrong in some of the Nachih interviews. It is possible that the interviewer, Marian, simply filled out these questionnaires himself and never interviewed the respondents whose names were on the questionnaire. Marian often came to work on the early truck at about five in the morning and had five or six interviews completed before I arrived. However, it seems unlikely that he could have gotten away with that much lying. It is more probable that the questions were asked rapidly and monotonously and the respondents did not understand the questions. Perhaps the competition that developed between the interviewers to see who could complete the most interviews resulted in high speed and low quality. The trouble with this explanation is that I monitored many of the interviews conducted by Marian later in the day and did not detect anything wrong. What happened remains a mystery.

Once I discovered that the responses of many of the men from Nachih were suspect I decided to have these men interviewed a second time. The respondents to the original interview were separated into two groups, 'Nachih One,' which included 120 men whose responses seemed normal, and 'Nachih Two,' consisting of the 112 men whose responses to the paired comparison questions included long strings of selecting the first (or second) pair. A cut-off point of five identical consecutive responses was used; not one respondent from Apas reached this cut-off point.

Some explanation had to be given to the interviewers about why half the Nachih interviews had to be repeated. I told Marian the truth:

that many of the people he had interviewed had answered a long series of questions the same way, regardless of the content of the questions. I discovered the unfortunate result of my comments when I stood hidden near the door of Marian's office and listened in on some of his repeat interviews. Marian was clearly influencing his respondents to alternate between selecting the first of a pair of phrases and selecting the second.

Two empirical tests confirm these suspicions about the second interview of the Nachih Two respondents. First, a comparison of the mean norm scores for Apas, Nachih One and Nachih Two shows that the Nachih Two scores are quite different from the others (the Nachih Two data are from the second interview of those Nachih respondents whose responses to the first interview were suspect). The table in this Appendix gives the unadjusted mean norm scores for each of the nine clusters. Pairs of scores that are significantly different at the .05 level are joined by brackets. The top part of the table shows that for the four Good norm clusters there are no significant differences between Apas and Nachih One, while Nachih Two differs from these two groups on each of the four scores. For the five Bad clusters, the largest number of significant differences is between Nachih One and Nachih Two. Second, in the responses to the association question, Apas and Nachih One are very similar, while Nachih Two is different from both of them. Both measures indicate that the Nachih Two data are different from the rest.

The reason for these peculiar results from the Nachih Two interviews does not seem to be simply interviewer bias. The bottom part of the table shows that the mean scores for Nachih Two are often different from all the other groups regardless of whether the second interviews were done by Marian or Manvel. For example, the norm scores from Nachih Two are higher on Political and Economic and lower on Religious than all other groups, regardless of interviewer. The possibility that the Nachih Two respondents were younger and poorer and therefore more susceptible to interviewer bias was also examined. However, the data show very small differences between Nachih One and Two on these variables. For age, Nachih One has $\bar{x} = 39.6$, s.d. = 10.9, Nachih Two has $\bar{x} = 39.1$, s.d. = 13.5; for wealth, with '1' representing the poorest octile and '8' representing the richest, Nachih One has $\bar{x} = 4.5$, s.d. = 2.3, Nachih Two has $\bar{x} = 4.4$, s.d. = 2.50. The possibility that some of the differences could be explained by the effects of being given the same interview twice could not be checked out.

Appendix Table 3 Differences of mean norm scores for Nachih Two second interview and other respondents

	n	Political	Religious	Economic	Kin-ship	Violent	Lazy	Incom-petent	Crafty	Irre-ligious
					Mean norm scores°					
Apas	142[+]	*7.1	7.6	5.8	2.5	6.2	6.4	2.4	4.7	4.3
Nachih One	120	7.3	7.4	5.6	2.7	6.6	5.4	3.3	4.5	4.1
Nachih Two	112	7.9	6.2	6.7	2.2	6.7	6.6	2.6	4.6	3.5
Between Interviewers										
Nachih Two Marian	51	8.1	6.3	6.1	2.6	6.6	5.8	3.6	4.4	3.6
Manvel	61	7.7	6.2	7.2	2.0	6.7	7.2	1.8	4.7	3.5

[+]Total population, including those under twenty-five years old

°These mean scores are not adjusted for the maximum possible score, which varies from 7 to 12, for different norm clusters.

*Brackets connect pairs of mean scores that have a difference large enough to produce a critical ratio 2.0. Standard deviations for the norm scores range from 1.3 to 2.0.

APPENDIX 4

Association of norms with action

THE FOLLOWING THREE tables summarize the responses to the individual association questions. Each table considers one of the three modern activities: farming far away, going to school, and going to the doctor. The tables list the individual normative statements that were associated with the modern behavior by at least 65% of the subjects. This calculation excludes individuals who responded that both behavior alternatives were 'the same' in the extent to which they were associated with the normative statement. Norms are starred if one response was given by 65% of *all* the subjects, including those who have 'the same' responses, and they are preceded by '°' if the proportion of subjects who responded 'the same' was smaller than 11%. The highest proportion of 'the same' responses in both hamlets was 26% for the question associating 'respects God' with farming far or near.

In those cases where a Good norm was associated with the traditional behavior or a Bad one was associated with the modern behavior, this is indicated by '(−)' after the cluster name. A *'DOES NOT'* is placed before normative statements that were associated with the traditional behavioral alternative, since the tables are constructed to show the attributes associated with the modern behavior. The tables show, in parentheses, after the cluster label, the origin of those norms that originally represented one cluster, but were shifted to another in calculating the association scores, in order to have a larger number of items for the score.

Appendix Table 4   Association between norm clusters and action alternatives
Statements associated with behavior by 65% of subjects

I. A person who farms far, as opposed to near, has these attributes:

Cluster	Normative statement	
	Apas	Nachih
Political	*knows Spanish better	°*knows Spanish better
Economic	*better corn farmer	*better corn farmer
Economic	*better farm leader	*better farm leader
Economic	+richer	*richer
Lazy	°*is less lazy	°*is less lazy
Religious	takes religious offices	*takes religious offices
Religious (orig. Irrel.) (−)	DOES NOT help relig. officers	—
Kinship	°*does more favors	does more favors
Kinship	—	better heart
Crafty	—	DOES NOT change sides

+This statement was not counted as part of the Economic cluster in calculating the association scores.

* = response given by 65% of all respondents, including those who answered 'the same'

° = fewer than 11% 'the same' responses

II. A person who goes to school has these attributes:

Cluster	Normative statement	
	Apas	Nachih
Political	°*knows Spanish better	°*knows Spanish better
Political	°*settles disputes better	°*settles disputes better
Political (orig. Incomp.)	°*speaks to officials	°*speaks to officials
Economic	°*better farm leader	°*better farm leader
Economic (orig. Lazy) (−)	°*DOES NOT work for others	*DOES NOT work for others
Crafty	°*DOES NOT change sides	°*DOES NOT change sides
Kinship	°*does more favors	*does more favors
Economic (−)	DOES NOT farm corn well	—
Economic	—	*richer
Violent	—	DOES NOT sep. from wife
Kinship	—	has a better heart

* = response given by 65% of all respondents, including those who answered 'the same'

° = fewer than 11% 'the same' responses

III. A person who goes to the doctor has these attributes:

Cluster		Normative statement	
		Apas	Nachih
Political		°*knows Spanish better	°*knows Spanish better
Political (orig. Incomp.)		°*speaks to officials better	°*speaks to officials better
Religious	(−)	*DOES NOT respect God more	*DOES NOT respect God more
Religious	(−)	*DOES NOT take relig. offices	*DOES NOT take relig. offices
Religious (orig. Irrel.)	(−)	*DOES NOT help relig. officers	*DOES NOT help relig. officers
Economic (orig. Lazy)	(−)	DOES NOT work for others	—
Economic	(−)	—	*DOES NOT farm corn well

* = response given by 65% of all respondents, including those who answered 'the same'

° = fewer than 11% 'the same' responses

APPENDIX 5

Correlations among norm clusters

THE MATRIX OF correlations among the scores for the nine norm clusters, in Apas and Nachih, are presented below. The correlations between two Good clusters or two Bad clusters are based on a recalculation of the norm scores, so that the two scores are independent. Given the original method of calculating the norm scores, the scores for the four Good clusters were not independent, nor were the scores for the five Bad clusters. For example, the Political and Religious norm scores were based on four of the same questions, those that compared political and religious norms. The interdependence would produce a negative correlation, since a respondent who had selected the political norm in these four questions could not have selected the religious norms. Therefore, new scores were computed so that for each correlation between two clusters, there was no overlap in the questions used to measure each cluster.

The tables below show that there are few correlations among norm scores. In Apas, none of the correlations among Good clusters, and only one of the correlations between Good and Bad clusters, is greater than .15. Of the correlations among Bad clusters, only those involving the unstable Irreligious cluster are strong. The single consistent relationship among clusters that is suggested by the table is between religion and economics. The Religious and Economic clusters have a higher positive correlation than any other pair of Good clusters; the related Bad clusters, Irreligious and Lazy, have the highest correlation among the Bad clusters.

There is no reason to be surprised about this absence of relationships among clusters, except for the two cases in which a Good cluster is uncorrelated with a Bad cluster that seems to be its opposite. One would expect a strong positive correlation between the Religious and Irreligious clusters, and between the Economic and Lazy clusters, but the correlations are zero in both hamlets. These results show that Good and Bad clusters that appear to be two poles of a single dimension may in fact be independent.

Appendix Table 5   Correlations (Tau B) along norm clusters in Apas

	Pol.	Rel.	Econ.	Kin.	Viol.	Lazy	Inc.	Crafty	Irrel.
Political	.09	−.02	.03	−.15	−.03	.00	.10	.05	
Religious		.12	−.15	.00	−.10	.09	−.09	.03	
Economic			.10	.01	.03	−.09	−.13	.15	
Kinship				−.02	.25	−.02	−.07	−.03	
Violent					.04	−.07	.14	.21	
Lazy						.06	−.06	.50	
Incompetent							.04	.20	
Crafty								−.07	

*Adult population, $n = 114$

Correlations (Tau B) among norm clusters in Nachih

	Pol.	Rel.	Econ.	Kin.	Viol.	Lazy	Inc.	Crafty	Irrel.
Political	.01	−.09	.19	.19	−.08	.16	.13	−.09	
Religious		.41	−.20	−.01	.13	−.06	.05	.04	
Economic			.14	.08	−.01	−.14	−.16	.10	
Kinship				−.21	.03	.12	−.07	.11	
Violent					.12	−.30	.13	.20	
Lazy						.24	.11	.14	
Incompetent							−.10	.01	
Crafty								.03	
Irreligious									

*Adult Population, $n = 108$

APPENDIX 6

Correlations of norm scores and action alternatives

THE FOLLOWING TABLES show the correlations between the norm scores and actions, in Apas and Nachih. There are nine major norm scores, one for each of the norm clusters. In addition, there are seven revised norm scores, each of which is based on a subset of some of the normative statements used to define one of the original nine norm scores. These revised scores were calculated because the sorting tasks indicated that some of the norm clusters could be subdivided further, and the survey data suggested that some of the sub-clusters or revised clusters related to different kinds of behavior.

Seven revised clusters were identified, and revised norm scores were computed for each of them. For example, the original Political cluster was split into two revised clusters: Leadership with Ladinos, measured by the norms about knowing Spanish and getting people out of the San Cristobal jail (which requires knowing Spanish and dealing with officials), and Internal Leadership, measured by the single norm about settling disputes within the community. This split in the Political cluster is suggested in both the first and the second sorting tasks, as can be seen by examining the cluster diagrams. The first table shows which normative statements were used to define each revised cluster. The norm scores for these clusters were determined in the same way as the original ones, on the basis of responses to the paired comparison questions that contained the relevant norms.

The measures of behavior that were used to compute the correlations on the following tables are described at the beginning of Appendix 7 and in Chapter 8. 'Doc/cur' refers to the index of relative frequency of going to the doctor, as opposed to going to the curer.

Appendix Table 6-1 Norms used for the original and revised norm scores*

Original clusters	Norms in original clusters	Revised clusters
1. Political	knows Spanish releases from jail	Leadership with Ladinos
	settles disputes	Internal Leadership
2. Religious	takes religious offices Ritual Advisor	Religious Offices
	respects God	General Religious
3. Economic	grows corn grows beans	Good Farmer
	farm leader	
4. Kinship	good heart does favors gifts for mother-in-law	
5. Violent	fights when drunk separates from wife	Revised Violent
	murders	
6. Lazy	lazy farmer children hungry	Revised Lazy
	won't work for others	
7. Incompetent	can't talk to bureaucrats deaf	
8. Crafty	changes sides informs	
9. Irreligious	won't help religious office holders won't take religious offices	

*Lines separating norms indicate what norms were included in the revised clusters.

Appendix Table 6-2 Correlations (Tau B) of norm scores and actions for Apas

Norm scores	Wealth	Farm far	Ed. son	Ed. daughter	Doctor	Doc/cur	Relig. offices	Age
1 Political	.11	.02	-.24	.06	.00	.04	-.14	-.07
Rev. 1 Ladino Leadership	.19	.05	-.18	.06	.02	.03	-.07	.02
Rev. 1A Internal Leadership ('settles disputes')	-.08	.00	.12	-.07	.01	.06	.07	-.13
2 Religious	.16	-.05	.30	-.14	.15	.09	.40	-.01
Rev. 2 Religious Offices	.15	.05	.30	-.06	.06	-.02	.06	.04
Rev. 2A Gen. Relig. (respects God')	.08	-.15	.58	-.32	.15	.10	.42	.10
3 Economic	-.04	.05	-.39	-.02	-.09	.00	.13	.01
Rev. 3 Good Farmer	-.17	.01	-.04	-.02	-.18	-.19	.15	.16
4 Kinship	.07	.09	.00	.06	.10	.13	-.20	.10
5 Violent	-.03	-.25	.07	.10	-.16	-.15	-.06	.17
Rev. 5 Rev. Violent (w/o 'murders')	-.04	-.14	.06	.19	-.08	-.16	.13	.05
6 Lazy	-.08	-.08	-.06	-.14	.12	.22	-.06	-.03
Rev. 6 Rev. Lazy (w/o 'won't work')	.01	-.09	-.22	-.06	.14	.17	-.20	.04
7 Incompetent	.06	.04	.29	-.15	-.15	-.25	-.13	.19
8 Crafty	.05	.02	.00	-.01	-.04	-.05	.00	-.01
9 Irreligious	-.04	.34	.02	-.06	.08	.13	.15	-.16
n	114	102	28	47	112	71	30	114

Appendix Table 6-3 Correlations (Tau B) of norm scores and actions, for Nachih

Norm scores	Wealth	Farm far	Ed. son	Ed. daughter	Doctor	Doc/cur	Relig. Offices	Age
1 Political	-.01	.02	-.30	.33	-.07	-.02	-.16	.09
Rev. 1 Ladino Leadership	-.12	.04	.13	.50	-.04	.05	-.06	-.01
Rev. 1A Internal Leadership ('settles disputes')	-.01	-.04	-.50	-.22	.00	-.08	-.02	.03
2 Religious	.05	-.02	-.31	.08	.06	.00	-.01	-.04
Rev. 2 Religious Offices	.01	-.09	-.21	.33	.06	.02	-.05	.08
Rev. 2A Gen. Relig. ('respects God')	.01	-.06	-.22	-.08	.11	.01	.02	.01
3 Economic	-.03	.01	.33	-.27	.08	.10	.37	-.08
Rev. 3 Good Farmer	-.08	-.06	-.05	-.33	-.06	-.01	.27	-.03
4 Kinship	.03	-.05	.31	-.16	-.02	-.02	-.31	-.02
5 Violent	.06	.00	-.13	.25	.20	.00	.14	.02
Rev. 5 Rev. Violent (w/o 'murders')	-.03	.00	.05	.16	.18	.00	.02	.07
6 Lazy	.00	.02	-.05	.00	.00	.00	-.24	.01
Rev. 6 Rev. Lazy (w/o 'won't work')	-.04	.06	.02	.09	-.05	.04	.15	-.06
7 Incompetent	-.16	-.21	.44	.25	-.31	-.16	.02	.04
8 Crafty	.03	.08	-.12	-.16	.12	.00	-.54	.01
9 Irreligious	.23	.02	-.03	.17	.18	.11	.22	.19
n	108	102	23	24	108	80	22	108

APPENDIX 7

Intercorrelations of measures of action and social position

THE TWO TABLES below show the intercorrelations in Apas and Nachih, among eight variables: going to the doctor sometimes v. never; going to the doctor when sick v. going to the curer; sending sons currently aged eight to fourteen to school v. not sending them; farming far away v. nearby; taking expensive religious offices v. taking none or inexpensive ones, for men currently aged fifty or more; and wealth and age (see Chapter 8 for a description of each measure).

The two tables show a substantial number of moderate correlations among the behavior variables. A few of these correlations are the same in both hamlets. In Apas and Nachih, wealthy people are older and take more expensive religious offices than poor people, and there is a positive correlation between sending sons to school and taking offices.

In all the other correlations, the two hamlets are different. In Apas, wealth is positively associated with the modern activities of going to doctors and sending children to school, while in Nachih, wealth is negatively correlated with 'modern' actions. However, if age is controlled, then the relationship between wealth and modernity turns out to be similar. In both hamlets, there is a positive relationship between wealth and daughters' education among the older men only; and in both hamlets, the relationship between wealth and going to the doctor is more positive or less negative among the older men.

Other differences between the hamlets concern farming far away or nearby. The elite of Nachih – the wealthy and those who take expensive religious offices – tend to farm far away, while in Apas, the elite do not farm far away. These findings are not surprising, given the great variation between the two hamlets in distance to the nearest farmland.

Finally, older men in Nachih are more likely to send their daughters to school, while in Apas, younger men are more likely to send them. In both hamlets, controlling for age strongly affects the relationships between the education of daughters and other variables. In both hamlets, daughters' education is positively related to wealth and farming far, among the older men only. Among younger men only, their education is negatively related to going to the doctor. The effect of age, in turn, changes when wealth is controlled. In both hamlets, age is more positively related to daughters' education and going to the doctor among the rich than among the poor.

A few generalizations can be made about this network of intercorrelations. First, there does not seem to be a coherent 'modernization' dimension tying together the four types of modern v. traditional behavior. Going to the doctor, sending children to school and farming far away are generally unrelated in Nachih and negatively related in Apas. Second, in both hamlets, the three social position variables of wealth, religious offices and age are positively intercorrelated. Third, the relations between the social position variables and the modern behavior variables differs in the two hamlets, although many of the differences become relatively weak when age or wealth is held constant. In Apas, farming far tends to be negatively correlated with the social position variables, while in Nachih it tends to be positively correlated. In Apas, the doctor and schooling variables tend to be positively related with the social position indicators. In Nachih the relation is negative, but, except for the education of sons, it is not negative for the older men.

These findings thus suggest that the four 'modern' behaviors have little in common, and that farming behavior, in particular, is different from the other three. They also show major differences in the behavioral implications of social position in the two hamlets.

Appendix Table 7   Intercorrelations (Tau B) of actions and social position in Apas

	Farm far	Ed. son	Ed. daughter	Doctor	Doc/cur	Relig. offices	Age
Wealth	−.07 (n=102)	.18 (n=28)	−.02 (n=47)	.12 (n=112)	.25 (n=71)	.27 (n=30)	.12 (n=114)
Farm far		−.28 (n=27)	.10 (n=40)	.04 (n=100)	−.05 (n=63)	−.19 (n=27)	−.20 (n=102)
Ed. son			[−.33] (n=15)	−.13 (n=28)	[−.02] (n=13)	.21 (n=20)	−.20 (n=28)
Ed. daughter				−.15 (n=45)	−.16 (n=33)	[.25] (n=14)	−.14 (n=47)
Doctor						−.06 (n=30)	.09 (n=112)
Doc/cur						[.21] (n=15)	.09 (n=71)
Relig. offices							all over 50

*Correlations are bracketed if fewer than 17 cases.

Intercorrelations (Tau B) of actions and social position in Nachih

	Farm far	Ed. son	Ed. daughter	Doctor	Doc/cur	Relig. offices	Age
Wealth	.19 (n=102)	−.21 (n=23)	−.17 (n=24)	−.05 (n=108)	−.24 (n=80)	.22 (n=22)	.26 (n=108)
Farm far		.03 (n=23)	.00 (n=24)	.03 (n=102)	.03 (n=75)	.31 (n=20)	−.01 (n=102)
Ed. son			[.35] (n=9)	.04 (n=23)	[.16] (n=14)	[.23] (n=14)	−.14 (n=23)
Ed. daughter				.08 (n=24)	[.23] (n=16)	[.61] (n=5)	.43 (n=24)
Doctor						.02 (n=22)	.06 (n=108)
Doc/cur						[−.09] (n=15)	.02 (n=80)
Relig. offices							all over 50

*Correlations are bracketed if fewer than 17 cases.

APPENDIX 8

? = glottal stop
' = glottalized consonant
x = sh
¢ = ts
c = ch

Good norms

1.	P1	*lek sna? xk'opoh ta kastiya*	he knows how to talk Spanish well
2.	P2	*lek sna? xlok'esvan ta cukel*	he is good at getting people released from jail
3.	P3	*lek sna? smel¢anel mulil*	he is good at settling disputes
4.	P4	*lek xk'ot yal rason huhun nopohel*	he is good at making intelligent, reasonable statements at meetings
5.	P5	*lek xal mantal ta kavilto*	he is good at giving orders at the town hall
6.	P6	*lek sna? sp'is ta vinik preserente*	he is good at respecting and obeying the president of Zinacantan
7.	P7	*lek xc'un mantal ta slumal*	he is good at accepting orders and doing his duty in his community
8.	P8	*lek xcanoh vun*	he has learned to read and write well
9.	P9	*task'an taspas sba ta hkaxlan*	he wants to become a Ladino (a non-Indian)

179

10. R1 *lek sna? kahvaltik*   he respects God and performs
                                        his religious duties well

11. R2 *lek xc'un totilme?il*   he is good at accepting the duties
                                        of Ritual Advisor

12. R3 *lek sna? spas ?abtel*   he takes religious offices and
                                        performs them well

13. R4 *lek stoy yabtel*   when he has a religious office,
                                        he is good at performing the
                                        rituals at the fiesta of San
                                        Sebastian

14. R5 *pasaro xa lek ?ispas*   he has taken all four religious
        ?abtel   offices and performed well in
                                        them

15. R6 *lek xc'un ?anil ka? ta*   he is good at accepting the duty
        huhun k'in   of riding a horse for fiesta
                                        rituals

16. R7 *lek sc'un c'amunel*   when religious office holders ask
        skwenta hpas ?abtel   his help, he is good at
                                        accepting this duty

17. R8 *lek hvabahom ta yolon*   he is a good musician at the
        yok kahvaltik   rituals of the religious office
                                        holders

18. R9 *lek stih kampana ta*   he is good at ringing the church
        spixkalil   bell when he is sacristan

19. R10 *lek sna? xak' xlimoxna*   he is good at paying the tax for
        yu?un k'in   fiestas

20. E1 *lek sna? sȼ'un cenek'*   he is good at growing beans

21. E2 *lek xtun ta baltioal*   he is good at being the
                                        representative of a group of
                                        farmers

22. E3 *lek sna? scabah*   he is a good corn farmer

23. E4 *lek smak'lan yah ?abtel*   he feeds his workers well
                                        (primarily farm workers)

24. E5 *lek xak' ta c'om stak'in*   he is good in lending people
                                        money

25. E6 *lek xk'uxubin povreetik*   he treats the poor well

26. E7 *lek hk'uleh*   he is good and rich

27. E8 *lek sna? k'usitik sȼ'un*   he is a good farmer and gardener

28. K1 *talel talel smotontak*   he receives many presents (of
        yu?un yamikotak   liquor) from all his friends
                                        (who come to ask him favors)

29. K2	*lek yo?on mu sna? xkap*	he has a good heart and doesn't get angry
30. K3	*lek xak'be presko sni? me?el*	he is good at giving soda to his mother-in-law
31. K4	*ta lek ?ismak yahnil*	he conducted a proper courtship for his wife
32. K5	*lek sna? sk'uxubin yahnil sci?uk xc'amaltak*	he treats his wife and children well
33. K6	*lek sk'uxubinoh xc'ul c'amal*	he takes good care of his god-child
34. K7	*lek sk'opon skumpare*	he is friendly with his ritual kinsmen
35. K8	*lek xtohob ta hak'olal*	he is a good, successful go-between, for arranging marriages
36. K9	*lek svaxan sba ta k'oponel*	he calmly listens and hears the truth in what is said
37. K10	*mu sna? snuȼlok'el hak'ol ȼna k'alal xhak'bat sȼebe*	he doesn't chase the go-between out of his house when his daughter is asked for in marriage
38. K11	*toh lek yo?on xk'opoh*	he talks with a very good heart (kind, generous, friendly)
39. 01	*lek smak ?ak'ben camel*	he is a curer good at stopping sickness due to witchcraft
40. 02	*lek xc'un ?ilolal*	he is good at accepting the duties of being a curer
41. 03	*lek sȼ'akubtas sba xanav*	he is a well dressed man, his clothes are clean and well made
42. 04	*lek sna? stoh yil*	he is good at paying his debts

Bad norms

1. V1	*toh tol sa? k'op xyakub*	he picks fights too much when he's drunk
2. V2	*tol sc'ak yahnil*	he separates from his wife too much
3. V3	*tol xmilvan k'u ca?al hurio*	he murders people too much, like a Jew
4. V4	*tol x?utvan*	he reprimands others too much

5. V5	*mu skol x?ilolah*	he is a curer but can't cure sickness
6. V6	*h?ak' camel*	he is a witch and makes others sick
7. V7	*tol xyakub*	he gets drunk too much
8. V8	*?ocel ?ocel ta cukel*	he is always getting put in jail
9. V9	*xtuket sk'oplal slo?iltael*	there is a lot of bad gossip about him
10. V10	*?iskob skumale*	he had intercourse with his ritual kinswoman
11. V11	*tol sȼak ?anȼ*	he chases after women too much
12. V12	*tol xak' ?elav xyakub*	he makes a public spectacle of himself when he gets drunk
13. V13	*tol smah yahnil*	he beats his wife too much
14. V14	*ba'ȼi hlosvaneh ta mahel*	he's always hitting people
15. V15	*tol slaȼbe ?arsial xc'amal*	he whips his children too much
16. L1	*toh c'ah ta cabahel*	he is a lazy corn farmer
17. L2	*mu xve? yu?un xc'amaltak*	his children don't have enough to eat
18. L3	*mu sk'an xkoltavan ta ?abtel*	he doesn't want to help people out by working for them
19. L4	*toh tol xti?olah ta ?abtel*	he is too lazy, and unhappy when he works
20. L5	*solel mu hunuk sentavo stak'in*	he doesn't have a penny
21. L6	*mu sna? stoh yil*	he doesn't pay his debts
22. L7	*tol xvay ta k'ak'altik*	he spends the day sleeping
23. L8	*mu sna? x?atin*	he doesn't wash himself (he's dirty)
24. L9	*tol sk'elan xc'amaltak mu sk'an s'ȼites*	he gives away his children; he doesn't want to raise them
25. L10	*ȼ'isbentik sk'a? k'u xanav*	he walks around in mended old clothes
26. N1	*makal xcikin mu xa?i k'op*	he is deaf and can't understand when people talk
27. N2	*mu sna? sk'oponel ministerio toh sonso*	he doesn't know how to talk to Ladino bureaucrats, he's too stupid (doesn't know Spanish)
28. N3	*ȼyak sba yok canav muxtohob ta xanbal*	he stumbles and can't walk well

29. N4	*mu sna? stihel vob*	he can't play stringed instruments (violin, harp, guitar)
30. N5	*yec xt'elt'on ta xi?el k'alal xk'opoh ta kavilto*	he just shakes with fear when he talks at the town hall
31. C1	*tol stik'be sk'ak'al xci?il*	he informs too much on people's wrongdoings
32. C2	*tol shoyp'in sk'op*	in a dispute he changes sides, according to which side is winning
33. C3	*tol xmaǥ'anvan ta cukel*	he gets people put in jail too much
34. C4	*tol xtuc' ta be k'op*	when disputes are being settled, he interferes and disrupts the settlement
35. C5	*tol snop k'op*	he lies too much
36. C6	*tol xlo?lovan*	he deceives and tricks people, goes back on his word
37. C7	*tol xlabanvan*	he criticizes and mocks others too much
38. C8	*ȼkahȼanbe smul xci?il*	when someone does wrong, he lies and gets them into worse trouble, falsely accuses them
39. C9	*tol spohbe yosil xci?il*	he cheats his relatives out of their land (steals their land)
40. I1	*mu sk'an spas ?abtel*	he doesn't want to take a religious office
41. I2	*mu xc'un c'amunel yu?un hpas ?abtel*	when asked to help a religious office holder, he refuses to accept this duty
42. I3	*tol stoy sba ta ten kamaroal*	he is arrogant and uncooperative when he has the position of setting off firecrackers
43. I4	*mu xak' ta c'amunel stak'in*	he won't lend people money
44. I5	*mu sna? xak' yul ta yabtel*	he doesn't give out corn gruel properly when he has a religious office
45. I6	*mu sk'an stoh yah ?abtel*	he doesn't want to pay his workers

46. I7	*mu sna? kahvaltik*	he doesn't respect God and perform his religious duties
47. 05	*tol xelk'an ka?*	he steals horses too much
48. 06	*tol xelk'an gol*	he steals squash too much
49. 07	*mu sna? rason*	he can't talk or listen with reasonable intelligence, with reason
50. 08	*mu sna? smelganvan*	he doesn't know how to settle disputes
51. 09	*mu sna? stuk'ulan sba*	he doesn't know how to take care of himself (poor clothes and undignified behavior)
52. 010	*mu sna? xic'sba ta muk'*	he doesn't care how he looks or behaves
53. 011	*mu sna? xnic'nah yu?un ?ag'am ?at*	he can't have children because he is sterile
54. 012	*mu sk'an malalinel*	he doesn't want to get married
55. 013	*mu xc'unbe smantal stot*	he doesn't obey his father
56. 014	*mu sna? ta yo?on ti mi ?ip xci?ile*	he doesn't care if his relatives or friends are sick
57. 015	*tol ssutes sni? mu xak' sgeb*	he rejects his daughter's suitors too much
58. 016	*mu sk'an nupbel sk'ob*	he doesn't want people to bow to him

Translation of new normative statements for second sorting task

Good norms

1. PP1	*p'ih ta rason*	he is an intelligent leader, good at giving orders and settling disputes
2. PP2	*lek xic'be stuk'il k'op*	he settles disputes well, without getting mad or changing sides
3. PP3	*lek xtun ta komite yu? un ?osil*	he serves well on the *ejido* land committee
4. RR1	*lek spas k'in krus ta Mayo*	he celebrates the May fiesta well
5. RR2	*lek sna? xcabi biernex santo*	he respects the rituals and taboos of Good Friday
6. EE1	*lek xconolah ta c'ivit*	he is good at selling things at the market

7. EE2 *sak p'ehan xanav* — he is well dressed, clean, has well made clothes

8. EE3 *lek sna? sʒ'unel sakil nicim* — he knows well how to grow flowers (for sale)

9. EE4 *lek spas kanal* — he is good at looking for work, making money

10. EE5 *ba'ʒi sobik xlok'staria* — he finishes his portion of farm work very quickly

11. EE6 *ʒoʒ vinik* — he is strong and fearless

12. EE7 *baxbol ta ?abtel* — he is an industrious worker

13. KK1 *lek smanbe slurse xc'amal* — he is good at buying candy for his children

14. KK2 *lek spoʒbe yot hvula?al* — he is good in giving food to visitors

15. KK3 *lek sk'opon slak'natak* — he is friendly with his neighbors

16. 001 *mu sna? stik'mulil* — he doesn't inform on people

17. 002 *mu sna'xac'van ec'el ta cukel* — he doesn't drag people off to jail, he doesn't have people put in jail

18. 003 *hutuk sna? xyakub* — he doesn't get drunk much

19. 004 *mu sna? sa? smul* — he doesn't do bad things (steal, lie, get mad)

Bad norms

1. VV1 *baʒ'i xti?et xhol k'alal xk'oponate* — he is grumpy and annoyed when he's spoken to, irritable

2. VV2 *xlabk'elvan nox* — he watches people from a distance with evil intentions, without speaking

3. VV3 *xalbe hyoket hol yan krixciano* — he calls other people stupid

4. VV4 *tol sk'ak'al yo?on sci?il* — he is too angry and envious

5. VV5 *naka ta kantina xk'ot slahes stak'in* — he spends all his money at bars

6. VV6 *tol xmahvan* — he hits people too much, beats them up

7. VV7 *tol xalbe ta stik'be bala sci?il* — he threatens people that he's going to shoot them too much

8. VV8 *tol xut sme?elal* — he scolds, reprimands his wife too much

9. LL1 *mu sna? sʒ'un nicim* — he doesn't know how to grow flowers

10. LL2 *ȼtam ec'el yok ta pinka skoh sc'ahil* — he ran off to work on the plantations because he is lazy

11. LL3 *xpaȼet shol mu sna? xak' ta lok'el* — his hair is wild, he never has it cut

12. NN1 *yec nox sȼunet shol* — he is dumb, stupid, wild-haired

13. NN2 *nelix* — he is cross-eyed

14. NN3 *mu sna? vun* — he doesn't know how to read or write

15. CC1 *baȼ'i hlo?iltavaneh* — he is always spreading gossip

16. CC2 *tol smuk'ibtas k'opetik* — he intensifies disputes

17. II1 *mu xtun ta totilme?ilal* — he is no good as a Ritual Advisor

18. II2 *tol stoy sba ta vabahel* — he is arrogant and uncooperative when he has the position of musician at rituals

19. 005 *mu xak' ta muk'ta ?ilel yahnil* — he doesn't have big curing ceremonies for his wife

20. 006 *toh t'ut'* — he is too stingy

21. 007 *mu sk'an smanbe skinya xc'amal* — he doesn't want to buy bananas for his children

22. 008 *mu sna? xc'un mantal* — he doesn't obey orders and do his duty

23. 009 *mu sk'an ci?inel ta k'in* — he doesn't want his family to accompany him to fiestas

APPENDIX 9

Translation of questionnaire

Name _____

Interviewer_____

Other identification _____

Hamlet _____

Well, first we shall talk about what good men are like, what good things they do.

A. If there are two men,
    the first has performed well in the religious office of first *alcalde*
    the other is good at growing potatoes
    which one is better, which one is more respected?
B. There are another two men
    the first takes good care of the sick
    the other is an industrious worker
    which one is better, which one is more respected?
    1. There are another two men
       the first is good at getting people released from jail
       the other is good at growing beans
       which one is more respected?
    2. There are another two men
       the first is good at being the representative of a group of far-
       mers
       the other has a good heart and doesn't get angry
       which one is more respected?
    3. There are another two men
       the first is good at getting people released from jail

the other takes religious offices and performs them well
which one is more respected?

4. There are another two men
   the first is good at accepting the duties of Ritual Advisor
   the other receives many presents (of liquor) from all his friends
   (who come to ask him favors)
   which one is more respected?

5. There are another two men
   the first takes religious offices and performs them well
   the other is good at being the representative of a group of farmers
   which one is more respected?

6. There are another two men
   the first receives many presents from all his friends
   the other is good at settling disputes
   which one is more respected?

7. There are another two men
   the first takes religious offices and performs them well
   the other is good at growing beans
   which one is more respected?

8. There are another two men
   the first is good at getting people released from jail
   the other is a good corn farmer
   which one is more respected?

9. There are another two men
   the first is good at getting people released from jail
   the other respects God and performs his religious duties well
   which one is more respected?

10. There are another two men
    the first is good at growing beans
    the other receives many presents from all his friends
    which one is more respected?

11. There are another two men
    the first is good at accepting the duties of Ritual Advisor
    the other is a good corn farmer
    which one is more respected?

12. There are another two men
    the first knows how to talk Spanish well
    the other is a good corn farmer
    which one is more respected?

13. There are another two men
    the first respects God and performs his religious duties well

the other is good at giving soda to his mother-in-law
which one is more respected?

14. There are another two men
the first has a good heart and doesn't get angry
the second knows how to talk Spanish well
which one is more respected?

15. There are another two men
the first is good at being the representative of a group of farmers
the other is good at giving soda to his mother-in-law
which one is more respected?

16. There are another two men
the first knows how to talk Spanish well
the other respects God and performs his religious duties well
which one is more respected?

17. There are another two men
the first takes religious offices and performs them well
the other is good at giving soda to his mother-in-law
which one is more respected?

18. There are another two men
the first is good at settling disputes
the other is good at being the representative of a group of farmers
which one is more respected?

19. There are another two men
the first is a good corn farmer
the other receives many presents from all his friends
which one is more respected?

20. There are another two men
the first is good at settling disputes
the other is good at accepting the duties of Ritual Advisor
which one is more respected?

21. There are another two men
the first has a good heart and doesn't get angry
the other is good at getting people released from jail
which one is more respected?

22. There are another two men
the first respects God and performs his religious duties well
the other is good at being the representative of a group of farmers
which one is more respected?

23. There are another two men

the first is good at giving soda to his mother-in-law
the other is good at settling disputes
which one is more respected?
24. (repeat of item 13)

Now we shall talk about what bad men are like, what bad things they do.

A. If there are two men
   the first hits people too much
   the other doesn't know how to read
   which one is worse, which one is less respected?
B. There are another two men
   the first behaves like a crazy man
   the other steals potatoes too much
   which one is worse, which one is less respected?
   1. There are another two men
      the first picks fights too much when he's drunk
      the other is a lazy corn farmer
      which one is less respected?
   2. There are another two men
      the first murders people too much
      the other doesn't want to take a religious office
      which one is less respected?
   3. There are another two men
      the first one's children don't have enough to eat
      the other refuses to accept the duty of helping a religious office
      holder
      which one is less respected?
   4. There are another two men
      the first is a lazy corn farmer
      the other informs too much on others' wrongdoing
      which one is less respected?
   5. There are another two men
      the first is deaf and can't understand when people talk
      the other picks fights too much when he's drunk
      which one is less respected?
   6. There are another two men
      the first murders people too much
      the other doesn't want to help out people by working for them
      which one is less respected?
   7. There are another two men
      the first doesn't want to take a religious office

the other informs too much on others' wrongdoing
which one is less respected?

8. There are another two men
   the first separates from his wife too much
   the other informs too much on others' wrong doing
   which one is less respected?

9. There are another two men
   the first is a lazy corn farmer
   the other doesn't know how to talk to Mexican officials, he's
   too stupid (doesn't know Spanish)
   which one is less respected?

10. There are another two men
    the first changes sides in a dispute, according to which side is
    winning
    the other is deaf and can't understand when people talk
    which one is less respected?

11. There are another two men
    the first separates from his wife too much
    the other one's children don't have enough to eat
    which one is less respected?

12. There are another two men
    the first doesn't want to help out people by working for them
    the other changes sides in a dispute, according to which side is
    winning
    which one is less respected?

13. There are another two men
    the first doesn't know how to talk to Mexican officials, he's too
    stupid
    the other murders people too much
    which one is less respected?

14. There are another two men
    the first refuses to accept the duty of helping a religious office
    holder
    the other is deaf and can't understand when people talk
    which one is less respected?

15. There are another two men
    the first is a lazy corn farmer
    the other doesn't want to take a religious office
    which one is less respected?

16. There are another two men
    the first separates from his wife too much
    the other refuses to accept the duty of helping a religious office

holder
which one is less respected?

17. There are another two men
the first one's children don't have enough to eat
the other is deaf and can't understand when people talk
which one is less respected?

18. There are another two men
the first one's children don't have enough to eat
the other changes sides in a dispute, according to which side is
winning
which one is less respected?

19. There are another two men
the first is deaf and can't understand when people talk
the other separates from his wife too much
which one is less respected?

20. There are another two men
the first picks fights too much when he's drunk
the other one's children don't have enough to eat
which one is less respected?

21. There are another two men
the first doesn't want to take a religious office
the other doesn't know how to talk to Mexican officials, he's
too stupid
which one is less respected?

22. There are another two men
the first picks fights too much when he's drunk
the other refuses to accept the duty of helping a religious office
holder
which one is less respected?

23. There are another two men
the first changes sides in a dispute, according to which side is
winning
the other picks fights too much when he's drunk
which one is less respected?

24. There are another two men
the first doesn't want to help out people by working for them
the other doesn't know how to talk to Mexican officials, he's
too stupid
which one is less respected?

Well, we have finished the questions about who is better, who is worse.
Now we shall talk about what people are like who have their corn field

far away in a hot country; are they the same as people who have their corn field nearby in a hot country or are they different?

A. Who is a more industrious worker?   the man who has his
   the man who has his field far away in a   field nearby in a hot
   hot country   country
   1. Who knows how to talk Spanish bet-
      ter?
      has his field far away   has his field nearby
   2. Who is better at taking religious of-
      fices and performing them well?
      has his field far away   has his field nearby
   3. Who is a better corn farmer?

      has his field far away   has his field nearby
   4. Who has a better heart and doesn't
      get angry?
      has his field far away   has his field nearby
   5. Who is better at settling disputes?

      has his field far away   has his field nearby
   6. Who respects God more and per-
      forms his religious duties better?
      has his field far away   has his field nearby
   7. Who is better at being the represen-
      tative of a group of farmers?
      has his fields far away   has his field nearby
   8. Who receives more presents from all
      his friends?
      has his field far away   has his field nearby
   9. Who helps out people more by
      working for them?
      has his field far away   has his field nearby
   10. Who is better at talking to Mexican
      officials?
      has his field far away   has his field nearby
   11. Who picks fights more when he's
      drunk?
      has his field far away   has his field nearby
   12. Who changes sides more in disputes,
      according to which side is winning?
      has his field far away   has his field nearby

13. Who separates more from his wife?

    has his field far away   has his field nearby

14. Who is a lazier corn farmer?

    has his field far away   has his field nearby

15. Who informs more on others' wrongdoing?
    has his field far away   has his field nearby

16. Who is richer?

    has his field far away   has his field nearby

17. Who is better at accepting the duty of helping a religious officer holder?
    has his field far away   has his field nearby

18. Who is better at looking for work and making money?
    has his field far away   has his field nearby

Now we shall talk about what people are like who have been to school; are they the same as people who haven't been to school or are they different?

A. Who obeys his father's orders more?   haven't been
   been to school
    1. Who knows how to talk Spanish better?
       been to school   haven't been
    2. Who is better at taking religious offices and performing them well?
       been to school   haven't been
    3. Who is a better corn farmer?

       been to school   haven't been
    4. Who has a better heart and doesn't get angry?
       been to school   haven't been
    5. Who is better at settling disputes?

       been to school   haven't been
    6. Who respects God more and performs his religious duties better?
       been to school   haven't been

7. Who is better at being the representative of a group of farmers?
   been to school   haven't been
8. Who receives more presents from all
   his friends?
   been to school   haven't been
9. Who helps out people more by
   working for them?
   been to school   haven't been
10. Who is better at talking to Mexican
    officials?
    been to school   haven't been
11. Who picks fights more when he's
    drunk?
    been to school   haven't been
12. Who changes sides more in disputes,
    according to which side is winning?
    been to school   haven't been
13. Who separates more from his wife?

    been to school   haven't been
14. Who is a lazier corn farmer?

    been to school   haven't been
15. Who informs more on others'
    wrongdoing?
    been to school   haven't been
16. Who is richer?

    been to school   haven't been
17. Who is better at accepting the duty
    of helping a religious office holder?
    been to school   haven't been
18. Who is better at looking for work
    and making money?
    been to school   haven't been

Now we shall talk about what people are like who mostly use native
curers when they are sick; are they the same as people who go to the
(Western) doctor, or are they different?

A. Who respects God more?   go to the doctor
   mostly use curers

1. Who knows how to talk Spanish better?
   mostly use curers   go to the doctor
2. Who is better at taking religious offices and performing them well?
   mostly use curers   go to the doctor
3. Who is a better corn farmer?

   mostly use curers   go to the doctor
4. Who has a better heart and doesn't get angry?
   mostly use curers   go to the doctor
5. Who is better at settling disputes?

   mostly use curers   go to the doctor
6. Who respects God more and performs his religious duties better?
   mostly use curers   go to the doctor
7. Who is better at being the representative of a group of farmers?
   mostly use curers   go to the doctor
8. Who receives more presents from all his friends?
   mostly use curers   go to the doctor
9. Who helps out people more by working for them?
   mostly use curers   go to the doctor
10. Who is better at talking to Mexican officials?
    mostly use curers   go to the doctor
11. Who picks fights more when he's drunk?
    mostly use curers   go to the doctor
12. Who changes sides more in disputes, according to which side is winning?
    mostly use curers   go to the doctor
13. Who separates more from his wife?

    mostly use curers   go to the doctor
14. Who is a lazier corn farmer?

    mostly use curers   go to the doctor

15. Who informs more on others' wrongdoing?

mostly use curers   go to the doctor

16. Who is richer?

mostly use curers   go to the doctor

17. Who is better at accepting the duty of helping a religious office worker?

mostly use curers   go to the doctor

18. Who is better at looking for work and making money?

mostly use curers   go to the doctor

We have finished talking about what people are like who go to curers, what people are like who go to doctors. Now we are going to talk about how men work on their corn farms.

1. Do you grow corn? yes_____ no_____

2. Where did you grow corn this past year?
   How many years have you farmed at (name of ranch)?
   Did you farm at another place when you were farming at (name of ranch)?
   Where did you farm before you farmed at (name of ranch)?

Year	Ranch A	Ranch B
1		
2		
...10		

(Questions 3 through 11 are part of Frank Cancian's study of corn farming [1971] and are not discussed in this book.)

3. Of all the places where you have farmed, which was the best?

4. Have you heard of any better place? yes_____ no_____
   Where? _____
   Have you been there? yes _____ no_____
   Who told you about it? _____

5. Who was the representative of your group of farmers this past year?
   Ranch A: name _____ hamlet _____
   Ranch B: name _____ hamlet _____

6. How many of you were represented   Ranch A: _____
   by him?   Ranch B: _____

6a. Where are you farming this year?   Ranch A: _____
                                            Ranch B: _____

6b. Who is the representative of your group of farmers this year?
    Ranch A: name_____   hamlet _____
    Ranch B: name _____   hamlet _____

7. How many years have you been working apart from your father?

8. Do you hire workers to work on your cornfield?
   yes_____ no_____

9. Do you work on other people's cornfield?
   yes_____ no_____

   How many years since you last worked for someone else? _____

10. Where did you sell your corn last year? Two, three, four, five years ago?

Year	alone	reseller	government warehouse	hot country	speculator
1					
... 5					

11. Now we will talk about where the government corn warehouses are.

	is there one in	have you seen it
Acala		
Chiapa de corzo		
Soyatitan	(in fact none)	
Flores Magon		
Venustiano Carranza		
Colonia Viente de Noviembre		
Chiapilla	(in fact none)	

12. Has your father taken a religious office?   yes_____ no_____
    Which offices has he taken?   _____
                                    _____
                                    _____
                                    _____

13. Has your father already asked for a future religious of-
    fice?   Yes_____ no_____
    Which office has he asked for? _____

14. Have you taken a religious office?   yes_____ no_____
    Which offices have you taken?   _____
                                     _____
                                     _____
                                     _____

15. Have you already asked for a future religious office?
    yes_____ no_____
    Which office have you asked for? _____

16. Do you have any children?   yes_____ no_____
    How many children do you have?_____

| | | | | will be sent to school when |
Name	age	been to school	years at school	older

17. Is your wife expecting a baby?   yes_____ no_____
18. Have you been to school?   yes_____ no_____
19. Do you know Spanish?   yes_____ a little_____ no_____

(Question 17 was inserted for George Collier's study of infants. Questions 18 and 19 did not relate to any of the norm or behavior measures.)

Now we will talk about curing sickness.

20. Do you use a curer when you get sick?   yes_____ no_____
    When is the last time you looked for a curer? _____
    Who was sick? _____
    How many times have you looked for a curer since the end of the
    fiesta of San Lorenzo? _____

21. Do you go to the pharmacy to buy medicine?
    yes_____ no_____
    When is the last time you went to the pharmacy? _____

What did you buy? _____

Who was sick? _____

With what sickness? _____

22. Do you go to the doctor?   yes_____ no_____

When is the last time you went to the doctor? _____

Who was the doctor? Where did you find him? _____

Who was sick? _____

How many times have you been to the doctor since the end of the
fiesta of San Lorenzo? _____

23. Gift choice _____

REFERENCES CITED

ALBERT, ETHEL M. (1956). 'The classification of values.' *American Anthropologist* 58:221-48.

ALEXANDER, C. NORMAN, Jr, and G. KNIGHT (1971). 'Situated identities and social psychological experimentation.' *Sociometry* 34:65-82.

ALEXANDER, C. NORMAN, Jr, and PATRICK LAUDERDALE (1972.) 'Situated identity and the definition of social reality.' Unpublished paper, Stanford University.

ALLPORT, GORDON W. (1935). 'Attitudes.' Pp. 798-844 in C. M. Murchison (ed.), *Handbook of Social Psychology.* Worcester, Mass., Clark University Press.

BALES, ROBERT F. (1970). *Personality and Interpersonal Behavior.* New York, Holt, Rinehart and Winston.

BANFIELD, EDWARD C. (1958). *The Moral Basis of a Backward Society.* Glencoe, Ill., Free Press.

BECKER, HOWARD S. (1963). *Outsiders.* New York, Free Press.

BENITEZ, JOSE CONRADO (1971). 'Educational Institutionalization.' Ph.D. dissertation. School of Education, Stanford University.

BERGER, PETER (1967). *The Sacred Canopy.* New York, Doubleday.

BERGER, PETER and THOMAS LUCKMANN (1966). *The Social Construction of Reality.* New York, Doubleday.

BERGESEN, ALBERT J. (1973). 'Political Witch-hunts: a cross-national study of deviance.' Ph.D. dissertation, Stanford University.

BIERSTEDT, ROBERT (1963). *The Social Order.* New York, McGraw-Hill.

BLAKE, JUDITH and KINGSLEY DAVIS (1964). 'Norms, values and sanctions.' Pp. 456-84 in R. Faris (ed.), *Handbook of Modern Sociology.* Chicago, Rand-McNally.

BLUM, ALAN F. and PETER McHUGH (1971). 'The social ascription of motives.' *American Sociological Review* 36:98-109.

BROOM, LEONARD and PHILIP SELZNICK (1963). *Sociology* (3rd Edition). New York, Harper and Row.

BRYAN, JAMES H. (1970). 'Children's reactions to helpers.' Pp. 61-73 in J. Macaulay and L. Berkowitz (eds.), *Altruism and Helping Behavior.* New York, Academic Press.

BURLING, ROBBINS (1964). 'Cognition and componential analysis: God's truth or hocus-pocus'? *American Anthropologist* 66:20-8.

CAMPBELL, DONALD T. (1961). 'Social attitudes and other acquired behavioral dispositions.' In Koch (ed.), *Psychology: A Study of a Science,* Vol. 6. New York, McGraw-Hill.

CAMPBELL, DONALD T. and JULIAN C. STANLEY (1966) *Experimental and Quasi-Experimental Designs for Research.* Chicago, Rand McNally.

CANCIAN, FRANCESCA M. (1964). 'Family interaction in Zinacantan.' *American Sociological Review* 29:540-50.

(1971). 'New methods for describing what people think.' *Sociological Inquiry* 41:85-93.

(n.d.). 'Norms and behavior,' in J. Loubser *et al.* (eds.), *Explorations in General Theory in the Social Sciences.* New York, Free Press. In press.

CANCIAN, FRANCESCA M. and LYNNE JONES (1972). 'The Stanford Woman in 1972.' Report of the Committee on Education and Employment of Women in the University. Stanford University.

CANCIAN, FRANK (1963). 'Informant error and native prestige ranking in Zinacantan.' *American Anthropologist* 65:1068-75.

(1965). *Economics and Prestige in a Maya Community.* Stanford, Stanford University Press.

(1972). *Change and Uncertainty in a Peasant Economy.* Stanford, Stanford University Press.

CAPRIATA, JORGE (1965). 'Economic and social behavior of Zinacanteco corn middlemen.' Unpublished manuscript, Harvard Chiapas Project.

CHEIN, ISIDOR, MORTON DEUTSCH *et al.* (eds.) (1949). 'Consistency and Inconsistency in Intergroup Relations.' *Journal of Social Issues* 5.

CICOUREL, AARON V. (1972). 'Basic and normative rules in the negotiation of status and role.' Pp. 229-58 in D. Sudnow (ed.), *Studies in Social Interaction.* New York, Free Press.

COLBY, BENJAMIN N. (1966). 'Ethnographic semantics.' *Current Anthropology* 7:3-32.

(1967). 'Psychological orientations.' M. Nash (ed.), *Handbook of Middle American Indians,* Vol. 6. Austin, University of Texas Press.

COLEMAN, JAMES S. (1961). *The Adolescent Society.* New York, Free Press.

COLLIER, JANE F. (1968). 'Courtship and marriage in Zinacantan, Chiapas, Mexico.' Middle American Research Institute Publication 25:139-201. New Orleans, Tulane University.

(1973). *Law and Social Change in Zinacantan.* Stanford, Stanford University Press.

COOK, STUART W. and CLAIRE SELLTIZ (1964). 'Attitude measurement.' *Psychological Bulletin* 62:36-55.

DAHRENDORF, RALF (1968). 'The origin of inequality.' Pp. 151-78 in *Essays in the Theory of Society.* Stanford, Stanford University Press.

D'ANDRADE, ROY G. (1965). 'Trait psychology and componential analysis.' *American Anthropologist* 67:215-28.

(1970). 'Cognitive structures and judgment.' Paper read at C.O.B.R.E. Workshop on Cognitive Organization, 16-21 August, Huntington Beach, Calif.

De Fleur, Melvin and Frank Westie (1958). 'Verbal attitudes and overt acts.' *American Sociological Review* 23:667-73.

Deri, S., D. Dinnerstein *et al.* (1948). 'Diagnosis and measurement of intergroup attitudes.' *Psychological Bulletin* 45:248-71.

Deutscher, Irwin (1966). 'Words and deeds.' *Social Problems* 13:235-54.

Devereux, Edward C. (1961). 'Parsons' sociological theory.' Pp. 1-63 in M. Black (ed.), *The Social Theories of Talcott Parsons*. Englewood Cliffs, N.J., Prentice-Hall.

Douglas, J. (ed.) (1970). *Understanding Everyday Life*. Chicago, Aldine.

Durkheim, Emile (1933). *The Division of Labor*. New York, Macmillan.

Ehrlich, Howard J. (1969). 'Attitudes, behavior and the intervening variables.' *American Sociologist* 4:29-34.

Erikson, Kai (1966). *Wayward Puritans*. New York, John Wiley.

Fendrich, J. M. (1967). 'A study of the association among verbal attitudes and overt behavior in different experimental situations.' *Social Forces* 45:347-55.

Fishbein, Martin (1967). 'Attitudes and the prediction of behavior.' Pp. 477-92 in M. Fishbein (ed.), *Readings in Attitude Theory and Measurement*. New York, John Wiley.

Fishman, Joshua and Robert Cooper (1971). 'The inter-relationships and utility of alternative bilingualism measures.' Pp. 126-42 in W. H. Whiteley (ed.), *Language Use and Social Change*. Oxford University Press.

Flavell, J. H. and E. H. Flavell (1959). 'One determinant of judged semantic and associative connection between words.' *Journal of Experimental Psychology* 58:159-65.

Flavell, J. H. and D. J. Stedman (1961). 'A developmental study of judgments of semantic similarity.' *Journal of Genetic Psychology* 98:279-93.

Foster, George (1960). 'Interpersonal relations in peasant society.' *Human Organization* 19:174-78.

Frake, Charles O. (1964). 'Further discussion of Burling.' *American Anthropologist* 66:119.

Garfinkel, Harold (1967). *Studies in Ethnomethodology*. Englewood Cliffs, N.J., Prentice-Hall.

Gibbs, Jack P. (1965). 'Norms: the problem of definition and classification.' *American Journal of Sociology* 60:586-94.

Goffman, Erving (1967). *Interaction Ritual*. Chicago, Aldine.

Goldschmidt, W. and R. Edgerton (1961). 'A picture technique for the study of values.' *American Anthropologist* 63:26-47.

Greenberg, Joseph H. (1966). 'Language universals.' Pp. 61-112 in T. Sebeok (ed.), *Current Trends in Linguistics*. The Hauge, Mouton.

Gross, Neil, Ward Mason and Alexander McEachern (1958). *Explorations in Role Analysis*. New York, John Wiley.

Gusfield, Joseph R. and Michael Schwartz (1963). 'The meanings of occupational prestige.' *American Sociological Review* 28:265-71.

Hall, Katherine P. (1972). 'Sex differences in initiation and influence in decision-making among prospective teachers.' Ph.D. dissertation. School of Education, Stanford University.

HARDING, J., B. KUTNER, H. PROSHANSKY and I. CHEIN (1954). 'Prejudice and ethnic relations.' Pp. 1021-61 in G. Lindzey (ed.), *Handbook of Social Psychology*. Cambridge, Mass., Addison-Wesley.

(1969). 'Prejudice and ethnic relations.' Pp. 1-76 in G. Lindzey and E. Aronson (eds.), *Handbook of Social Psychology*, Vol. V. 2nd Edition. Reading, Pa., Addison-Wesley.

HARTSHORNE, H. and M. A. MAY (1928). *Studies on the Nature of Character*, Vol. I. New York, Macmillan.

HAVELAND, JOHN (1971). 'Gossip, gossips and gossiping in Zinacantan.' Ph.D. dissertation. Department of Social Relations, Harvard University.

HOLLINGSHEAD, AUGUST (1949). *Elmtown's Youth*. New York, John Wiley.

HOMANS, GEORGE (1950). *The Human Group*. New York, Harcourt, Brace and World.

(1961). *Social Behavior*. New York, Harcourt, Brace and World.

HOPKINS, TERENCE K. (1964). *The Exercise of Influence in Small Groups*. New York, Bedminster Press.

HYMES, DELL H. (1964). 'Discussion of Burling.' *American Anthropologist* 66:116-19.

INKELES, ALEX (1969). 'Making men modern.' *American Journal of Sociology* 75:208-25.

JOHNSON, HARRY (1960). *Sociology*. New York, Harcourt, Brace and World.

JOHNSON, STEPHEN C. (1967). 'Hierarchical clustering schemes.' *Psychometrika* 32:241-54.

KAHL, JOSEPH A. (1968). *The Measurement of Modernism*. Austin, University of Texas Press.

KATZ, JOSEPH (1969). 'Career and autonomy in college women.' In J. Katz *et al., Class, Character and Career*. Institute for the Study of Human Problems, Stanford University.

KENKEL, WILLIAM F. (1963). 'Observational studies of husband-wife interaction in family decision making.' Pp. 144-56 in M. Sussman (ed.), *Sourcebook in Marriage and the Family*. Boston, Houghton-Mifflin.

KIMBERLEY, JAMES C. (n.d.). 'Relations between status, power and economic rewards.' In J. Berger et al. (eds.), *Sociological Theories in Progress*, Vol. II. Boston, Houghton-Mifflin, forthcoming.

KLUCKHOHN, CLYDE (1954). 'Values and value-orientations in the theory of action.' Pp. 388-433 in T. Parsons and E. Shils (eds.), *Towards a General Theory of Action*. Cambridge, Mass., Harvard University Press.

(1958). *The Scientific Study of Values*. Toronto, University of Toronto Installation Lectures.

KLUCKHOHN, FLORENCE R. (1960). 'A method for eliciting value orientations.' *Anthropological Linguistics* 2:1-23.

KLUCKHOHN, FLORENCE R. and FRED STRODTBECK (1961). *Variations in value orientations*. New York, Row, Peterson.

KOHN, MELVIN (1969). *Class and Conformity*. Homewood, Ill., Dorsey Press.

KUTNER, B., C. WILKINS and P. R. YARROW (1952). 'Verbal attitudes and overt behavior involving racial prejudice.' *Journal of Abnormal and Social Psychology* 47:649-52.

LABOVITZ, SANFORD and ROBERT HAGEDORN (1973). 'Measuring social norms.' *Pacific Sociological Review* 16:283-304.

LAING, R. D. (1968). *The Politics of Experience.* New York, Ballantine Books.

LAPIERE, RICHARD T. (1934). 'Attitudes vs. actions.' *Social Forces* 13:230-7.

LAUGHLIN, ROBERT (n.d.). *Tzotzil – English, English – Tzotzil Dictionary.* Smithsonian Museum, Washington, D.C.

LEARY, TIMOTHY (1957). *Interpersonal Diagnoses of Personality.* New York, Ronald Press.

MACCOBY, ELEANOR (1966). 'Sex differences in intellectual functioning. Pp. 25-55 in E. Maccoby (ed.), *The Development of Sex Differences.* Stanford, Stanford University Press.

McGUIRE, W. J. (1969). 'The nature of attitudes and attitude change.' Pp. 136-314 in G. Lindzey and E. Aronson (eds.), *Handbook of Social Psychology,* Vol. III. 2nd Edition. Reading, Pa., Addison-Wesley.

MERTON, ROBERT (1957). *Social Theory and Social Structure.* Glencoe, Ill., Free Press.

METZGER, DUANE and GERALD E. WILLIAMS (1963). 'A formal ethnographic analysis of Tenejapa Ladino weddings.' *American Anthropologist* 65:1076-101.

MEYER, JOHN W. (1970). 'The charter: conditions of diffuse socialization in schools.' In W. Scott (ed.), *Social Processes and Social Structures.* New York, Holt, Rinehart and Winston.

MEYER, JOHN and BARBARA SOBIESZEK (1972). 'Effects of a child's sex on adult interpretations of its behavior.' *Developmental Psychology* 6:42-8.

NAROLL, RAOUL and RONALD COHEN (eds.) (1970). *A Handbook of Method in Cultural Anthropology.* New York, Doubleday.

NEWCOMB, THEODORE (1943). *Personality and Social Change.* New York, Dryden Press.

OLSON, DAVID H. (1969). 'The measurement of family power by self-report and behavioral methods.' *Journal of Marriage and the Family* 31:545-50.

OPLER, MORRIS E. (1945). 'Themes as dynamic forces in culture.' *American Journal of Sociology* 51:198-206.

OSGOOD, CHARLES (1964). 'Semantic differential technique in the comparative study of cultures.' Pp. 171-200 in A. Romney and R. D'Andrade (eds.), 'Transcultural Studies in Cognition,' Part 2 of *American Anthropologist* 66.

PARSONS, TALCOTT (1937). *The Structure of Social Action.* Glencoe, Ill., Free Press.
    (1951). *The Social System.* Glencoe, Ill., Free Press.
    (1961). 'An outline of the social system.' Pp. 30-79 in Parsons *et al.* (eds.), *Theories of Society.* New York, Free Press.

PARSONS, TALCOTT, *et al.* (1954). *Towards a General Theory of Action.* New York, Free Press.

PITTEL, S. and G. MENDELSOHN (1966). 'Measurement of moral values.' *Psychological Bulletin* 66:22-35.

REEVES, WILLIAM J. (1973). 'Structural uniformity in formal organizations.' Dissertation prospectus, Stanford University.

ROKEACH, MILTON (1968). 'A theory of organization and change within value-attitude systems.' *Journal of Social Issues* 24:13-34.

——— (1969). *Beliefs, Attitudes and Values.* San Francisco, Jossey-Bass.

ROMMETVEIT, RAGNAR (1960). *Selectivity, Intuition and Halo Effects in Social Perception.* Oslo, Oslo University Press.

——— (1968). *Social Norms and Roles.* Oslo, Universitets Forlaget.

ROMNEY, A. KIMBALL (1972). 'Multidimensional scaling and semantic domains.' *The Study of Man,* Vol. I.

ROMNEY, A. K., R. SHEPARD and S. NERLOVE (eds.) (1972). *Multidimensional Scaling,* Vols. I and II. New York, Seminar Press.

ROSALDO, RENATO I. (1968). 'Metaphors of hierarchy in a Mayan ritual.' *American Anthropologist* 70:524-36.

ROSEN, BERNARD C. (1971). 'Industrialization, personality and social mobility in Brazil.' *Human Organization* 30:137-48.

SAENGER, GERHART and EMILY GILBERT (1950). 'Customer reactions to the integration of Negro sales personnel.' *International Journal of Opinion and Attitude Research* 4:57-76.

SCHOONHOVEN, C. KAYE and KATHRYN GROSS (n.d.). 'The relationship between norms and behavior with social structure as an intervening variable.' Unpublished paper. Stanford University.

SCOTT, JOHN FINLEY (1971). *Internalization of Norms.* Englewood Cliffs, N.J., Prentice-Hall.

SCOTT, WILLIAM A. (1959). 'Empirical assessment of values and ideologies.' *American Sociological Review* 24:299-310.

——— (1965). *Values and Organizations.* Chicago, Rand McNally.

SHERIF, CAROLYN, M. SHERIF and R. NEBERGALL (1965). *Attitude and Attitude Change.* Philadelphia, Saunders.

SIMPSON, MILES (n.d.) 'Particularism vs. modernity: Parsons' societal typology reconsidered.' Unpublished manuscript. Stanford University.

SMITH, DAVID H. and ALEX INKELES (1966). 'The O-M scale: a comparative sociopsychological measure of individual modernity.' *Sociometry* 29:353-77.

STAR, SHIRLEY A., R. WILLIAMS Jr. and S. STOUFFER (1958). 'Negro infantry platoons in white companies.' Pp. 596-601 in E. Maccoby *et al.* (eds.), *Readings in Social Psychology.* 3rd Edition. New York, Holt, Rinehart and Winston.

STINCHCOMBE, ARTHUR L. (1963). 'Some empirical consequences of the Davis – Moore theory of stratification.' *American Sociological Review* 28:805-08.

STOUFFER, SAMUEL A. (1949). 'An analysis of conflicting social norms.' *American Sociological Review* 14:707-17.

STRODTBECK, FRED L. (1951). 'Husband – wife interaction over revealed differences.' *American Sociological Review* 16:468-73.

STURTEVANT, WILLIAM C. (1964). 'Studies in ethnoscience.' Pp. 99-131 in A.

Romney and R. D'Andrade (eds.), 'Transcultural Studies In Cognition,' Part 2 of *American Anthropologist* 66.

SWANSON, GUY, A. F. C. WALLACE and JAMES COLMAN (1968). 'Review Symposium on Studies in Ethnomethodology by Harold Garfinkel.' *American Sociological Review* 33:122-30.

TITTLE, CHARLES R. and RICHARD J. HILL (1967). 'Attitude measurement and prediction of behavior.' *Sociometry* 30:199-213.

TYLER, STEPHEN A. (ed.) (1969). *Cognitive Anthropology*. New York, Holt, Rinehart and Winston.

VOGT, EVON Z. (1969). *Zinacantan: A Maya Community in the Highlands of Chiapas*. Cambridge, Mass., Harvard University Press.

(1970). *The Zinacantecos of Mexico: A Modern Maya Way of Life*. New York, Holt, Rinehart and Winston.

VOGT, EVON Z. and ETHEL ALBERT (eds.) (1966) *People of Rimrock*. Cambridge, Mass., Harvard University Press.

WALLACE, ANTHONY F. C. (1970). 'A relational analysis of American kinship terminology.' *American Anthropologist* 72:841-45.

WALLACE, DAVID L. (1968). 'Clustering.' Pp. 519-24 in *International Encyclopedia of the Social Sciences*, Vol. II.

WALLACE, WALTER L. (1966). *Student Culture*. Chicago, Aldine.

WELLER, LEONARD and ELMER LUCHTERHAND (1969). 'Comparing interviews and observations on family functioning.' *Journal of Marriage and the Family* 31:115-22.

WHITE, RALPH K. (1951). *Value Analysis*. Manual published by Society for Psychological Study of Social Issues.

WHYTE, WILLIAM FOOTE (1955). *Streetcorner Society*. Chicago, University of Chicago Press.

WICKER, ALLAN W. (1969). 'Attitudes vs. actions.' *Journal of Social Issues* 25:41-78.

WILLIAMS, ROBIN M. Jr (1960). *American Society*. New York, Alfred Knopf.

(1961). 'The sociological theory of Talcott Parsons. Pp. 64-99 in M. Black (ed.), *The Social Theories of Talcott Parsons*. Englewood Cliffs, N.J., Prentice-Hall.

(1968). 'The concept of norms.' Pp. 204-8 in *International Encyclopedia of the Social Sciences*, Vol. II.

WILSON, BRUCE and STEPHEN OTTO (n.d.). 'Between theory and social reality: the effects of firing a professor on faculty norms.' Unpublished paper. Stanford University.

INDEX

achievement, *see* work ethic
action: Parsons' concept of, 107, 142;
behavior, 109; survey measures of,
117-21, 176-8; and meaning, 145-7. *See
also* consistency of norms and action;
norms; social identity approach
age in Zinacantan: and social status, 35; and
attitudes to Ladinoization, 61; and
schooling, 118-19; knowledge of, 121;
and relation of norms and actions, 133
Albert, Ethel, 15, 17-18
Alexander, Norman, 44, 151
Allport, Gordon, 110
Apas: description of, 122; v. Nachih, 72,
126, 150, 166, 170-1, 174-5
appearance of Zinacantecos, *see* clothing
association questions, 126-7; as measures of
generality of clusters, 101-3; results of,
167-9
attitudes, norms and action, 109-12

Bad norms, *see* Good–Bad
Bales, R. Freed, 19
Banfield, Edward, 20-1
behavior, *see* action
behaviorist approach to norms, 8-9, 152
Benitez, Jose, 155
Bierstedt, Robert, 7
Blake, Judith, 4, 7, 8, 105, 112
Broom, Leonard, 8

Campbell, Donald, 9, 111
Cancian, Frank, 24, 29-30, 64, 117-18, 120,
123
cargo system, *see* religious offices
central v. peripheral norms, 83, 93-7
change of norms: in Parsonian theory 108,
139; and socialization, 107-9; in social
identity approach, 139-41; research on,

153. *See also* social identity approach;
internalization
Chein, Isidor, 115
Cicourel, Aaron, 4
clothing in Zinacantan, 28, 35, 45
cluster diagrams, 47, 50-2, 58-68, 86-92; and
structural differentiation, 74-5; accuracy
in interpreting, 82-3, 84, 87-8, 92, 103; as
measure of centrality, 96; as basis of
questionnaire, 116. *See also* generality of
norm clusters; reliability, of frame-sorting
method
Colby, Benjamin, 22
Coleman, James, 18-19
Collier, Jane, 32-4, 66
commitment to norms and identities, *see*
conformity
Compadrazgo, *see* kinship
conflict, *see* violence; craftiness
conformity to norms: in Parsonian theory
107-8; in social identity approach, 139-41
consensus: on hierarchy of norms, 72, 100-1;
in social identity approach, 137-8. *See
also* norms, consensus in
consistency of norms and action: types of,
114-15; Zinacantan survey on, 125-31,
172-5
Cook, Stuart, 110
corn farming, *see* farming
costumes, *see* clothing in Zinacantan
craftiness and intrigue in Zinacantan, 35. *See
also* Crafty norm cluster
Crafty norm cluster, 67, 90. *See also*
craftiness
curing ceremonies and medical practices of
Zinacantecos, 32, 34; as measured in
survey, 120; association of norms with,
167 8